1,001 Days in the Bleachers

1,001 Days
in the
Bleachers

A Quarter Century of Chicago Sports

Ted Cox

 Northwestern University Press
Evanston, Illinois

Northwestern University Press
www.nupress.northwestern.edu

Printed in the United States of America

10   9   8   7   6   5   4   3   2   1

Library of Congress Cataloging-in-Publication Data

Cox, Ted.
    1,001 days in the bleachers : a quarter century of Chicago sports / Ted Cox.
    p. cm.
    ISBN 978-0-8101-2868-2 (pbk. : alk. paper)
    1. Professional sports—Illinois—Chicago—History. 2. Chicago White Sox
(Baseball team) 3. Chicago Cubs (Baseball team) 4. Chicago Bulls (Basketball team)
5. Chicago Bears (Football team) 6. Chicago Blackhawks (Hockey team) I. Title.
II. Title: 1001 days in the bleachers. III. Title: One thousand one days in the bleachers.
GV584.5.C4C68 2013
796.04′40977311—dc23

                                                                                    2012031400

⊚ The paper used in this publication meets the minimum requirements of the
American National Standard for Information Sciences—Permanence of Paper for
Printed Library Materials, ANSI Z39.48-1992.

To my mother and father

And to my grandfather

Contents

Foreword by Tony Fitzpatrick   ix

1. No Joy in Mudville—Until . . .

Southpaw   5
Community   9
Tragic Heroes   13
A Bad Case of Cubosity   18
Celebrants   22
History   27
Spirit of '69   31
Requiem for a Ballpark   37
The End of Some Things   42
"Don't Worry About Getting Hurt"   47
Bartman: The Fans' Complicity   54
Better Lucky Than Good   64
Destiny, Ability, and Camaraderie   68
Denying Our Own Eyes   73

2. Running with the Bulls

Basketball in Black and White   79
The Shot   84
Rising Bulls   90
The Transformation   95
The Zen Triangle   101
Bringing It All Back Home   106
Three-peat: The Jordan Is Mighty and Shall Prevail   113
The Comeback   121
Head Games   127
Father's Day, Bloomsday, Championship Day   133

Tanned by the Spotlight   139
Doo-Doo and Shit   144
A Sense of the Familiar   150
The Last Shot   158

3. Setting Free the Bears

A Team as Great as Payton   169
Super Bears   174
Da Coach Outcoached   179
Bear Furnishings   184
Tale of the Tape   188
Soldier Field's Inner Beauty   193
Mensches of the Midway   198
Ridiculously Beautiful   201

4. Cold Steel on Ice (Metaphorically, Not Literally)

Hearing the Hawks   207
The Bleachers in Winter   211
Blacked-Out Hawks   215
Blackhawks Family Values   220
So Beautiful, So What?   225

5. Further Afield

Memories   233
Harbor Lights   237
That's Cricket   242
Tyson at the Auditorium   248
King Versus Simeon   255
Kevin Garnett   260
Chicago by Canoe   266
Bloom of the Rose   269

Acknowledgments   273

Foreword

Tony Fitzpatrick

HERE AND THERE, one runs across the unfortunate soul who hates baseball—the slack-jawed type who needs constant stimulation, the guy on the couch with his joystick. He needs things to blow up: bells, whistles, and car crashes. These are such pitiable creatures.

What these people fail to understand is that baseball—all nine perfect innings—is a novel, not a sketch. It rewards the attention span, the attentive viewer, those who wait for the story to reveal itself.

Sometimes it does so in fits and starts, and sometimes over the arduous pitchers' duel that unfurls increment by perfect increment.

You see, it was a game built to last.

This is the great reward of Ted Cox's stories about baseball. He understands the nuanced drama that plays out over 162 games. He writes wonderfully about other sports as well—but it is his baseball writing that most relays the joy of what he does, and the complicated American game that fascinates him.

I got a frantic e-mail from Ted once a couple of years ago:

"Tony, get to a television. Something very special is happening—something you may never see again in your life as a Sox fan." Well, hell, the White Sox had won a World Series a couple of years before. I wondered what it was.

By the time I got to the only bar in Bucktown where you could watch the Sox (the Charleston—make a note of it; the rest of these watering holes around here prefer the minor-league club in town, the Cubs) Mark Buehrle was putting the finishing touches on a perfect game. And Ted was right: one could go a whole lifetime and not see one—even a devoted fan. I've always been grateful for this.

I have more to be grateful to Ted Cox now: this marvelous collection of his columns, though I prefer to call them stories. Like the inventors and innovators of baseball, Ted Cox built these stories to last—like A. J. Leibling or the great *Sun-Times* writer John Schulian on boxing. Cox wrote his stories for the long haul—to be reread and treasured long after the Sox and most assuredly the Cubs have let us down.

Cox is a different kind of bird for this beat: a literate man in a game more and more crowded with disposable empty prose and the cheapest variety of boosterism. Ted is the thinking man's sports writer. In fact, he is a thinking man's writer, period. It just happens to be our good fortune that he writes about games that turn grown men into twelve-year-olds with one crack of the bat.

Here is a paragraph I wish I wrote; it has to do with the ever-present numbers and statistics that hold no small amount of poetry and sway in baseball:

> These are numbers with a certain value; they are baseball's immortal figures, part and portion of what one friend used to call the baggage we carry, the names, the nicknames, figures, and statistics that many of us (mostly grown boys) nestle and nurture in the backs of our minds the way some women keep their wedding dresses well preserved in the closet.

Cox certainly knows himself—the grown-boy fan—and he knows us. I carry around an unlimited number of numeric baseball factoids, but I can't remember my fucking PIN for my ATM. Cox knows that numbers are part of our great game's poetic engine. It is why the tattooed kid with a nose ring and the mathematics professor can both be baseball fans with equal rabid alacrity. It is why, despite the fact I don't much like the Cubs, Wrigley Field will always be the altar of baseball to me. We are contradictory types, we baseball fans, and Cox is one of us and luckily—unlike me—can explain us, the game, the people who play the games, and why they're all important.

I'm lucky that in my life I've been fortunate enough to read some of the greats: Red Smith, Roger Angell, Jerome Holtzman, and now Ted Cox.

This is a book I'll hang onto forever. Like Nolan Ryan, it's built to last way into the late innings—the goods.

1,001 Days in the Bleachers

1

No Joy in Mudville—
Until . . .

Southpaw

June 24, 1983

BRITT BURNS stands on the mound, shifts his weight from right leg to left. His arms hang from sloping shoulders, the ball in his left hand, behind his back, already hidden from the batter. He tilts his head and looks above the grandstand, squints, focusing—not on the sun, not on the pennants hanging above the grandstand, not on a bird, nothing so certain, but on the haze, the ozone, the ether, if such a thing is possible and if anyone should ever want to do it. He looks to the catcher with the same stare. His hands join in front of him and he rocks back on his right leg, raises his hands above and over his head, touching the glove to the nape of his neck. Then is beauty: the left foot turns perpendicular to home and accepts his weight, the right leg swings up and perpendicular to the body, the hands come down to the belt but do not pause. They separate: the left arm hangs loose and long behind the body, the right arm curls like the prow of a ship.

At this moment Britt Burns is the most frightening, the most graceful left-handed pitcher I've ever seen. Britt Burns is so fucking beautiful I can't believe it, and nothing he does the rest of the day will disturb that notion.

With the left arm following in the wake of his body, he takes one giant step down the pitching mound. It seems that easy. There is nothing the arm can do but come slinging over the shoulder as he turns to face home plate. The ball appears just to the side of his left ear; then it is free. His left leg drags behind like a tail, keeping his balance, as the hand continues down and brushes the dirt, as if pulling a window shade to its full length. The curveball flutters toward home, then, like the hat tumbling from his head to his feet, drops down, past the batter—whose swing connects with nothing and jerks his head around toward third base—and into Carlton Fisk's waiting glove.

It is not over, not yet, not even this tiny cycle. The ball itself is round; you come around to home. So the hand, already at his feet, reaches for the

5

hat. He rights himself, touches the cap to his forehead, presses the back down with his glove. As Fisk returns the ball and he catches it in the glove, the hand goes to the chest, clasps the tiny medal hanging there, and—thumb pulling open the neck of the jersey—deposits it inside for safekeeping, until the next pitch is thrown. He walks backward up the mound and stands atop it, above all the other players, at the center of the diamond, the focal point of the stands, and looks to the sky.

THIS WEEK, we abandon the editorial *we*—so much abused last time in a showing of solidarity—and choose instead the first-person *I*. E. B. White, driving from New York City to Martha's Vineyard in his Model T, makes a similar change and for similar reasons. "We went to the theater with our wife the other evening," he writes in "The Talk of the Town," and we understand, we empathize, for if we do not have a wife we are certainly familiar with the kind of man who does and who goes to the theater with her. He is a common enough sort. When Mr. White moves to the farm, however, he shifts to a self-conscious, apologetic *I*, realizing that we think him a bit strange, an aberration. Mr. White hopes we will find his lunacy interesting or—at very least—that we will feel fortunate that we have retained our sanity by remaining in the city.

Now, if I wrote that Britt Burns is not merely the best, but also the most aesthetically beautiful pitcher in Chicago, the one I would want to see on any given day, most baseball fans—even the die-hard box-score readers—would think me insane, that I had gone south for the summer. For in that very same box score, down at the bottom, is a figure marked *T*, which stands for "time," and on the days Britt Burns pitches, it is more likely that the figure will be over three hours than it is that Harold Washington and Eddie Vrdolyak will be on the evening news.

Every day Britt Burns pitches—no matter the weather—is a day of heat and humidity, of dust collecting in the veins of grass and hot dog wrappers rolling across the field of their own volition, like tumbleweeds in a horror movie. The wind stops, the numbers on the fence begin to shimmer, and if it's a night game cigarette smoke billows out of the stands and hangs in the lights like dust motes in a sunbeam.

Britt Burns, you see, is from the South, and if you have never heard his drawl that is not important, for every gesture speaks for him. He is a large man, listed at six feet five and 218 pounds in the program, and he walks slow, incredibly slow, as he does everything on the mound. He is said to be a heavy and long sleeper, which is not surprising, for on the mound he often seems in a state somewhere between sleep and aware- ness, as if this thin northern air were too light to sustain him. During one afternoon game in New York, he went behind the mound to rub up the baseball. As he put his glove back on and adjusted his hat (he wears large bobby pins to keep it on, unsuccessfully) the ball fell from his glove and landed between his feet. He looked at the sky, turned, and took the mound, in those slow, myriad southern steps. Carlton Fisk, squat- ting behind the plate, did not give him a sign, but this is not abnormal (Fisk too has a reputation for slow play, although his is the sloth of the New England longhair, always thinking in a daze, as opposed to Burns's southern metabolism), and it took the umpire, walking out from behind home and pointing at the mound, to make Burns recognize that some- thing was amiss. He tracked the ball down, picked it up as he would a nickel that had slipped through a hole in his pocket—not sure it's worth the effort—and rubbed it up again, continuing the game.

You see, I am hypnotized, in a state normally peculiar to Sunday after- noons spent with the paper. Halfway through a story buried in "The Week in Review," I find the words no longer have meaning, that I have been following their rhythms only, and I'm not sure I have the energy or the inclination to fix the drink that will make the words form sentences again. Britt Burns affects me in that fashion. As when watching someone hammer on a pier across a lake, the visual does not quite match the aural, and suddenly I am lazy and distant. Burns's motion, his body, his entire style is from another era.

His nickname is said to be "Hoss," and although I am not fond of nick- names—they seem contrived and deliberately xenophobic—this one is perfect, because Hoss is a classic baseball nickname, usually reserved for pitchers, and Burns is a classic baseball pitcher. He has a full stretch, touching the back of the neck, while most pitchers have gone to shorter, less complicated windups. He works at his own pace, while most pitchers have learned to work fast to keep fans interested and infielders on their toes. He throws straight overhand, while most pitchers nowadays throw three-quarters, somewhere between overhand and sidearm, to make their sliders crisp. Burns throws a slider, but his money pitch is a hard fastball that he throws with the same smooth motion, and that he sets up with a beautiful curve, the sort that can only be thrown overhand. I must admit that the description of his motion is not wholly original. In the '50s, before the slider came to dominate baseball, Charlie Dressen, the Brooklyn Dodgers manager, told his young pitchers that to throw a good curve they should imagine they were pulling down a window shade. Sliders, I suppose, are practiced with venetian blinds.

Baseball has its own measure of time, the inning, which can last from five to thirty minutes, and this open-endedness is one of its best qualities to fans and one of its major faults to detractors. It's a myth that baseball games used to move slower; they've never been as long as they are now. Yet, when Burns pitches, baseball time comes to life, and if in today's hectic world we have to exaggerate the qualities we like most to make them stand out, what's wrong with that?

Yes, Burns "labors like a monk over a manuscript," as Jim Kaplan wrote in *Sports Illustrated*, but the products of his labor are equally beautiful. An afternoon with Britt Burns is evanescent, but it is etched in my mind, and it will remain so until I figure out how someone so large can move so slowly and so gracefully while standing on one foot.

Community

September 23, 1983

I DON'T even remember the scoreboard going off. Harold Baines, with a cut barely stronger than a checked swing, chipped a fly ball into center field deep enough to score Julio Cruz, poised at third base, and as I saw the center fielder catch the ball and Cruz leap off third I stepped into the aisle and began moving toward left field. Ahead, the aisle was filling with people already, as I looked back over my shoulder and saw Cruz score, and the rising roar of the crowd reached a crescendo that would not subside for a half hour, and from behind the pushing began. I was hardly past third base, with no room ahead for the crowd, but the pushing was so strong that for a moment I was literally carried off my feet between the shoulders and bodies of those around me, and—as the scoreboard went off, I imagine, for it could have gone off at no other time without my notice—it was all I could do to remain standing, with or without my feet on the ground.

The Frains had blocked the aisles to the field well down past third base; it was understood from the night before that the infield was off limits. The first open aisle to the field, however, we poured to the right, went through the gate past a watching, helpless Frain usher, passed under a token rope run across the field at the foul line (the most dangerous part of the journey, for as some of us passed under the rope some of us were going over) and on out into the outfield, where we were screaming and jumping and howling and where you could high-five your way from left field to right and back again if you wanted, and some did. It didn't matter if you were there in a group or not because the White Sox had won the Western Division title with two weeks to spare and if you were a White Sox fan and had acknowledged pennant fever this was the reward. For if you had admitted that, yes, you wanted the White Sox to win more than you had ever wanted anything so stupid in all your life, you also had to admit that yes you were as happy as you had ever been and for the simple, silly, stupid reason that a team from Chicago—city of losers, city

9

of the greatest and most aggressively stoic fans in the world—the Chicago White Sox had finished first going away. Yes we said yes we will yes.

We had been out on the field the night before, but that was a different sort of occasion. With Floyd Bannister pitching as well as we had ever seen him, Baines broke a scoreless tie against the Seattle Mariners with a homer in the seventh. The Sox batted around in the eighth, scoring six runs, and Bannister coasted home with a little help from the home plate umpire for a shutout.

One by one, then, they came dripping over the outfield walls in defiance of an announcement asking everyone to keep off, an announcement that prompted a fan behind me to yell, "I want second base!" Although this was not to be (Frains and security roped off the infield), everyone in the park knew how absurd it was to expect forty thousand parched White Sox fans to control themselves in sight of the oasis, and many of us in the grandstand joined our more rash brothers and sisters from the bleachers and filed onto the field to watch the end of the Oakland A's–Kansas City Royals game, carried on the scoreboard television. The Sox, of course, had not yet won it. The Royals had to lose, and with Dan Quisenberry, the best reliever in the league, protecting a 6–5 Royals lead, we knew it probably would not happen that night, so we milled about as if at a drive-in movie without cars and hoped for a miracle. None occurred. The Royals won, the magic number was one, and we went home, vowing to return Saturday if at all possible.

The game began shortly after 8 P.M., following ninety minutes of rain that poured through long streaks of lightning that continued to light up the sky throughout the evening. Jerry Koosman, the forty-year-old veteran of the 1969 New York Mets, gave up an unearned run in the first, then settled down. The Sox tied it in the third and took the lead in the fourth, when Vance Law brought in Tom Paciorek from third on a suicide squeeze, one of manager Tony LaRussa's favorite plays and one he has rarely had the opportunity to use the way the Sox have been scoring runs, with homers and timely hitting. Kooz then fell into a groove, retiring the next ten Mariners in a row. He is a calm and seasoned pitcher, with a motion in which he sashays to the right, kicks to the left, and steps down the mound with a long stride typical of pitchers trained in the Mets farm system in the '60s. He still has the remains of the fastball that brought him to the majors, and mixes it with a slow, roundhouse curve in a manner that benefits both pitches, throwing the batter off. When Baines homered in the eighth inning for an insurance run, it looked as if the Sox, yes indeed, had won the game and the division. (The Royals were trouncing the A's, putting all the responsibility on the Sox, which is how everyone preferred it anyway.)

I was standing with others of my ilk behind the last row of seats in the grandstand, and planned to move down to the main aisle near the field after the Sox eighth. From standing room, you could see that everyone in the park (or at least the lower deck) could feel it coming, felt it so strongly that—before the Sox could finish their ups—"Na Na Hey Hey Kiss Him Good-bye" seemed to start itself in the lower left-field boxes, and the fans joined in all over the park. Now, singing has been a part of baseball since the Royal Rooters of the Boston Red Sox taunted the Pittsburgh Pirates with "Tessie" in the first World Series in 1903, but never has a song enriched the game the way "Good-bye" did that night. It was too early, we were too cocky, we knew it, but we couldn't help it. In fact, we flaunted it. Players' heads peeped out of the dugout in admonishment, but we continued singing.

What is it, I wondered, that brings this out in us? I could see it all around me and—worse yet—feel it in myself, but what was it that caused it? Because twenty-five guys who spend their summers in Chicago are the best group of baseball players around, does that mean the city should go crazy? I'm afraid of crowds, they're trouble, they're base, so why should I feel such a part of this one? The inning ended, I moved down into a forming crowd of standing people that filled the main aisle, where you could see the same wonder and fear on the faces of the players. If fans sometimes feel helpless because they try to help the players yet have no control over their performances, the players must feel even more helpless, in that their performance triggers the fans yet they have no control over the actions they elicit. And when a team wins a pennant in Chicago, everything comes apart, in a situation where no one has any real control over anything, and where the seemingly dangerous becomes beautifully harmless.

We were not yet there, however; we should have known better. In the ninth inning, every Chicago baseball myth manifested itself like a ghost and was, mystically, put to rest, as if we—all at once—did away with the old religion, the old fears. It was not an easy exorcism. Kooz allowed a hit to the leadoff man, and LaRussa came to the mound to remove him, bringing in Dennis Lamp. I've said all along I like the way LaRussa manages, but I've been a Chicago fan long enough to know you don't bring in an ex-Cub to protect the lead in the White Sox' pennant-clinching game. Lamp, true to myth, gave up two additional singles and a walk, allowing the Mariners to tie the score.

The Frains ordered us back to our seats, but I had no seat, so I ducked under one of the yellow railings along with a few others and sat against the cement just below the second level of seats. The attitude of the fans, on the whole, had not changed; we still felt the Sox would win. Yet, there was doubt lurking about. Would this ever end? Won't we ever win? Was it possible—in Chicago, if nowhere else—that a team could lose the last fifteen games and the pennant that was so certainly theirs? Mariners manager Del Crandall, however, played trump to our ex-Cub, bringing in ex-Cub Bill Caudill, who, miraculously, got pinch hitter Jerry Hairston to line out to first before succumbing to tradition and walking the next three batters, loading the bases for Baines, who made his small, safe, pennant-winning swing on the first pitch he saw.

Everyone was smiling in the outfield: we slapped each other, hugged each other, and ran through the field for the pure joy of sliding in the wet grass. I saw a ring of dancers, as in Milan Kundera's *Book of Laughter and Forgetting*, where they seem to raise themselves off the ground with each kick, except—on this occasion—Comiskey Park kept rising up to meet them. For Kundera, a Czech exile, the ascending ring of dancers he imagines is—on one level—a symbol of false community, of forgetting what's important in life. No, there is no real reason why the Sox should affect us so, but as I drove home past drivers who were courteous to one another, past blaring horns and people waving Sox pennants, up Lake Shore Drive where we continued to honk our horns at passersby, I thought that this sense of community—no matter how false, no matter how fleeting—will do for the next three weeks and, possibly, for some time after that, at least until something better comes along, and by that I do not mean the Bears making the playoffs.

Tragic Heroes

October 14, 1983

I REMEMBER reading, during the All-Star break, an interview with Ernie Banks in one of the Chicago papers. He was asked to name his greatest disappointment in sports. Of course, he replied that never appearing in the World Series was most disappointing. The reporter asked another question that made the first worthwhile: why was that most disappointing? Banks said that no matter how good you are, no matter how long you've been around, no matter how many home runs you've hit or games you've won, you never know how you'll play in the World Series, how you'll react to the pressure, unless you actually do it. Banks said he had retired without knowing how he would have responded—that would always remain a mystery to him.

I sometimes ask myself why it is that I spend so much time following a boy's game, why I spend so much time on sports in general. I'm not a frustrated athlete: you'll read no stories here of girls and catcher's mitts left behind at a minor league bus stop. Neither do I seek to recapture my youth (not yet, anyway). When I ask myself these things, the answer I most often come up with is that sport, in its finer moments, has all the drama and grace of any of the arts, high or popular, all the depth of any book; and baseball—because it isolates its athletes one or two at a time—has more fine moments than any other sport. It's simply a matter of knowing when to look and what to look for, finding out how the players deal with the pressure and themselves. If you didn't learn anything about human nature last Saturday, you were spending too much time trying to catch the eye of the beer vendor or bartender as he passed you by.

That's what I think in my finer moments, when I'm sitting in the dark working on my second gin trying to make sense of a season. Other times I feel just like any other Chicago sports fan: screwed again.

It all came down to the fourth game, not merely because the White Sox had to win to stay alive. In a short five-game series, the concept of momentum has a weight that it rarely carries during the regular season;

the series itself becomes more like a football game, with the tide turning one way and then the other, so that the last team to seize the momentum wins. Had the Sox won Saturday, they would have sent LaMarr Hoyt to the mound Sunday, and the Baltimore Orioles did not want to see Hoyt again after he had shut them down in game one, looking like Catfish Hunter returned, a great and determined money pitcher. Everyone in the park felt that if the Sox could save game four, in whatever fashion, game five would be theirs, and it was simply a matter of turning the momentum around.

Say what you will about the Sox: as bad as some of the players choked, some looked impressively cool, like Hoyt, Julio Cruz, Rudy Law before the last game, and—in that last game—Britt Burns.

Everyone knew that the fate of the Sox rested on Burns's wide yet sloping shoulders, but in the end everyone was wrong, for Burns pitched better than anyone could have expected, and in the end he lost the game. Over the course of the season, he became the most enigmatic figure on the pitching staff, a large, twenty-four-year-old man-child, a graceful professional one time out, a confused Baby Huey the next. John Schulian wrote one of his rich yet simple-minded columns saying that Burns lost the will to excel after the death of his father; *Sports Illustrated*, in its fine series on the Sox staff, explained additionally that Burns lost confidence after the shoulder injury of last year and the false injury of spring train-ing, when he caught a cold in his arm, was placed on the disabled list, and two days later felt right—and as cheerful—as rain. Certainly, he had something to prove, this man considered the ace of the staff a year and a half ago at the age of twenty-two, but certainly the odds and conditions were against him. His noted southern metabolism, responsible for his slovenly posture and lazy pitching style, adapts poorly to both day games and cold weather. As he warmed up in the fifty-degree chill of the last minutes of Saturday morning, you wondered just how he was going to pitch, if he—like Richard Dotson the night before—would fall apart and place the Sox in a deep hole before they even got a chance to bat.

He didn't. In the first, he faced the minimum three Oriole batters, get-ting the talented and glassy-eyed Cal Ripken Jr. to ground into a double play. For six innings he matched Storm Davis—a twenty-one-year-old clone of Jim Palmer who got the start over the original—almost out for out, as each allowed one base runner apiece in the fourth, fifth, and sixth, and had faced twenty-three batters going into the seventh.

The Sox, of course, were not hitting, for the Orioles had initially seized momentum in game two, when Mike Boddicker utterly destroyed their timing and waved away their confidence as if he were a sorcerer dispelling spirits. The quote on Boddicker, in case you hadn't heard, comes from Rod Carew, who said one night, "He threw me more garbage than I take out in a week." Boddicker pitched the sort of game that will send a fastball-hitting team like the White Sox into a slump for days, but the Sox didn't have days to recover, and for that reason he was named the most valuable player in the series. Yet, credit should also go to Orioles catcher Rick Dempsey, who kept pitchers Mike Flanagan and Davis on the slow and crooked path the following two days, calling for the curve when the Sox expected fastballs and vice versa. Throughout the series, Dempsey called for his pitchers to start out throwing the curve for strikes and end up throwing it for outs, and if they consistently got this oftentimes difficult pitch over the plate it was only because Dempsey convinced them it was the only way to beat the Sox—anything else was suicide. Davis and reliever Tippy Martinez so confounded Sox batters that of six strikeouts on Saturday, four were called by the umpire.

Three of those victims were Greg Luzinski, who gave Dempsey five put-outs alone by popping up to the catcher his other two times up. Luzinski was the dog if not the goat of the game, for not only was he a washout at bat, but he refused to talk to reporters after the game. Very bad form; this is Chicago, Bull, not Philadelphia.

Something else, however, was seriously wrong, for the star-crossed Harold Baines, coming off a torrid September, hit shots all through the series yet could not get a hit until late on Saturday. Baines, in fact, proved to be the symbol of the team's efforts to turn the series around, butting his head into nothing less than a wall of fate. The night before, with the team already down 4–0, he came up in the fourth with no outs and a runner on first—Ron Kittle, the victim of a too-tight pitch that aroused his anger and our emotions. Suddenly there seemed too much noise for the stadium to hold, and Baines jumped on the rattled Flanagan and hit the ball hard. It skipped savagely off the infield dirt, but second baseman Rich Dauer grabbed it like a greased pig as it passed him and turned it over quickly for the double play. Saturday, in the first inning, Baines hit a blue dart to shortstop Ripken, who threw to first to double up Carlton Fisk. Leading off the fourth, Baines hit one down the left-field line that Gary Roenicke caught diving to his right.

Call it fate, bad luck, just another playoff appearance by a Chicago team, but the Sox were not destined to win. Even when it appeared that there was nothing they could do but score in the seventh.

Put Jerry Dybzinski with the immortals. Add to the Merkle boner and the Snodgrass muff the Dybzinski blunder, although my first preference is to call it the Dybber's fuckhead catastrophe. In the seventh, Greg Walker led off with a hit. Mike Squires came in to run for him as Martinez, the Oriole bullpen ace, came in to relieve. Vance Law threatened to bunt the first pitch, then slapped one past the scurrying infielders to put runners on first and second, no outs. Dybzinski, given the start over Scott Fletcher at shortstop and team leader in sacrifice bunts, tapped one off the plate and into the hands of Dempsey, who threw Squires out at third by ten feet. This was unfortunate, but the worst was to come, for Dybzinski had been singled out by the gods.

Julio Cruz hit a line drive into left field. Roenicke fielded it quickly. There was never any question about Law trying to score from second; there was no way. Yet here came Dybzinski, allegedly one of the best base runners on the team—as he was the best bunter on the team—tearing around second base with his bowlegs pumping, making him seem fleet and five feet tall, when—halfway to third—he looked up and saw Vance Law looking him in the face.

Woe to him who does not guard against fate on all occasions, especially in the fourth game of the playoffs. I was sitting in the upper deck, above third base, and I could see his face clearly. He stopped dead. His eyes came out of his head. He stood straight up to his full six-two and saw that the gods had played a horrible, terrible trick on him, that whatever Chicago did way back when to deserve what it so obviously deserves, he should have known better than to challenge it, he should have stayed in Cleveland, he should have retired rather than come to Chicago and be the pawn in this cruel, indescribably hideous scheme. The Dybber had awakened to find himself cast as the Judas Iscariot of 1983. The rally was over. They had had their shot at Martinez and failed.

We all felt then it was only a matter of time. Burns felt it too, I think, which made his performance in the eighth and ninth all the more amazing. He would not give in to the will of fate. He loaded the bases with two out in the eighth, then got pinch hitter Dan Ford to pop to Cruz. As he trudged slowly from the mound (not redundant; Burns has two speeds: trudging and trudging slowly), I didn't think I could respect him more, but in the end I did.

As if foretold by a fairy godmother, Burns's 150th pitch, in the tenth inning, was a pumpkin that Tito Landrum, a minor league nobody two months ago, hit into the left-field upper deck. Burns pursed his lips in disgust. LaRussa came to the mound; Burns left the field, slowly, trudging. He was given the most somber, quiet, sustained applause I have ever heard at a sporting event. It was just hand claps, just applause, no shouts, no yells, I don't even remember hearing anyone near me talk as he walked from the field. We had seen a noble performance by a man who had tested himself while trying to beat the Chicago sports myth. It seemed as if there were already a gulf between the present and the future, that what we were watching was past and somehow being reexperienced. For a moment, Britt Burns was a tragic hero, and if that is not as desirable as being series MVP, it is certainly more fitting for a pitcher who spends six months of the year in Chicago.

A Bad Case of Cubosity

April 27, 1984

As a child, watching the Cubs from the suburbs on television, I envied the people living on Waveland and Sheffield who could watch the game simply by standing on the roofs of their buildings. That, for me, was paradise, dangled briefly before my eyes once or twice every game, a shot of a small group of people with their feet up on the edge of the building, drinking beer and idly watching the Cubs.

So Cubs opening day, 1984, was, for me, one of those rare occasions when a dream is realized, for at the end of last season, in an incredibly fortuitous occurrence that had little to do with the Cubs, I moved into an apartment across the street from Wrigley Field. Up on the roof of my building, looking down at the bleachers and the grandstand and a field I hadn't expected to see so clearly, I recalled how long I'd wanted to be able to climb my own back stairs to watch the Cubs—silly pipe dream—and suddenly I was there. I giggled stupidly at odd moments, laughed out loud, danced from foot to foot in the cold wind. I was, for a couple of hours, in paradise, and it didn't matter that it was so cold, or that the wind was strong enough to blow over a half-filled beer if you didn't hide it behind the cooler, or that the only scoreboard we could see was hopelessly messed up. The Cubs obliged with a victory, a win so decisive the score wasn't important after five or six innings. We had all brought beer, so the cooler was well stocked even when the game ended (too cold to work up a good thirst), and someone had brought a large bag of peanuts from one of the nut shops on Clark (but you had to take off your gloves to peel them, so those were left at the end of the game too). The conversation was good but did not often concern the Cubs, which was more than all right because it was, after all, only opening day, many more to go, and we weren't even in the ballpark. Yet, like box-seat fans, we cheered the early outs and yelled and stomped our feet when the Cubs rallied, proving a theory I've long held, that 99 percent of all baseball fans cheer only for themselves and those around them, not the players. It was, on the whole, a wonderful day, a fantasy come true, and as the summer arrives it can only get better.

So, having spent one of the great days of my life across the street from Wrigley Field, I am now ready to surrender myself to complete Cubosity and am picking the Cubs to finish first in the National League East.

Of course, I don't really expect the Cubs to finish first, but I am sincere about picking them to finish there. Only the foolish true believers expect miracles, and although these people are, traditionally, the most loyal of Cubs fans (I spent a few minutes on the bus bench at Clark and Addison one day with a crazy old chain-smoking woman with mascara drawn out from the corners of her eyes and up to her temples, who had a message written on the bottom of a grocery bag—"Here's the Beef! We want Buck!"—and she made sure to tell everyone who walked by about it too), the true Cubs fan takes pleasure in thinking he or she is independent and must be fooled somehow into thinking the Cubs have an actual chance. So here's the method (fooldja, didn't I?) behind the madness, and be sure to pay attention, because this is what they'll be saying come June and July.

At first, I thought about picking the Cubs because I couldn't bring myself to pick any of the other teams in the division. Not only is there no dominant team, there isn't even a complete but mediocre team among the other five. All have talent, but all have obvious holes, and the Cubs—to Dallas Green's credit—did the best job of spackling during the off-season and spring training.

Say what you will about them, the Cubs have a complete team—a mediocre team, but it is complete, especially if you consider the pitching staff better and bolstered, as I do. Steve Trout, I think, is the key, for he is the most fragile of the links in the staff and the one pitching coach Billy Connors has spent the most time with. Where Trout, a year ago, was showing a different motion on every pitch, a few days ago I watched him on television pitching his second straight complete game (he pitched the home opener too), and he looked very sharp and even. He's broken his motion down to its basics and is letting it throw the ball, and while he still looks like the ugly duckling—the most graceless player on the team, save for maybe Tom Veryzer—he seems a dependable pitcher who could win fifteen games or more if he gets an incredible case of confidence.

One of the good things about these early games in cold weather is that when there are only five thousand people in the ballpark, and half of those in the bleachers, that leaves an awful lot of box seats open, and I snuck down at a game last week and watched Scott Sanderson at close range and was quite impressed. He is a tall, long-legged pitcher with a simple motion—pump, kick, deliver—that looks as if it hasn't been altered since high school. He won only six games with the Montreal Expos last year because of a thumb injury, and rumor had it that the thumb was a convenient cover-up for a sore arm. He looks healthy and sharp, however, and before the season is over he could be the ace of the staff. It wouldn't take much.

Trout and Sanderson, Rick Reuschel and Chuck Rainey—the most malleable links; they must both win ten games—and Dick Ruthven: not a staff of impressive names, but try listing the pitchers on the 1975 Red Sox sometime. Tiant, Campbell, and uh-um—that's right. Teams with five good starters usually win pennants, but pennants are not usually won by teams with five good starters. To win the pennant, the Cubs need only one year of incredible luck, and I'm beginning to get the feeling that this team thinks that this is its last chance. The nucleus of the team— that nebulous something that contains its personality—has shifted from the Leon Durham–Lee Smith–Jody Davis youth axis to the Ruthven, Ron Cey, Larry Bowa, Gary Matthews experience axis without the one moving out the other (although Mel Hall and Joe Carter have suffered). Durham-Smith-Davis remain essential, but they no longer seem to reflect the personality of the team.

Ruthven, the Cubs' opening-day pitcher and therefore, at this point, the ace, strikes me as having this personality. He is thirty-three years old, he doesn't have a lot of stuff, and he hasn't had a really good year in some time. Yet he is a veteran of the 1980 world champion Phillies, as many players on the Cubs are, and every time he pitches I get the feeling he thinks this year is his last chance to have a great one. If the Cubs are developing a team character, this is it, because Green has mortgaged the immediate future for the immediate now, and if the team does not win this year they are not likely to win in the next few. Cey, at third, is thirty-six, Bowa, at short, is thirty-eight, and Matthews, the Cubs' only regular outfielder, will be thirty-four before the season is out. If these three share

ages above baseball's average life expectancy, they also share histories of
success and grace under pressure. They are Cubs now, but they haven't
always been, and sometimes memories are better than talent.

One thing is for certain: this is not a .500 ball team. They will come
close and win or come close and lose (because they do not, after all, have
the best team in the division and they are, after all, the Cubs) or they will
go into the toilet early, because Green has put together a team so filled
with divisions that only winning will sustain it (another reason to pick
the Cubs). Sometimes I think it might be better if the Cubs failed completely, so we could get rid of Green and return things to their normal
complacency. Yet Ruthven and Matthews—two players I was not very
fond of before the season started—are changing that, and I think an
actual ball team might be forming on the North Side as the spring turns
to summer.

One of the things I am asked the most is, what makes it unique to be
a Cubs fan? Is it the day games? Getting drunk in the bleachers? The fact
that they always lose and are therefore somehow comforting? Well yes,
all of those, but also the Cubs fan believes dreams can be realized, that
miracles can happen, and the miraculous thing about it is that the Cubs
fan maintains this belief even though miracles never happen. Standing
on my rooftop, watching the Cubs romp over the New York Mets, reinforced that belief, and after the last few years it needed reinforcement.

Oh yes, the San Diego Padres will win the West and beat the Cubs in
four games. Because every Cubs fan has a limit.

Celebrants

September 28, 1984

A WRITER can do his job without anyone knowing he's there, but a television camera changes people. So, Monday night, we went down the street to Bob's, at the corner of Clark and Waveland, kitty-corner from Wrigley Field, and left Murphy's behind. Murphy's is a large place with a rowdy audience of Cubs fans, and—ever since its days as Ray's Bleachers, before Murphy bought out Ray Meyer in 1979—it has been the party headquarters for Cubs fans. Bob's is a smaller place with a bigger television, a place where one can be among a crowd of Cubs fans and still talk with friends around a table. I was sold on Bob's the first time I went in, earlier this summer, when a friend and I were talking about Shawon Dunston and other Cubs minor league prospects and Bob himself chipped in from behind the bar with not only the names but the current batting averages and ages of every player with the Cubs' Iowa farm club. Here was a dedicated Cubs fan, a devout reader of *The Sporting News*, who had found his ideal place in the world, I thought, and when it came time to pick someplace to watch the Cubs clinch the East Division title there was really no competition.

Although this may sound like an advertisement, it's not intended as one. It's just that each of us had a choice to make last Monday, if we consider ourselves Cubs fans, and while the less confident stayed home to watch the Cubs clinch and some went to visit friends and the rowdier sorts went to Murphy's and some—for who knows what reason—went to Rush Street, we went to Bob's. In hindsight, it was the right choice. The minicams were at Murphy's long before the game was over, and if that wasn't enough Big Jim Thompson was there too, and he came this close to bringing George Bush with him. (The Secret Service nixed that idea.) That's the last thing any self-respecting Cubs fan wants to run into on the most important day in memory.

We got there at six, selected a table, and waited and watched the news. By 6:30, the game was on, the tables were filled, and spots at the bar were few and scattered. We scored in the first inning, and we cheered as if we were there. With the herky-jerky left-hander Larry McWilliams pitching for the Pittsburgh Pirates, Ryne Sandberg doubled to left field. ("Triple, triple," we yelled, because Sandberg was five hits, a homer, and a triple away from becoming the first person in major-league history to amass two hundred hits, twenty doubles, twenty triples, twenty homers, and twenty stolen bases in one year, an amazing if trivial feat.) Then, for the third straight game, Gary Matthews, the Sarge, got what would become the game-winning hit, driving Sandberg home with a single. Rick Sutcliffe had his lead.

Sutcliffe, throughout the incredible second half he has had, has only required a lead to win. At first, he was criticized as a lucky pitcher because the Cubs always scored runs for him, but even then he demonstrated an amazing toughness whenever he was charged with holding a lead, and in the last two months he has gripped one- or two-run advantages with intensity. Like the LaMarr Hoyt of 1983, Sutcliffe is determined not to let go once he has the victory in his back pocket. Against the Pirates, ahead early, for at least the fourth time this year he went through the order with perfection in the first three innings. In the fourth, he allowed the leadoff man to get one past Keith Moreland in right field, and Moreland proceeded to play it into a triple that produced a run, but by that time the Cubs had scored a run in each of the first three innings and were up 3–1, and Sutcliffe showed no sign of weakness.

He is a strange-looking pitcher at first and takes some getting used to. His motion is at once both smooth and jerky, and in the course of his windup he hesitates in positions as fixed and regular as the stations of the cross. He turns perpendicular to the plate and lifts his leg in position one, cocks his wrist back behind his body, giving the batter one quick glimpse of the ball, as he kicks in position two, leans back and holds his body behind his front leg as he moves down the mound with his left arm leading the way in position three, and lands hard on his front leg, causing his body and arm to come crashing over the top like a wave in position four. This is at once an aesthetic and practical motion: the hesitations suggest a baseball version of Duchamp's *Nude Descending a Staircase*, and in holding his body back he adds torque that gives his fastball and curve such sharp movement. A very pretty pitcher.

By the middle innings it was standing room only, and we cheered every out. Sutcliffe looked so solid that the only worry was that the New York Mets might lose before we won. The Mets went ahead 4–1, but the Philadelphia Phillies came back to tie. The games entered the top of the fifth inning at the same time (they showed the score on the screen), and although the Mets went ahead 5–4 the Phils again tied it. We got our last run in the fifth, but the Pirates brought in their relief ace, Kent Tekulve, and the game began to move along. Sutcliffe was dominant. He sometimes fooled Pirate hitters by throwing curves on a full count, sometimes blew them back to the bench with his fastball. As the game went on, he seemed to get stronger, and by the ninth inning we were wild with excitement, and the Mets—who would eventually win—were forgotten. (We cheered, "We want Ernie, activate Ernie, put in Ernie.") With two out in the ninth, he got ahead of the batter and then threw the fastball, a hellacious pitch for a busher just in from the minors to face, and the ball cut over the outside corner for strike three without the kid even twitching his bat. The Cubs had won 4–1, capturing the NL East title.

We slapped high fives and yelled and screamed, and a person waving a Cubs flag in the bar came very close to catching it in the ceiling fan, but that's to be expected. We watched the Cubs celebrate on the television for as long as it was interesting, then headed out into the street for our own celebration. Cars were honking and people were yelling, and we thought at first to go down to Murphy's, because this was one time to find a large crowd of Cubs fans, but we saw a large crowd forming already below the neon Cubs sign in front of the ballpark and headed in that direction.

The intersection was half blocked off. A TV truck was there, its bright lamps shining on the crowd and a camera positioned on its roof, and—in what would become standard behavior for the night—everyone faced toward the camera, shouting and gesturing, holding up one finger and slapping high fives. Cars were honking all around, and the ones that tried to slip through the intersection were pounded upon and yelled at: "Cubs win!" Up above, some people were already out on a roof across the street, climbing onto the Smirnoff's billboard to scream and yell in the bright lights. Firecrackers, bottle rockets, and Roman candles were going off all around, and when the cops arrived they simply parked their cars in the middle of the street with the lights flashing and stood on the edge of the crowd, smiling. You couldn't run into an unhappy person.

About this time, we got the idea that we'd head back to the apartment and watch the highlights on the news, but on the way we saw that Sheffield was blocked off to traffic so we walked on up to Murphy's and milled around there for a while. Again the intersection was filled and again everyone was pointed at the bright TV lamps atop the trucks. Arcs of beer foam were spraying in every direction and the cheering went on and on. The reporter Joan Esposito, doing a sound check for WLS TV on top of its truck, was soaked in beer and finally gave up, got off the truck, and moved down into the edge of the crowd. Back upstairs, we turned on the television and saw again and again Sutcliffe heaving that last pitch past the last stupefied Pirate.

We caught up with the celebrants around the city and right outside (saw Big Jim slapping high fives at Murphy's after the last out; we'd definitely selected the right bar) before being surprised with a little bit of magic in front of the global village's campfire. Here, suddenly, were the Cubs, out on the field, watching us celebrate on Three River Stadium's immense television, and we were watching them watching us. They were by this time pretty trashed, or, as Jody Davis said, "out of it in Pittsburgh."

Someone asked me how this compared to the White Sox clinching it a year ago, and I must say that this was as different and as similar as two such experiences could be. I remembered driving home from Comiskey Park, and how everyone had honked their horns and waved for cars to pull in front of them, and how the world, at the time, was just about the kindest place you'd ever want to spend a lifetime. The atmosphere around Wrigley Feld was like that. This television stuff, however, was something completely different from a year ago, when we took the field at Comiskey Park and watched the celebration in the clubhouse from the huge screen on the scoreboard. We had been part of the immediate experience then; we had watched the game and rooted the Sox on and felt a part of the victory. That feeling was absent Monday night until we saw that picture of the Cubs watching us on television. Then it became apparent that we were there and not there, that we had rooted them on in Pittsburgh from every bar in Chicago and had somehow been part of the outcome of the game. The celebration, this time, was much larger citywide—why, even the people in the stands at Comiskey Park had watched the Cubs clinch as the Sox were suffering through a seven-run sixth inning. Of course, the final and greatest difference is that not just a Chicago team but the most Chicagoan of all teams, the Cubs, the losingest of all the sports franchises in this city of losers, had finished first for the first time in thirty-nine years. The Chicago Cubs—the Chicago Cubs—have won the National League's East Division.

History

October 12, 1984

WRIGLEY FIELD was not originally built for the Chicago Cubs; at first, it was not even called Wrigley Field. It was constructed in 1914 for the Chicago Whales of the Federal League. The Feds made a short-lived attempt—one of the last—to form a third major baseball league, and they folded after two seasons, 1914 and 1915, but the Chicago franchise was, evidently, one of the stronger operations, winning the pennant in the final season. Its owner was able to build Wrigley at the cost of $250,000 in an effort to lure fans from the Cubs' West Side Park, on Lincoln, much in the same manner that failing franchises convince cities to build new ballparks nowadays, thinking that new stadia—like new shopping malls—come complete with customers.

It's an awfully cynical beginning for such a beautiful ballpark, to think that die-hard Cubs fans, even then, must have vowed never to set foot in such a monument to modernism. Yet, after the Feds failed, the Chicago franchise owner formed a group and bought the Cubs, and in 1916 the Cubs moved in. Still, it was not the ballpark we know today. In 1918, when the Cubs won the pennant, they played the World Series in the much larger Comiskey Park, the palace of baseball at the time. The bleachers were constructed and the park renamed in the '20s, the upper deck constructed late in the decade, and the bleachers reconstructed and the scoreboard added in the 1930s. Bill Veeck Jr. (his father had come to the Cubs when William Wrigley took control of the club after the 1918 season) added the vines, planting them himself in 1938.

Only Comiskey, Tiger Stadium in Detroit, and Fenway Park in Boston are older, and none is richer in history. Wrigley Field is where in 1917 the Cincinnati Reds' Fred Toney and the Cubs' Hippo Vaughn pitched a double no-hitter for nine innings before the Cubs and Vaughn blew it in the tenth, where Babe Ruth called his shot in the 1932 Series, where Gabby Hartnett hit the homer in the gloaming to win the pennant on the last day of the 1938 season, where Hank Borowy, the Rick Sutcliffe of his era, pitched three games in four days, two of them starting and both of them losses, in the 1945 Series against the Tigers, where Sandy Koufax pitched his perfect game in 1965, where Ron Santo clicked his heels, and where Ernie Banks hit his 500th home run off the Atlanta Braves' Pat Jarvis, and it was host to the World Series in 1929, 1932, 1935, 1938, and 1945. Entering Wrigley Field—or looking down upon it from the roofs across the street—we are in the grip of history, and today is, therefore, more memorable.

So it was that I was up on the roof a week ago last Monday, helping the landlord pound nails in preparation for the playoffs and World Series to come, and Wrigley Field was just about the most beautiful building I'd ever seen. Earlier in the day, I'd watched the Cubs and the San Diego Padres take batting practice and—between hits and pitches, conversations and questions—marveled at the beauty of the ball field: the very green grass, the ivy still flushed in green from the summer but showing a tinge of fall, the way the outfield wall softly curves in, 355 and 353 feet to the left- and right-field foul poles, but only 368 to the power alleys, which makes Wrigley the great hitter's park it is, the graceful ascension to the left- and right-field bleachers to the center-field section and the square scoreboard above and, beyond the fences, the brownstones across the street, the el tracks, and in the distance the high-rises. What a beautiful ball field, the Friendly Confines. Yet that is the view most of us are acquainted with, the view of the playing field, and it wasn't until I got up on the roof that Wrigley itself stood center stage. Decked out in red-white-and-blue bunting hanging from the upper deck, with the grandstand practically empty as the Padres continued to practice, Wrigley really was a host or hostess, the bride or the father of the bride (I couldn't make up my mind), and Tuesday, the beginning of the playoffs and the World Series to come, was what Wrigley Field was all about, what it had been created for. It was a very strange feeling, because—aside from my being a Cubs fan—I have no reason for being proud of Wrigley, even if you grant in the first place that pride is something one may feel about a ballpark, a large, concrete structure for accommodating fans. It was funny or maybe it was just my way of distancing myself from what was going on—the Cubs winning the division—so that if (when) the Cubs did fail it would not be the blow it could or would be (we Cubs fans have been known to develop some pretty complicated tricks to protect our psyches), but if that were the case in the end it didn't work.

All of us, I think, felt that something special was happening. It had something to do with Wrigley Field and something to do with finishing in first place for the second time in forty years and something to do with a team that at first seemed disjointed coming together and something to do with the Tigers and the Mets having good years at the same time and a great deal to do with Rick Sutcliffe and Ryne Sandberg. Those two are the sort of players only great teams, teams of destiny, are blessed with. Sandberg's attempt to become the first player with two hundred hits, twenty doubles, twenty triples, twenty homers, and twenty stolen bases in a single season and Sutcliffe's incredible second half placed us at once in two places—the present as here and now and the present as history in the making—and because of that the Cubs, for once, seemed destined to win, not lose.

When Sutcliffe pitched, we watched history—because he will never pitch so well again and it may be five, ten, or more years before a pitcher enjoys such a splendid second half as he did—and the first game of the playoffs was no exception. I had decided, at first, not to make any more predictions, but after watching the Cubs have a home run–hitting contest at their practice on Monday, while the Padres did their best slapping the ball around the green, I decided that—with the wind blowing out—the Cubs would blast the Padres out of Wrigley Field in the first two games and chase them down in San Diego, where a demoralized and fairly young team wouldn't have the mettle to even attempt a comeback. It was a perfect prediction except for the last part, for the Padres showed much more grit than anyone thought them capable of. Not only was Sutcliffe appropriately brilliant on Tuesday—even without his best stuff—but he hit a home run, and we stomped them 13–0. The weather was perfect, a gorgeous autumn day in Chicago, as it was for game two. Steve Trout—son of Dizzy Trout, who pitched for the Tigers against the Cubs in '45, for the Fates left hints of a Tigers-Cubs rematch everywhere—pitched superbly, Lee Smith got an impressive save, and we had a 2–0 lead in the series. The World Series was coming to Chicago, to be played during the day, where and when it has always belonged.

So when Sutcliffe's magic ended a week too soon and the roof came down and the Cubs lost, I felt sorry not for the Cubs and not for the fans and not for myself, but for Wrigley Field, a building, and came home Sunday night and sat on the balcony and played a Jimmy Yancey boogie-woogie record on the stereo, because Yancey—although he was a groundskeeper for the White Sox and not the Cubs—would have understood. With a slow number like "How Long Blues" to testify for him, he would understand.

Before I lived across the street from Wrigley Field, I lived next to churches, at two different addresses. I am not a religious person, but there was something to living next to churches. On Sunday, I would wake up and the sound of organ music would be coming in the window. I'd sit out on the balcony reading the Sunday papers, and the service would end, and the parking lot would fill with persons talking or saying good-bye or holding conversations over the hoods of their cars. During the week, the church would be empty, but in many ways it always felt the same to live nearby. Wrigley Field gives off the same sort of feeling, only doubled, tripled, a hundredfold, a strange and monstrous benevolence. In the winter, with the cold winds blowing through it, Wrigley Field remains the spirit of summer and the spirit of the Cubs, awful and capable of vindictive silence, yet for the most part kind and optimistic. The fans who recently gathered at Murphy's and the Cubby Bear and elsewhere nearby know the feeling; otherwise they wouldn't have come to the neighborhood to celebrate outside Wrigley Field's doorstep, and although they are gone they remain, in a sense, for Wrigley Field is the Cubs and it is baseball, and most important, it is in and of itself history. They gutted it this week, rolling up the grass to send back to the sod farm and throwing the scraps into a large orange dumpster just outside the right-field wall. Wrigley Field will be empty next week and the week after that, because the Cubs have ended their season just when it seemed they would not release it until the very end, but Wrigley Field remains. The day the Cubs lost, the leaves on the trees outside turned bright yellow overnight, and it is a long wait, it seems to me, until next summer, but Wrigley Field endures and so do the Cubs and so, in fact, do we. No surprise about that. Bring on the winter. We are ready. Wrigley Field invites the storm.

Spirit of '69

October 12, 1989

"Nineteen-sixty-nine—I've heard enough about it," said Don Zimmer. "And I've been asked enough about it, and my players have been asked enough about it, but in 1969 I was managing in Key West, Florida, in the Florida State League, and what happened to the '69 Cubs—the fans remember it, and the '69 players remember it, but these players wasn't on that club, and it didn't have no reflection on this ball club." The Cubs' manager stood at a lectern, answering reporters' questions during a pre-playoff workout a week ago last Tuesday at Wrigley Field. The interview session was held upstairs in the grandstand at the Stadium Club, and all the while, lurking on the wall behind Zimmer's left shoulder—quite humorous at the time, quite ominous now—was a framed poster of the 1969 Chicago Cubs.

What makes the Cubs' ensuing performance in the National League Championship Series so painful—what always makes it painful—is that they really should have won. Looking at the two teams preparing for play that bright, brisk, cloudless afternoon, one had the feeling that the Cubs were not only the better team—certainly the more balanced team—but also the better prepared team. Almost to a man, they gave off a feeling of quiet confidence; they seemed to take nothing for granted, not even their own proficiency as the East Division champions and as the win-ningest team in the league. With no dominant team running roughshod this year, this quality of subdued confidence, of professionalism first and foremost, might have been all the Cubs needed to finish first—in a penmanship contest, the one team to dot the *i*'s will win every time—and it made them even more endearing to the common fan than the Cubs usually are. At the workout, hushed, almost whispered interviews were common. Rick Wrona at the batting cage and Ryne Sandberg in the dugout both held forth with softly uttered statements, while reporters scurried and scuffled about trying to find a way to get their tape recorders close enough to pick up a few remarks. The statement of the day, however, was issued by Mark Grace, who was asked when it was that the Cubs knew they were the team to beat—if it was after the early September Saturday win over the Saint Louis Cardinals following the crushing defeat the day before, or perhaps after the sweep of the Expos, which followed immediately after. "No, it came much later than that," Grace said. "I think we finally realized that when they flashed that score, 4–1 Pittsburgh over Saint Louis, in Montreal on the night we won it." That was the confident humility that typified the Cubs from the moment they first realized they had a chance—Andre Dawson insisted they did when he went down with an injury early in the season—right on up into the series with the Giants.

As Zimmer put it, "I'm not too sure that they know yet they were in a race. They played that way all year."

There was one ominous note, though, going into game one. It came when Greg Maddux took the lectern at the official interview session. He said, to open the interview, "I think we're going to have fun," and he concluded his interview by saying, "I think it's going to be a lot of fun." If this falling back on a pet phrase didn't betray his underlying worries, his eyes—wide and white—did. When asked if he would approach the play-off games any differently than a regular-season game, he said, "I don't, I don't, I don't think it's any different."

The Giants, by turn, were subdued and not confident. Their pitching staff was beat up, and their manager, Roger Craig, encouraged speculation about the health of catcher Terry Kennedy's throwing arm. Don Robinson threw a simulated game that very day at the workout, testing a banged-up right knee that wore a large and noticeable brace under his uniform. His pitching was also noticeably subpar. (One of the great shames of the series was that the Cubs did not sufficiently pounce on Robinson's replacement in the rotation, Mike LaCoss, in game three, nor on Robinson himself when he entered the same game in relief.) Perhaps I should have suspected something when I found the team that had just been there, playing for the NL championship only two years ago, less confident than the fresh-faced team of wonder boys. But my head said Cubs in five, and my heart—being closer to the Cubs and naturally more aligned with the erratic thinking patterns of Don Zimmer—said Cubs in six.

Maddux, of course, was one of the Cubs' prime goats, but he was by no means the only one. Every great flop of the Cubs except those dictated by hubris (a crime the team has rarely been guilty of) has been marked by the embarrassment of one of the team's best and most popular players. Think of Ron Santo's pop-ups and double-play grounders in a year in which he nevertheless drove in 123 runs; the failure of both Rick Sutcliffe and Lee Smith to hold leads against the San Diego Padres; Ryne Sandberg's failure to glove a hard San Diego grounder of the sort he usually gets, and of course Leon Durham's flubbed fielding play in the same series. This year what made the series most painful of all was the ineptitude of Andre Dawson, the man who so wanted to be a Cub that he took a pay cut. Well, now he's a full-fledged member of this historic franchise: he choked, utterly, at the plate and in the field (fans of the White Sox were quick to point this out), leaving three runners on third base—one with only one out—and six runners stranded in game five alone; he also failed, like Sandberg, to make a great play in the field, dropping the ball and then missing the cutoff man on Will Clark's game-five triple, which allowed the Giants to tie the score 1–1 in the seventh inning as Mike Bielecki pitched the best postseason game thrown by a Chicago pitcher since Britt Burns's sullied masterpiece for the White Sox in 1983.

Dawson and Maddux will draw much of the attention and much of the blame for the Cubs' loss in the future. Forgotten will be the strange and unpredictable ways of Don Zimmer. Zimmer seemed so impressed with the team's attitude toward the series—just another set of games—that he adopted it himself. Of course it was not just another set of games, it was the height of the season, a fight for superiority between the two best teams in the league, and the Cubs were ill prepared for battle. The blame here goes right up to general manager Jim Frey, because whoever scouted the Giants either did not do his job or failed to make his conclusions strongly enough for Zimmer. Even a mere fan knows that the scouting report on the Giants begins with the line "Try not to let Will Clark or Kevin Mitchell beat you." Why, then, did Zimmer intentionally walk Brett Butler in game one, setting up a situation in which Clark—who already had a double and a homer on the night—would almost certainly come to the plate after the speedy Robby Thompson? The second line of the scouting report reads, "Don't throw Matt Williams any fastballs for strikes," because it's well known that Williams can't hit a curveball with the business end of a shovel. Why then did Maddux throw a fastball to Williams on the first pitch after walking Mitchell to load the bases in game four, and why did Steve Wilson stick consistently to fastballs, finally getting punished on the twelfth pitch when Williams hit the game-winning homer, later in the same game?

The playoffs are not just another series. The aggressive base running that paid the Cubs a bounty of breaks during the regular season only burned them against the Giants, a sound team fundamentally. It's a common problem, repeated every year or so, as to how an aggressive team should suddenly rein itself in during the postseason, but advice should have been given to the Cubs—again, by a knowledgeable scout. In almost every facet of the game, everywhere one looked, the Cubs sowed the seeds of their own defeat. They should have won—I still believe that— but in the end they got what they had coming.

In any case, the point is moot. The Oakland Athletics will win the World Series in four or five games. They have the best manager and the best slugger of the decade, as well as the best leadoff man in baseball history. Throughout their playoff series with the Toronto Blue Jays, they played a sharp, fundamentally sound brand of baseball. Compare the treatment the Athletics' pitchers gave Fred McGriff and George Bell to the treatment Clark, Mitchell, and Williams received from the Cubs' staff. And National League fans take note: both the Cubs and the Giants failed to break up double plays that cut off innings, while Rickey Henderson won game one in the AL series with a hard-nosed slide. This may be the team of the decade; for peak value, only the 1984 Detroit Tigers come close.

We were in Europe the last three weeks of the baseball season, feeling like a character out of Henry James—the sudden recipient of riches too great to quantify. Hemingway once said that James's novels were typified by two characters talking about the action while the real scene took place somewhere else, outside the range of the reader, and that too was typical of our trip as it related to the Cubs. The character who arrives to discuss the action without adding anything to it was played on our trip by USA Today and the International Herald-Tribune, and day by day we would hunt them up for news of the Cubs. We had left on a Friday, the day after seeing the play *Bleacher Bums*, the very day Mitch Williams—as forecast in the drama—gave up a game-winning homer to the Saint Louis Cardinals (to Pedro Guerrero, however, not Tom Brunansky), cutting the Cubs' first-place lead to half a game. Of course we wrote them off, but the following week, when we heard from a group of Chicagoans that the Cubs had gone on to win both the remaining games of that series (Saturday's game, in which Luis Salazar played the decisive role in a comeback, was probably the game of the pennant race for them), and had followed that up with a win over the Montreal Expos, and then later on that week we saw in *USA Today* that they had swept the Expos and had pushed the lead back to five full games, well, we started planning our return—tentatively, wishfully, but expectantly just the same.

This distant version of the pennant race is told not to add to the drama of the Cubs' finishing in first place (read that phrase again and ask, "What could?"), but because, boring as it is, in drama and excitement it nevertheless rivals many versions of the pennant race we heard on our return. There was an essential divergence in the tale tellers, we noticed: those who were absent from Chicago in 1984 were much more excited—and, it seemed, much less reliable—than those who saw the 1984 team finish first. In fact, more than once, veteran campaigners who observed the 1984 fiasco firsthand described the 1989 race as "anticlimactic." Indeed, once the Cubs had padded their lead back to five games, no team got back within three games the rest of the season. This was the impression we received in Europe, where each day we checked the standings first thing, only to find the lead the same as it had been the day before.

The most compelling and entertaining statement about the Cubs' divisional triumph was issued, for us, by Wrigley Field itself. We walked past it late last week, and there were groups posing for photos in front of the large neon sign at Clark and Addison, as well as a cigar-smoking father walking four children. He held the hand of one, a toddler, but when the group came within sight of the large Cubs logo painted on the wall near the door of the administrative offices, the three older children all ran to the wall and hugged it, rubbing their hands all over the logo, saying, "Cubs, Cubs," and the father released the toddler, who joined the older kids literally embracing Wrigley Field in celebration. This scene left no doubt about where the Cubs had finished; we could have been just in from Turkestan, with no news of baseball whatsoever, and known what it meant. We leave with a picture of Wrigley Field, dressed up again in its bunting and pomp. Where five years ago she looked like a dowager, returning to society with more grace than anyone thought possible, this time she seemed an aged actress—with her tiaralike lights and whalebone sky boxes—outfitted again for a great role on opening night. In the end, isn't it always what we fall back on—Wrigley Field?

Requiem for a Ballpark

October 4, 1990

IT WAS A beautiful day for a wake—and for a birthday, our friend Neil (now and forevermore thirty-nine) reminded us as we drove down to Comiskey Park last Sunday morning. There wasn't a cloud in the pale blue sky, only a certain cool slant to the sunlight, reminiscent of college football games. On the way, along Monroe Harbor, we passed the festive balloon arches of the AIDS Walk Chicago—an occasion in keeping with the spirit of the day even if it wasn't on our agenda. We arrived early in the Comiskey neighborhood, shortly after 11, more than two hours before game time, but the streets and sidewalks were already bustling, with a hive of activity just north of the stadium, near a tent put up by SportsChannel to both encourage and monitor the celebrations. We parked in one of the new lots surrounding the new ballpark, then walked back past the tall, nut-brown stadium—still under construction—to the center attraction, Comiskey Park.

Comiskey's last days elicited such a range of responses that it was sometimes hard to believe everyone was referring to the same place. There were the usual complaints about obstructed views, about the awful sight lines from the corners, about the wasted seating in the upper-deck bleachers, as some adopted an attitude of "glad to see it go." Others went too far in the other direction, taking Comiskey as the be-all and end-all, the Platonic form upon which all other stadia should be modeled, while turning a blind eye to its obvious faults. The *Tribune*'s Alan Solomon took both sides, saying Bill Veeck "corrupted" it with his concessions to the masses—the exploding scoreboard of his first administration and the "fairgrounds" atmosphere of his second—and harking back to when Comiskey was an unsullied ballpark. The truth is that skinflint Charles Comiskey cut corners on his "Baseball Palace," just as he cut corners on all things, and that he, himself, is responsible for most of the park's inherent design flaws—which date back to its opening in

1910. (Wrigley Field and Fenway Park, built within years of Comiskey, managed to avoid many of the same sight-line problems.)

It was, nevertheless, built to last, and last it did, and that became its main charm. Viewed from the traditional spot, behind home plate in the grandstand, Comiskey had the solid, unadorned look Chicagoans have come to take a perverse pride in: the way the blocky, two-tiered bleachers fit into the grandstand gave the stadium an appearance of wide shoulders, and, as those seats were always so difficult for batters to reach, the park always seemed big, as big and boxy as one of Al Capone's suits.

The response most often triggered by Comiskey's last days, however, was simple reverie, of days gone by and occasions remembered. What could we say about the place where we saw our first baseball game? It was a night game in 1968, so hot and muggy the Baltimore Orioles' first baseman, Boog Powell, sweated right through his heavy gray road jersey and had to change into another in the seventh inning.

There was that peculiar mix of smells found in the picnic sections, where the aromas of cut grass and fried food moiled, and where before a game the pitchers would trot past so close we could hear the crunch of their spikes on the gravel of the warning track. There were fifty thousand people filling the place for a bat day double header—twenty-five thousand of them kids tapping the bats persistently against the concrete, demanding a rally. (How did our parents endure that?) There was the night when Baltimore pitcher Jim Palmer changed speeds so adroitly, spun his curveballs and sliders so sharply, that what was so difficult for the batters to fathom suddenly became obvious to us, and a whole new realm of the game opened up.

That was on one of Bill Veeck's "fairgrounds" nights, when tickets were available for half price for anyone with a musical instrument, and we drove up with a rebellious high school friend, we with a harmonica, he with a comb and a piece of paper, and the man at the window made him play a little on it before selling us seats three rows behind home plate for what must have been $2.50 or $3 apiece—still some of the best seats we've ever had for a ball game.

Later, armed with a press pass, we'd enter the ballpark early, with the ushers and the vendors, and watch the Sox take batting practice—savoring the extra-crisp sound of bat on ball in an empty stadium.

There were the wonderful winning ways of the 1983 Western Division champs, ending in the playoffs with the greatest game we've seen, Britt Burns's tragic masterpiece, marred by Jerry Dybzinski's seventh-inning baserunning boner (the Dybber's fuckhead catastrophe) and the tenth-inning homer by Baltimore's Tito Landrum. There was the best game we've seen pitched, LaMarr Hoyt facing twenty-seven Yankees in 1984, with a bloop single by New York's Don Mattingly (erased by a double play) the only blot on the scorecard.

Comiskey's last days prompted similar thoughts on the part of all Sox fans; it triggered a process in which they tried to define themselves, determining what made them different from fans of the Cubs. This produced a real consensus, quite unlike the varying feelings about the ballpark itself. Sox fans came to describe themselves as baseball connoisseurs, intolerant of losers, people able to appreciate a well-pitched game stressing speed and defense. Comiskey—no matter its faults—was celebrated, quite rightly, for emphasizing those qualities.

Throughout the last month, everyone—from manager Jeff Torborg to the meanest fan—was citing the team's renaissance this year as the revival of classic White Sox baseball. There was a staff of young, promising pitchers coming of age, a quality of all the great White Sox teams, even the 1977 South Side Hit Men (who included double-figure winners Francisco Barrios, Ken Kravec, and Chris Knapp, as well as fifteen-game-winner Steve Stone). There was speed up and down the lineup, but most of all in the outfield, where Ivan Calderon, Lance Johnson, and Sammy Sosa all stole thirty bases on offense and stole extra-base hits from the opposition on defense. There was heady coaching by Torborg and his staff, especially defensive spotter Joe Nossek, now the leading in-house candidate for new general manager. The Sox defensive alignment deposed that of the Oakland Athletics as the most unusual—and successful—in baseball. Combined with pitching taught to play to these alignments, the Sox improved their earned run average to one of the best in the league. In one instructive night in Milwaukee, they played their outfield like so against Robin Yount: left field to pull, center field to slice, and right field almost on the foul line. With the Sox pitching him outside, Yount hit a pair of would-be doubles straight at Sosa, who didn't have to move a step to catch them.

There were Walt Hriniak–style slash hitters up and down the lineup, turning good pitches, low and on the outside corner, into base hits by going to the opposite field. There was yet another great season from Carlton Fisk, who in an early season run-in with the Yankees' Deion Sanders established himself as the definitive professional, part cranky New England Yank, part South Side Chicago curmudgeon. Unfortunately, there was also a stronger, better team in the same division. The distant second-place finish for the Sox, even with their ninety-plus wins, sent fans back to the '50s for parallels with the Go-Go Sox, ever overshadowed by the Yankees until 1959. But finally, there was the August arrival of rookies Alex Fernandez—yet another promising young pitcher—and Frank Thomas.

Thomas, a huge first baseman, arrived from Class AA Birmingham with stats that would make him *Baseball America*'s Minor League Player of the Year. He got better with almost every big-league game and fixed himself in the cleanup spot for what appears to be years to come. Through the last game at Comiskey Park, he hit .343 with seven homers and thirty RBI—power figures that translate to more than twenty homers and ninety RBI over a full season. What was most impressive was his swing. Everything about it seemed an attempt to rein itself in—to not overextend itself—but with his size and strength it couldn't help being a mighty cut. He began in a crouch, almost hiding, then his swing opened up in the manner of one of those startling bursts of time-lapse photography in which a flower blooms like a skyrocket. His attempts to make his swing both controlled and delayed directed most of his power to right field and right center—Punch-and-Judy power—but last Friday night he turned on a pitch. He watched the Seattle Mariners' tall and talented lefty Randy Johnson diddle himself behind in the count 2–0 with a pair of off-speed pitches. The next pitch would be a fastball, and Thomas pounced on it, hitting it well up into the left-field lower deck for what would be his first and only Comiskey Park homer—in fact, the last to set off fireworks.

It figured, however, that the last game at Comiskey Park would be a pitchers' duel. Our Jack McDowell locked up with Seattle's Rich DeLucia Sunday for five shutout innings before McDowell staggered in the sixth, allowing a triple down the right-field line to Ken Griffey Jr. and sending him home with a wild pitch. Lance Johnson, however, opened the bot-tom half of the inning with his own triple and scored on a single up the middle by Thomas, who then scored on a bad-hop triple by Dan Pasqua, who slapped the ball into left field, where it bounced up and off the shoulder of Ken Griffey Sr. and rolled to the wall. (Like the White Sox' father-and-son ballparks, the Mariners have father-and-son outfielders.) McDowell pitched courageously out of jams in the seventh and eighth before allowing Bobby Thigpen to finish. Thiggy came on to earn his fifty-seventh save—easily a major league record.

Afterward, an amazing display of police kept anyone from entertain-ing any thoughts of getting onto the field. The final out was made, cops poured out of the grandstand from every aisle, the center-field fence opened, and out came more cops on horseback and in paddy wagons to stand guard all around. It was insulting. Sox management was so guarded about keeping its precious ballpark intact—a park it used first as an excuse to threaten leaving, then, this season, as a cash cow—that it took no chances. A postgame video played on the scoreboard and the Sox themselves slipping between the cops to get to the center of the field to wave good-bye to the fans only struck us as bones thrown to keep us from charging. Stadium organist Nancy Faust played one final "Na Na Hey Hey Kiss Him Good-bye" and then "Auld Lang Syne" and it was over.

We remember watching on television once when a fire in one of the grandstand grills sent fans out onto the field. The fire was soon put out, but while the smoke cleared the fans ruled the grass, with a line forming to run from third to slide into home. After a few minutes the fans were told to clear the field for play, and the game resumed. In 1983, the Sox clinched a tie for first, and we went out on the field. The Kansas City Royals were the only other team still alive in the West—and they were losing. The Royals' game was broadcast on the scoreboard television, and when we watched them rally we left the field. If anyone tried to grab a fistful of turf, there was always another fan there saying, "Hey, save it for after the World Series." That was also the case the following night, when the Sox won to clinch and we went out on the field whooping and hollering and thinking, as we would later joke,

Yes we said yes we will yes.

Not this time. Never again.

The End of Some Things

October 21, 1993

THE MAIN arteries leading to Bill Veeck Stadium were clogged with traffic before the start of game one of the American League Championship Series. Cars inched their way toward parking lots that were already filled. Ticket holders who had managed to ditch their cars somewhere along the route strutted past the traffic in a way that must have truly infuriated those who were simply, hopelessly stuck. Not me. I parked on Halsted north of 35th, locked the doors, and fed the meter to get it at least close to the 9 P.M. cutoff. Then I walked down to Kattouyia's Hot Dogs for a killer Polish sausage (literally: it was deep fried and made my heart murmur with surrender even as it went down). Then I walked across the street to Puffer's, a delightful little Bridgeport tap, where spots were opening at the bar as local ticket holders left for the game. The televisions were tuned to the pregame coverage, but the sound was down; Tito Puente was on the bar stereo. "George Bell would feel at home here," said the bartender. In spite of the October cold—a cozy, homey sort of baseball chill, in contrast to the brisk ripeness of opening day—the front windows were open. The whole neighborhood was buzzing with good wishes and high expectations. It was there I heard that Michael Jordan was retiring from basketball.

A *Tribune* article on where to watch the playoffs lumped Puffer's in with other Bridgeport sports bars, but that was wrong, a misguided journalist's attempt to grant the place some instant stigma. Puffer's is a natty, neighborly little shotgun tavern, with a wide wooden bar and, opposite, small and intimate tables rather than booths, an arrangement that gives the place a deceptive width. It is owned, in part, by a high school friend of a friend of mine, and it has a selection of beer and spirits to shame any NorthSiders who think they have a lock on the city's alcoholic sophistication. I started with a Fuller's, a heavy Scottish ale, and moved on, before the night was over, to a Golden Prairie, a malty, pleasantly busy lager from a microbrewery on Clybourn, and Legacy, another local lager, somewhere between the previous two in taste and texture. The bartendress asked if I wanted a "Smoke a Jay" button, referring to the White Sox' opponents, the Toronto Blue Jays, and for a dollar I bought one and pinned it on. Down the bar, a few regulars clinked glasses with the toast "To ourselves." Up the bar, under the television, another regular caught a glimpse of a helicopter shot of the area surrounding the ballpark, and slipping into a hokey, self-deprecating accent said, "There it is—da South Side." A scalper wearing a CCCP warm-up jacket wandered through selling tickets at face value and found no takers. The bartender caught sight of a meter maid sauntering past, eyeing a car parked right in front, and shouted, "Hey, who's got the white Taurus? Anybody got the white Taurus? You gotta feed the meters till nine o'clock." A few people scuttled out of the bar to their cars, and the meter maid shot the bartender a hostile glance. On the television, they showed a quick replay of Michael Jordan throwing out the first pitch.

In hindsight, giving short shrift to the ceremonial first pitch was the blunder of the night. This was Jordan's first public appearance in Chicago since his father's death, and it was loaded with drama—even before the heart-stopping report that would follow within two hours. A friend of mine at the game said later that even those in attendance had been surprised by the brusqueness of the ceremony. He noticed a curious applause in the moments before the game was to begin, and suddenly looked up to see Jordan on the field. To sustained cheers and clapping, Jordan made the toss, turned down Ron Karkovice's request that he autograph the ball (it was later reported in the newspapers), and was gone. Back at Puffer's, I wrote in my notebook: "MJ relegated to replay. ARGH!"

The music was turned off, the TV sound was turned on, and Jack McDowell got leadoff hitter Rickey Henderson to fly to right for the first out. There were cheers and clapping, and a guy down the bar said, "Twenty-six more to go!" The Sox threatened early but couldn't push a run across. Robin Ventura struck out with Frank Thomas on third in the bottom of the first. "Ohhhh," went the sound of the bar. Ellis Burks popped down the left-field line with runners at second and third to end the third; Henderson caught the ball next to the stands and shook it at nearby fans.

Then came the three quick punches of the game and, of course, the knockout of the night. The Jays scored in the fourth on a two-run, two-out double by Ed Sprague. The Sox came back in the bottom of the inning on a two-run single by Ozzie Guillen, who stole second and scored the go-ahead run on a single by Tim Raines. Then the Jays counterpunched. They scored three runs in the fifth, the big blow John Olerud's two-out, two-run double to center. As with Sprague's double—and as with several of the Jays' big hits in the series—it seemed the result of a Sox scouting report that was accurate and detailed, but out of sync with itself. The Sox, as always, had their defenders placed where the odds said the Jays would hit the ball. The Sox pitchers were throwing the ball where the Jays didn't like it. But, with the pitches where they were, the Jays were hitting it where they usually didn't. Sprague dropped the bat on a low, inside McDowell split-finger fastball and sent it down the right-field line; Burks, shading him to center, just missed catching up with it. Olerud laced a McDowell pitch to right center; Lance Johnson had been shading him to left, and again just missed catching up with it. Then CBS's Pat O'Brien and Jim Gray broke in, from one of the photographers' wells along the field, with the report that Jordan was retiring.

All five stages of death were run through in Puffer's that night. The first two, denial and anger, came at once. "I can't believe they'd interrupt the game with that crap," said the fellow sitting next to me. But CBS showed Jordan leaving the game without issuing a statement. Then came resistance, in the form of rooting for the Sox. But McDowell just didn't have it, and gave up a two-run homer—again with two outs—to Paul Molitor in the seventh. Then came resignation. "This is weird, man," said the fellow sitting next to me. "The night is getting very strange. It's weird." A bad moon rose over the buildings across the street. And finally came acceptance. Tito Puente went back on the bar stereo. Said the bartendress, as the game ended and the clientele began to leave, "Well, Michael Jordan has fucking ruined the playoffs."

That might be a bit harsh, but it captured the feeling of many Sox fans I spoke with over the next few days. And the Sox played as if they were shell-shocked the following afternoon. Errors by Dan Pasqua (manager Gene Lamont's lame attempt at playing a hunch) and Joey Cora (I don't know how many times I heard him compared to "a deer in the headlights" during the playoffs, but it was at least five, from five different sources) led to two unearned runs, which cost Alex Fernandez the game.

The Sox were reborn in Toronto, winning the third game behind Wilson Alvarez and the fourth behind Tim Belcher out of the bullpen, with unexpected offensive power provided in the latter by Johnson (who gave the Sox the lead with his first homer of the year in the second and their final lead with a two-run triple in the sixth) and long-awaited power from Thomas (who tied the game ahead of Johnson with a homer in the sixth). Yet McDowell was thumped again in game five (newspaper rumors have it that he was tipping his pitches), and the Sox came home facing elimination a week ago Tuesday.

There was cause for optimism. The Sox had their two hottest pitchers lined up, in Fernandez and Alvarez. Yet, on the whole, the mood of the city was that of a death watch. A friend called up in midafternoon with an extra skybox seat and said I was the tenth guy he'd offered it to (no offense, none taken). And although I had planned to watch again at Puffer's, I parked for the last time this season on State Street, just north of 35th, in a half-legal spot next to a bus stop, and walked over and met him at the el station.

We were stuck in a skybox with a bunch of suits (my friend had only been offered the tickets himself earlier in the day). I was the only one taking the trouble to keep score, but to their credit they did have the skybox windows open, even on this cold night. (There was no distinction to be made between April and October cold on this evening; it was just plain frigid.) Yet Fernandez, supposedly a cold-weather pitcher, started colder than the weather. He walked the leadoff batter in the second, hit the next man, and following a sacrifice bunt and another walk allowed a two-run single. The Sox countered with two in the third (there was a bases-loaded walk to Thomas), but that's all they would get while the game was in doubt. Dave Stewart, the old Oakland Athletics ace—even now unbeaten in eight lifetime decisions in the playoffs—looked as if he had been thawed out for the occasion. Returning to the locker room while the Jays batted, checking with manager Cito Gaston that he would remain in the game, he allowed only two hits after the Sox' third-inning uprising before leaving for the Jays' bull pen closer, Duane Ward, in the eighth.

Simply put, the Jays proved themselves the better team. Their lineup was solid with all-stars through the seven slot, and eight and nine were filled by time-tested pressure players, Sprague and Pat Borders (he got the two-run single off Fernandez in the second). Gaston used the same nine players in each game and did not make a single nonpitching substitution during the entire series. The Sox, meanwhile, sniped at one another in the media, hit erratically in the clutch, booted the ball around in the field (Toronto's lead run in the fourth in the deciding game was, of course, unearned), and—with ace McDowell getting bombed in both his games—pitched poorly overall. It was the sort of performance that made one loath even to think about next year.

The fans went silent after the Blue Jays were first to score, and they got involved in the game only sporadically after that. Some booed before leaving. Others remained to the very end, clapping diligently as the Jays celebrated on the field and the Sox relievers and backup catchers trudged in from the bull pen. The season was over, winter was coming, and this year, quite suddenly, there was no Michael Jordan to look forward to.

Losses are not death, not even when they end seasons, and neither are retirements. In general, I agree with the title character in Richard Ford's novel *The Sportswriter*, who thinks that one of the few things to be learned from sports is that "there are no transcendent themes in life. In all cases things are here and they're over, and that has to be enough." But Jordan's retirement had the feeling of a violent or sudden death in that one had to come to terms with the idea that either one had savored Jordan in flight or missed him altogether; there was to be no last opportunity to save up memories, no adequate chance to say good-bye. The greatest athlete any of us is ever likely to see was here, and then he was gone. May he have a long, satisfying, and peaceful retirement. Life goes on; sports goes on. But sometimes "wait till next year" is more hollow than even a cliché has any right to be.

"Don't Worry About Getting Hurt"

October 9, 2003

THIS YEAR'S Cubs are a breed apart. They're different from the Cubs of the past—even the relatively successful Cubs of 1984, '89, and '98—in that they're less lovable but more steely and determined. That attitude is epitomized by Mark Prior, who established himself as the team's ace in the second half of the season by going 10–1 with a 1.52 earned run average. That was after spending three weeks on the disabled list because of a July collision with Atlanta Braves second baseman Marcus Giles in a baserunning gaffe at Wrigley Field.

With his cap pulled low on his forehead, leaving only his jaw to jut out of the shadows as he delivered a mid-nineties fastball and a biting curve, Prior took the Cubs beyond where even manager Dusty Baker had led them. It was no coincidence that he had a critical role in two of the wildest days—and nights—in memory at Wrigley Field: the Central Division–clinching double header two Saturdays ago and the game three victory over the Braves last Friday. On each occasion the scene was familiar—most reminiscent of the two games the Cubs won to open the 1984 play-offs, which they went on to lose to the San Diego Padres—but also radically new. These Cubs seemed to expect to win, as the championship-era Bulls had. These Cubs, as embodied by Prior, didn't elicit a fan's love and mere jubilation at good fortune, but rather admiration and respect—an unusual sensation at the Friendly Confines.

Though the sparse crowd, slow to arrive for the early start, roared with surprising strength from the moment he emerged from the dugout, Prior was typically stoic as he walked to the bullpen to warm up for the opener of that double header with the Pittsburgh Pirates. The Cubs had entered the final weekend in an identical tie for first with the Astros at 86–73, but had been rained out on Friday while the Astros were losing to the Cubs' regional rivals—and sudden best friends—the Milwaukee Brewers. Everyone knew that if the Cubs won both games and the Astros lost again the Cubs would clinch the division title, though that seemed highly unlikely.

Prior came out throwing a ninety-four-mile-an-hour fastball. After allowing a hit to the leadoff man, he dropped a couple of lovely curves on Pittsburgh's dangerous Jason Kendall before fanning him with a fastball, then struck out ex-Cub Matt Stairs with a curve to end the frame.

Dark-bottomed clouds like those at the start of *The Simpsons* rolled slowly across the sky, and the bleachers filled quickly while the grandstand gradually packed. The fall afternoon was placid only on the surface. Every fan watched the hand-operated scoreboard for signs of life behind the shuttered slots, and when the Astros scored in the bottom of the first there was a sense that, well, that was expected. But when the Brewers put two on the board in the third, there was a sudden rise of energy in the crowd; people could almost smell it, the potential for something grand and historic to happen.

In the fourth, Prior left a high fastball out over the plate, and Craig Wilson pounded it into the left-field bleachers. Prior didn't look sharp. He was making a lot of pitches and seemed to be overthrowing. Usually his motion is so compact and efficient that the ball flies out of his hand like a fighter jet catapulted off the deck of a carrier, but he seemed to have to work to throw it hard on this day—a bad sign and perhaps a dangerous one, as he'd been averaging 130 pitches a start in September, heavy use for someone just turning twenty-three and finishing his first full season in the majors. Still, he always made the pitch he needed to get himself out of the moderate trouble he'd gotten himself into, and the Cubs came to his rescue in the fourth and fifth.

Mark Grudzielanek led off the fourth with a hit, and Sammy Sosa and Moises Alou followed with walks from former White Sox phenom Josh Fogg. Aramis Ramirez grounded to short, but Alou went in hard at second to break up the double play as Grudzie scored. "Aloooooo!" the crowd yelled. Randall Simon used his buggy-whip swing to loft a fly to left that scored Sosa and put the Cubs in front, 2–1. Minutes later Wes Helms homered for the Brewers in Houston, only moments before Cubs catcher Damian Miller responded in kind, putting both teams up 3–1. I was watching in the press box and saw the Helms homer on TV, but all the fans had to go on that something was up in Houston was a pitching change announced on the scoreboard. Prior followed Miller's shot with a single and came around to score on a Sosa sacrifice fly. The Cubs led 4–1, and then the scoreboard put up a 3 for the Brewers in the sixth, making it 5–1 in Houston. Excitement was building in the fans like steam in a kettle, and even in the press box one reporter—I swear it wasn't me—gasped "Yes!" at a Prior strikeout, prompting Cubs media relations director Sharon Pannozzo to utter the familiar admonition "There is no cheering in the press box" over our speakers.

After giving up a run in the sixth, Prior walked a man with two out in the seventh on his 133rd pitch, prompting Baker to remove him for Kyle Farnsworth. Farnsworth finished the inning, but then walked the leadoff man in the eighth—a cardinal sin with a 4–2 lead. But he worked through it, and turned the game over to closer Joe Borowski in the ninth. The Astros, meanwhile, scored a run in the seventh but then went quietly. When the 5–2 final went up on the scoreboard, fans went ape. Here it was, the chance to make history. "Let's go, Cubs!" they chanted. Borowski got into some two-out trouble in the final frame, but Kendall popped to Grudzie to end the game. The Cubs had clinched a tie for first, and needed only to win one of the final two against the Bucs to claim first outright.

Yet it wasn't that simple. If the chin-bearded Matt Clement lost the nightcap, the Cubs would have to send Kerry Wood to the mound in the regular season finale. If they clinched with a sweep, they could save Wood for the Tuesday opener of their series with the Braves. Clement stepped purposefully on the foul line—ignoring all baseball superstitions—in taking the mound and proceeded to mix a ninety-mile-an-hour fastball with a hanging slider that got him into trouble but bit just often enough to get him out of it. He allowed hits in each of the first three innings but managed to keep the Pirates from scoring, and by that time the game was blessedly in hand.

Sosa started things off—as he so often did this season—with a gargantuan homer in the first. He crushed a low pitch from fireballer Ryan Vogelsong and, hopping almost out of his shoes, sent it up, up, and away, over the shrubbery of the hitting background and into the refreshment stand at the base of the deep-center-field bleachers. The fans roared; they could feel it. When the Cubs opened the second with four straight hits—Ramon Martinez's scooted under the glove of the second baseman like a mouse under a kitchen counter to score Ramirez—the call went forth across the North Side. The Cubs scored five that inning to open a 6–0 lead, and it was just a matter of time.

A few pockets of fans had vanished after the first game, but after that no one left. The rooftops all around filled as the evening came on, and word circulated that the cops were closing down the streets in every direction. In the middle innings Clement's fastball began to sink, and he mowed down the Pirates. Expectation built. He gave up a couple of runs in the seventh and departed, but Mike Remlinger ended the inning and Dave Veres came in to mop up the final outs.

By that time Alou had added a shot onto Waveland Avenue to make it 7–2, and I'd moved down into some unoccupied seats in the lower deck behind home plate. Everyone was standing in the ninth, shouting and screaming. A guy in front of me was listening to the game on the radio on headphones, and I asked him how Ron Santo sounded. "Real crazy!" he shouted, with a lunatic grin of his own. Santo, I later heard, was saying it was the best he'd ever felt, and I think many fans would have echoed that. When Veres got the last outs on a double-play grounder after a walk, the place went mad—but reservedly so. The players clustered so that no one could make out individuals; it was their wives and children, ushered onto the field and hugging and dancing with one another when they weren't watching their men celebrate, who offered the best visual expression of the team's jubilation. The Cubs finally broke it up and circled the field for a victory lap, the fans all screaming and yelling; then a few players went into the dugout and emerged with champagne from the clubhouse and started spraying one another.

I was watching the beginning of the scene in the clubhouse when Baker came in, started congratulating everyone he met, and then was turned around by Pannozzo and headed toward the media interview room. I hightailed it after them and wound up following Baker across the infield as thirty-five thousand fans—and more on the rooftops—cheered his name. He had insisted all along, since taking the job last fall, that this scenario, as unlikely as it seemed after ninety-five years without a championship, was possible, and now here it was—reality. The players said they couldn't have done it without him.

"Dusty told us, respect the history, but it has no bearing on us," Eric Karros said afterward.

"Feel free to believe in us," Remlinger added. "Don't worry about getting hurt."

What odd advice for Cubs fans!

I don't know if it was the air of purposeful confidence the Cubs gave off—the feeling that getting there was not enough, as it had been in 1998, that there was still work to be done—or just the drain of watching two exciting ball games, but the celebration inside and outside the stadium wasn't as raucous as it had been in 1984, when the Cubs clinched on the road and we all went pouring out of the neighborhood bars and into the Wrigleyville streets. Yet it didn't take long to reach that fever pitch when the Cubs returned to Wrigley last Friday for the third game of their series with the Braves. The Cubs had won the opener in Atlanta on a masterful performance by Kerry Wood. The only hit he gave up when the game was in doubt was a homer to Marcus Giles on an inside fastball Giles somehow got around on without hitting it foul. Carlos Zambrano lost the second game, as the Cubs' offense scored two but left the bases loaded in the first inning and then sputtered to a halt. Yet now the Cubs had Prior going again, on a full four days' rest, and even though he was facing turncoat Greg Maddux, the craftiest pitcher of his generation, confidence rather than dread reigned supreme.

Traffic was snarled all around the park in the dark, misty chill after a day of rain, and the crowd was slow to arrive. (Baker later talked of how fans seemed to have "dropped out of the sky" at the start of the game.) Oddly enough, Prior emerged from the dugout just as public-address announcer Paul Friedman was starting to give the lineups, so the usual roar of greeting as Prior walked down to the bullpen was swallowed by the larger set of cheers. Prior worked methodically through his stretching and long tossing before taking the bullpen mound, while the older Maddux was already warming up on the Braves' side in the cold. That was when I looked up into the stadium lights and saw the swirling mist form tangible raindrops that fell from the sky in larger and larger sizes. Prior and Maddux scurried to their dugouts, and the start of the game was delayed thirty minutes. The disruption seemed to affect Maddux more than Prior, who hadn't really begun to warm in earnest before the

rain. Prior's control was off, as he walked four men in the first four innings and whacked another, the Braves' dangerous Gary Sheffield, with
an errant pitch in the sixth. But through seven innings he allowed only
a single hit, to Giles, and no runs. Maddux, meanwhile, twinged a calf
muscle in the process of warming, halting, and warming anew, and gave
up two runs in the first. Kenny Lofton, the Cubs' second-half spark plug,
led off by slashing a cut fastball into right field and went to second when
Grudzie reached on an eely bunt that eluded slipping first baseman
Robert Fick. Maddux got Sosa and Alou and seemed about to work out
of it when Simon—who makes life hard for a pitcher of Maddux's craft
because "I always swing at everything and I hit everything," as he later
explained—swished one down the right-field line to score two. Those
were all the runs Prior would need.

He was something to watch, relying on his mid-nineties fastball early
and an increasing number of curves later in the game as he regained a
feel for the pitch. The crowd of 39,982 rose to its feet every time he got
two strikes on a batter with two out—and then just whenever he got two
strikes. He received a huge ovation hitting in the seventh but gave up a
run in the eighth on a double by pinch hitter Mark DeRosa, who came
around to score on a sacrifice fly. The Cubs got it right back in the bottom
half, as Alou singled, stole second, and scored on a Ramirez double off
Atlanta reliever Kevin Gryboski. Baker never seemed to seriously consider taking Prior out. Having thrown 115 pitches, he took the mound to
raucous applause in the top of the ninth and mowed the Braves down on
nineteen more tosses, actually retiring four batters: Javier Lopez struck
out but reached base when a biting curve got past Miller. When Fick
popped to Grudzie for the final out, Prior pumped his fist slowly, raised
it above his head as the catch was made, and pumped it again. Before he
was pulled aside for a postgame TV interview on the field, he tipped his
cap to the fans in the grandstand. Gods may not answer letters, but they
do sometimes acknowledge applause.

Clement couldn't finish the job the way he had against the Pirates.
Starting the fourth game at Wrigley last Saturday—as men, women, and
children wore muffs on their chins in a show of support—he struggled.
Handed a 1–0 lead, he gave up a run in the third and three in the fourth
as Chipper Jones hit a two-run homer. Jones added another two-run shot

off Mark Guthrie in the eighth, negating two solo homers by Karros. The final was 6–4, with Sosa hopping as his long fly off John Smoltz died on the warning track for the final out.

Wood took the mound in Sunday's deciding game back in Atlanta. Which Wood would he be—the one who threw too many pitches early in the season and routinely turned games over to the bullpen, or the one who toughened and responded to Prior's challenge for the title of staff ace late in the year? Sporting a "Mark Prior" baseball mitt, Wood made it clear from the outset he was the latter. The Cubs gave him a run in the first on a Lofton double and an Alou single, and another in the second on a homer by Alex Gonzalez—who always seems to have a role in critical situations—and they were all he'd require. Ramirez hit a two-run homer in the sixth to make the score 4–0, and even though an umpire's muffed call cost Wood a run in the bottom half, he turned a 5–1 lead over to Borowski in the ninth.

Make no mistake, the Cubs wouldn't have approached the playoffs without Baker as manager. But I don't believe they'd have advanced to the National League Championship Series without Prior. The example he set was a statement that making the playoffs was not sufficient, that nothing was worth playing for but the championship, and it was contagious. If the Minnesota Twins had ponied up the money to draft him in 2001, they'd be playing this weekend for the World Series, and the Cubs would still be looking for their first postseason series victory since 1908.

Bartman: The Fans' Complicity

October 24, 2003

WHEN I CLIMBED the steps into the grandstand before the first game of the National League Championship Series, Wrigley Field appeared more beautiful than I had ever seen it. After a full day of Indian-summer sun the park was warm and welcoming—even if Sammy Sosa, taking batting practice, had already settled into fall fashion and sported a blue watch cap. The wind wafted out to straightaway center, and the ball carried well, each crack of the bat echoing off the grandstand with a little extra crispness in the thin autumn air. The setting sun, low on the horizon, gave everything a rosy glow, and the ivy on the outfield walls was just beginning to hint at another color. Indeed, reserve catcher Josh Paul would soon take to calling this team "the red-ivy Cubs," for how late they played into the season. So, before we advance to the inevitable realization that red ivy is also dying ivy, before we grant that the Cubs' demise on October 15 came too soon even if it was the latest game ever played at Wrigley, let's preserve that image of the Friendly Confines as if under a massive glass dome. In great beauty lay the seeds of great tragedy.

The story of this season's Cubs was, of course, a tragedy, full of curses and omens, heroes and goats, and both players and fans complicit in the team's collapse simply because they acted according to their natures. As Terry Eagleton pointed out in *Sweet Violence*, his fine recent book, the postmodern world is not conducive to tragedy, full as it is of colorful irony and a moral spectrum that tends toward a prevailing gray. But I think most Chicago fans experienced the end of the season as pure tragedy—pure as one can have without the intrusion of an actual death.

The other memory worth preserving is the unique feel of playoff baseball, the way the sport builds slowly toward a series of climaxes, and how the smallest details—misjudgments, mistakes, great plays, perfect pitches—combine to determine the final victor. Baseball aficionados champion the game as the best of all sports for this very quality, that so much is left to chance—to who's up when, to a perfectly if accidentally

54

placed hit—yet everything comes down to the performance of each individual. The same mixture of fate and self-determination is present in April baseball, but it's refined in the playoffs, becoming headier and more intoxicating the deeper one goes toward the World Series. In the end, of course, it's whether those intangibles result in winning or losing that defines a team—and its fans.

The upstart Florida Marlins came into the series a young, loose, effervescent club unburdened by history or expectations; they were fearless, even after falling behind 3–1 in the best-of-seven series, and populated with characters ranging from the revitalized veteran catcher Ivan "Pudge" Rodriguez to pesky center fielder Juan Pierre, who wore his cap askew with the sandlot insouciance of the Minnesota Twins' Torii Hunter, as well as to familiar, fresh-faced Kane County Cougars alumni Luis Castillo (class of '95), Josh Beckett ('00), and Miguel Cabrera ('01). This year's Cubs, by contrast, were hyperaware of history; one of the encouraging things about them was the way everyone acknowledged it. Manager Dusty Baker's mantra was that the players must respect the team's ignominious past yet it had nothing to do with them. Meanwhile, Cubs management trotted out familiar symbols of past debacles—Ryne Sandberg of the 1984 squad and Fergie Jenkins from 1969 both threw out ceremonial first pitches in the NLCS—and Cubs theme songs were revived without dread: "Hey Hey, Holy Mackerel" (1969), "Go Cubs Go" and Van Halen's "Jump" (1984), and even KC and the Sunshine Band's "Get Down Tonight" (1998). These Cubs seemed to be the group steely and determined enough to confront and finally overcome the team's past. They were five outs from the World Series. Yet suddenly they succumbed, becoming perhaps the single greatest expression of that legacy of losing. That's what is most frustrating—the lovable losers seemed about to become victors. Yet they turned out to be Cubs after all, and there was something both reassuringly secure and bitterly disappointing in that.

The first game might have warned everyone what was to come, because in many ways it was the series in miniature. The Cubs pounded across four runs in the first inning when Beckett inexplicably left his curveball in the bullpen. Kenny Lofton walked. Mark Grudzielanek showed bunt, then hammered the ball over Pierre's head for a triple, and Moises Alou hit a towering shot just inside the left-field foul pole that set off the first of several melees involving fans chasing balls on Waveland Avenue. Aramis Ramirez tripled on another Beckett fastball and scored on a double by Alex Gonzalez.

Yet, handed a 4–0 lead, Carlos Zambrano became the first of the Cubs' young pitchers to give way to the strain of working more than two hundred innings this season. His velocity was in the mid-nineties, but his pitches had no movement, and he gave up five runs in the third when three of four straight batters homered. Rodriguez mashed a fastball to drive in his first three of what would become an NLCS record ten runs batted in, Cabrera homered on another fastball, and Juan Encarnacion whacked a changeup into the left-field bleachers. Cabrera scored again in the sixth, with the help of a Paul Bako passed ball, to make it 6–4, but the Cubs tied the game in the bottom half when Randall Simon doubled on a Beckett fastball and Gonzalez hit one into the right-field basket. When the Cubs squandered a leadoff double by Damian Miller in the seventh, the momentum swung back to the Marlins, and helped along by Grudzie's misplayed grounder they scored two runs in the ninth off Joe Borowski. With Florida closer Ugueth Urbina coming on, the game seemed over. But Lofton doubled to get Sosa to the plate with two out, and on a 1–2 count—mighty Casey territory—he smashed an Urbina slider into the darkness of Waveland. There was joy in Wrigleyville, and if the Cubs lost anyway when Mark Guthrie gave up a homer to Mike Lowell in the eleventh, it promised to be a long, good series. The fans were quieted but unbowed. All through the park, one could hear the Marlins slapping hands near the pitcher's mound, but one fan behind their dugout called out, "Celebrate now, boys! It'll be the last time you do!"

Dusty Baker called the loss "disheartening" but quickly added, "We come back with our horses the next two games," meaning Castor and Pollux aces Mark Prior and Kerry Wood. As I walked home from the bus stop that night, I saw a guy sitting on the front steps of his apartment building, his head literally in his hands.

"Cub fan?" I said.

He growled an affirmative.

"I was there," I said. "I saw Dusty. He said we have our two horses going the next two games. They'll go in games six and seven."

He looked up. "Thanks, man," he said.

See, everyone felt these Cubs were different. We believed.

What saps.

Yet Prior justified that optimism the following night. Displaying the grit that seemed to separate him from all other Cubs aces, he worked out of jams in the first and second innings, then cruised, as the Cubs gave him two runs in the first, three in the second—two of them on a gargantuan Sosa homer off the top of the camera shack deep in the center-field bleachers—and three more in the third. Fueled by chants of "Let's go Prior!" clap, clap, clapclapclap, and tinkering, he later admitted, with his changeup to keep himself engaged, he coasted to a 12–3 victory. A full yellow moon was rising over the Sheffield Avenue apartment buildings that night, and as I walked home I looked up at it to see a V of honking geese heading south—like the Cubs for Florida.

Chicagoans took to the city's bars en masse for the third game. My little group couldn't find seats in one Ashland Avenue tavern, so we went up the street to a restaurant and watched on the bar TV there, dining all the while with a small but devoted group of fellow fans. It was another tense eleven-inning affair, won by the Cubs this time, an outcome that distracted from what could later be recognized as the first cracks in the team's facade. Lofton led off the game with a single off the soft-tossing lefty Mark Redman, went to second on a Grudzie bunt, and scored on a Sosa single to give the Cubs the lead. Wood himself padded it with a sacrifice fly in the second that scored Eric Karros, but gave back a run in the bottom half and after that struggled to maintain the 2–1 lead. He totally lost his rhythm in the fifth with two out, walking the pitcher, giving up a hit to Pierre, and walking Castillo to load the bases, but pulled himself together to fan Rodriguez on three straight breaking pitches. He wasn't so lucky in the seventh, getting himself in a jam and then giving up run-scoring singles to Castillo and Rodriguez on low, straight fastballs. Baker worked a bit of magic in the eighth, calling on Tom Goodwin and Simon to pinch-hit back-to-back at the bottom of the order. Goodwin tripled, and Simon followed by lashing a first-pitch fastball off Chad Fox into the right-field seats. Yet Borowski couldn't nail down the save, and the game went into extra innings tied at four. There it stood until the 11th, when Lofton singled with one out, and Baker worked what would turn out to be his last trick of the year. He sent Doug Glanville up to pinch-hit and called a hit-and-run. Glanville slapped the ball directly through the spot in the infield vacated by the shortstop covering second, and the ball scooted past left fielder Jeff Conine all the way to the wall for a run-scoring triple. In a last bit of good fortune, Ramirez booted a game-ending grounder to third in the bottom half, only to find Castillo running from second straight toward him. Ramirez tagged him for the final out. The Cubs had won, 5–4, and led the series 2–1. Their horses had held on, if not entirely by themselves.

The chin-bearded Matt Clement faced former Cubs farmhand Dontrelle Willis—the player he was traded for last season—in the fourth game. Willis, of the ebullient demeanor epitomized by his leg kick, was nervous in the first inning, and it cost him. He gave up a leadoff hit to Lofton and walked Sosa and Alou before surrendering a grand slam to Ramirez on a low, inside fastball. At that moment, when the ball went up and we all waited to see if it would stay fair and the TV camera settled on an empty section of seats just right of the left-field foul pole, we all of us knew that this was it, this was the team that would go to the World Series and perhaps even win it against either a less-than-stellar New York Yankees team or a Boston Red Sox squad that was all hitting and no pitching. Staked to the big lead, Clement worked efficiently into the eighth and turned the game over to Kyle Farnsworth, who mopped up the 8–3 win. The Cubs were up 3–1 and needed only one more victory, with two games scheduled at home and "the horses" lined up—if need be.

Yet before they left Florida, the Cubs ran into a buzz saw in the form of a refocused Beckett. Loyal readers will recall I wrote about him three years ago (though they might remember that column better as the one about finding a yard to park my dog in before I could see him pitch), and this was the game where he delivered on all the promise he showed in Kane County. Mixing the mid-nineties fastball and the biting curve he had even then with a wicked, drifting ninety-mile-an-hour "changeup," he mowed the Cubs down to claim a 4–0 two-hit shutout. Zambrano was gritty but weary in giving up two runs, and he got little support from relievers Dave Veres and Mike Remlinger. Even so, the Cubs were coming home, where Prior would no doubt settle things, thus setting Wood up for the first game of the World Series with Prior himself available for the second game.

Hours before game time, thick groups of fans made their way on foot to Wrigley Field—some to attend the game, some to watch in Wrigley-ville bars, some just to stand on Waveland Avenue and wait for the grand celebration. Not even during the Bulls' championship runs had I experienced anything quite like the anticipation of the crowd going into the sixth game. It was like the first two games of the 1984 NLCS against the San Diego Padres, only doubled or tripled, because the confidence was the same but this time the coup de grace would be administered here at Wrigley. Prior received a huge ovation in the pregame introductions and cheers all down the left-field grandstand as he made his way to the dugout after warming up in the bullpen. From the first pitch—a ninety-four-mile-an-hour fastball—the crowd chanted, "Let's go Cubs!" As in game two, Prior struggled early to gain mastery over his pitches—and the Marlins—but he worked out of a jam with runners at the corners in the first and after that limited the Marlins to a base runner an inning through the first five. Sosa, meanwhile, once again drove in Lofton for a go-ahead run in the first, deflecting a slider from the angular Carl Pavano down the right-field line. The crowd roared, and I wrote in my notebook what no doubt many were thinking: "My God, it's here. It's finally here." An anxious calm settled over the fans in the middle innings, just as Prior found the touch on his curve, striking out Rodriguez and Cabrera in order with it while retiring eight straight batters.

Pavano maintained the 1–0 deficit into the sixth, when he allowed Sosa to reach third. Florida manager Jack McKeon called on Willis to relieve, but Willis threw a wild pitch to bring the run home. The Cubs pushed across another in the seventh, when Bako led off with a single, went to second on a Prior bunt—Prior received a standing ovation trotting back to the dugout—and scored on a two-out single by Grudzie off reliever Chad Fox.

"Let's go, Prior!" the fans chanted to start the eighth, and Mike Mordecai popped up to become the eighth straight hitter he'd retired.

"Every out—elation—CLOSER CLOSER," I jotted.

Mordecai would be the last man Prior retired this year.

Pierre slapped a 2–2 fastball into left field for a double, and with that Prior seemed to have lost his out pitch. The count went full on Castillo, then he fouled two off, and on the eighth pitch of the at bat he sent a high pop down the left-field line. Most fans in the grandstand could see Alou in hot pursuit and with a possible play, but that was lost on Steven Bartman, sitting in the first row of seats and listening to headphones that no doubt muffled the crowd reaction. Just as Alou leaped to make the grab at the top of the wall, Bartman reached out, blocked the ball, and deflected it into the crowd.

He didn't even make the catch.

Alou was irate, and a noticeably miffed Prior argued fan interference—to no avail. The chant of "Ass-hole! Ass-hole!" began in the right-field bleachers and soon circled the stadium, and by that time Bartman was shriveling in his seat as the realization no doubt came to him that his life would never be the same. It would never be the same because Prior threw a wild pitch with his next delivery, walking Castillo and sending Pierre to third. He got two strikes on Rodriguez but then left an 0–2 curve out over the plate, and Rodriguez lined it into left to score Pierre. Then, in the most critical play of the game, Cabrera grounded a first-pitch curve to short, where Gonzalez had made a mere ten errors all season. Yet he booted the ball trying to backhand it, and everyone was safe. Derrek Lee, hog-tied by Chicago pitching all series and 0–3 on the night, hit a first-pitch fastball into the left-field gap for a double, tying the game and chasing Prior. After he left the game, 39,577 fans went utterly silent as the Marlins pushed five more runs across the plate against Farnsworth and Remlinger. The Cubs went meekly in the last two innings, with Urbina not even breaking a sweat, leaving him ready to go again in game seven, when Beckett would be available out of the pen.

Baker was less than inspirational afterward. "History had nothing to do with this game—nothing," he insisted, but admitted to being stunned by Gonzalez's error, "because he doesn't miss anything. And then after that we couldn't stop the bleeding."

McKeon, projecting a cranky cool that was part Charlie Weaver and part Robert Forster, declared that this was the Marlins' modus operandi. "Give us an opening and we'll come through," he said. "We're coming out here playing nice and loosey-goosey, and whatever happens tomorrow night happens. We're not putting any pressure on ourselves."

He'd leave that to the Cubs.

Walking home after the sixth game, again I heard the honk of geese overhead. They were crossing the sky not in a V formation but in a ragged line, unable to settle on a leader, heading dead west. It was like an omen out of Macbeth.

All through the second half of the season, Wood had followed Prior's lead in pitching with steely determination. When Prior crumbled, Wood did too. Gripping his curve too tight and throwing it repeatedly in the dirt in front of the plate, he gave up a leadoff triple to Pierre on a fastball with no movement on it. An out and a walk later, he threw a low, inside, straight fastball to Cabrera on a 1–2 count, and Cabrera lined it into the left-field bleachers for a 3–0 Florida lead. Even then, the Cubs were able to torment their fans with a couple of final thrills. The bottom of the order tied the game off Redman with three runs in the second, two of them coming on a home run by Wood himself. That sent 39,574 fans jumping up and down, waving their hands over their heads—they looked like computer-generated animation in a video game—not to mention the thousands more packing Waveland. When Alou mashed a 1–0 fastball into the left-field bleachers with Sosa on in the third, putting the Cubs up 5–3, optimism surged through the crowd. We were going after all. But Wood went flat again in the fifth. He walked the leadoff man and Castillo one out later, and grooved a first-pitch curve to Rodriguez, who lined a double into left field for his tenth RBI of the series. Baker for some reason played the infield back, and Cabrera's grounder to first scored Castillo with the tying run. Lee then lined a first-pitch fastball into right field to score Rodriguez and put the Marlins up 6–5.

In the bottom of the fifth McKeon did as I feared and called on Beckett. If he could get three shutout innings from Beckett and two more from Urbina, the Cubs would be toast. As it was, he got four good innings out of Beckett—with only a Troy O'Leary pinch solo homer to interrupt the twelve outs—and one from Urbina. And the homer became meaningless after the Marlins touched Wood and Farnsworth for an insurance run in the sixth and scored two more—all the action coming with two out—in the seventh. In the bottom of the eighth Sosa took a Beckett fastball on the outside corner for strike three, and when Alou followed with an inning-ending groundout the crowd again went utterly silent. When the

Marlins won 9–6 and started celebrating on the field, their shouts and slaps could be heard throughout Wrigley Field. At first very few people left, and after a few moments a chant of "Cubbies! Cubbies!" broke out behind the Cubs' dugout. But no player emerged to take a curtain call; no one acknowledged the applause. More than half an hour later, after Baker had briefly waved to the remaining fans while crossing the field going to and from the interview room, dozens of individuals still sat in their seats, as if stunned into paralysis.

Cubs fans: the largest documented mass outbreak of Stockholm syndrome.

The prevailing mood, reinforced by the spin Baker tried to put on the defeat afterward, had it that this was a young team with a nucleus of Prior, Wood, and Zambrano that was taking its first steps toward a championship. I'm not so sure. Baker worked those three very hard this season, given the youth of Prior and Zambrano, and Wood's previous elbow surgery. After the seventh game, I had a long talk with *Baseball Prospectus* writer Will Carroll, an expert on baseball health, who had already written that, even if the heavy workload those three were put under this season didn't harm them right away, it might have an adverse effect that shows up next year or in seasons soon to come. We agreed that we'd already seen such an effect: Wood and Zambrano were noticeably less effective in their last starts of the season, and even Prior saw his stuff go all at once in the sixth game. Baker rode his horses hard, and they gave out on him on the border of the promised land.

So we come to the matter of culpability. It is my strong belief that if Alou had been able to make that catch down the left-field line Prior would have ended the threat with minimal damage, carrying the Cubs into the World Series against the Yankees. If Steven Bartman obeyed instinct by trying to catch the ball, he prompted the Cubs to obey their seemingly innate compulsion to self-destruct.

That was what was most frustrating. This year's Cubs promised a change, a transformation, a refusal to accept the status quo. When they returned to their old ways they taught a bitter lesson to those of us who'd resolved never to settle for such paltry pickings again. We were right to want and expect more, and we weren't going back to being lovable losers.

Even so, a century from now, if the Cubs still haven't won a World Series, every Chicago fan will know the name of Steven Bartman. In an instant he became the Fred Merkle, the Don Young, the black cat of baseball fans. I'm not glorying sadistically in that; simply stating a fact. Like the Cubs, he now must live with history and the consequences of his actions. Yet given the Cubs' official response in support of him, and given the way the team trots out Sam Sianis and his billy goat on an annual basis, and given the acceptance of most Cubs fans, I think we can look forward to the day when Bartman is called upon to throw out the first pitch at a Cubs playoff game, as the team continues to confront its past in anticipation of the time when someone—Prior or Wood or Sosa or some player yet unborn—comes along with the ability and the determination to free us all from the dull acceptance of the way things supposedly are meant to be.

Better Lucky Than Good

October 20, 2005

JOSH PAUL looked elated, and why not? After years of scuffling just to make the opening-day rosters of the White Sox and Cubs, he was in the playoffs as the Angels' third-string catcher. Born in Evanston and still a Naperville resident in the off-season, Paul was all smiles as he took batting practice at White Sox Park before the first game of the American League Championship Series. When a Chicago reporter asked him about the hair sprouting on his face, he said, "Playoff beard, just like the NHL guys—grow until you're done."

He's done.

Paul, as all fans know by now, played an unfortunate role in the pivotal play of the series. The Sox had lost the opener 4–3 and were lying prone at the feet of the Angels' bullpen when A. J. Pierzynski struck out to send the second game into extra innings knotted at 1–1. Paul rolled the ball back to the mound, the way all good catchers do, and Pierzynski turned and broke for first base as if the third strike had been dropped. Had it? Paul's actions made that possibility look unthinkable, and it looked as if home plate ump Doug Eddings had made both a strike call and an out call. But Pierzynski flummoxed the umps into seeing it his way, and once he got to first base he stayed there—over manager Mike Scioscia's fierce protest—until Sox manager Ozzie Guillen sent in Pablo Ozuna to pinch-run. Ozuna stole second, and then Joe Crede jumped all over a hanging split-finger fastball from Kelvim Escobar—who'd struck out five previous hitters, including Pierzynski, on splitters that had dived like a falcon after prey—and lined it into the left-field corner to win the game.

The Sox never looked back. They won four straight games to reach the World Series for the first time since 1959, in the process overcoming the curse of the 1919 Black Sox, last discerned in the 1994 baseball strike that aborted a potential championship and earlier in what I call "the Dybber's fuckhead catastrophe" of the 1983 championship series.

Baseball has a long, rich history, and many fans and analysts drew parallels with previous immortal gaffes. To my mind, however, the Pierzynski-Paul phantom–trapped third strike most resembled the infamous "Merkle boner" of 1908. Fred Merkle was a teenager with the New York Giants, who were locked in a fierce pennant race with the Cubs late in September, and he was on first base when Al Bridwell delivered what appeared to be a game-winning single with two out in the ninth. Except that Merkle, a scrub accustomed to running from the dugout to the center-field clubhouse after games at the Polo Grounds, took off for the clubhouse without touching second. The Cubs' Johnny Evers tracked down the ball in the crowd swirling onto the field and headed for second to force Merkle and end the inning without the run counting. But third-base coach "Iron Man" Joe McGinnity seized the ball from him and threw it into the stands. Evers apparently touched second with another ball, at which point Chicago manager Frank Chance dragged out the umpires and argued that Merkle should be out and the game ruled a 1–1 tie. They sided with him. The game would be replayed, if necessary—and after the Giants dropped five key games down the stretch, it was. The Cubs won and went on to what remains their last world championship.

"I'd rather be lucky than good," Guillen said after the second game of the Angels series, and it's a common sentiment in every sport. Ability you either have or you don't. Luck can be conjured. I'd made up my mind not to cut my hair until the Sox were done—in spite of the winged Paulie Walnuts sideburns—and my Sox pal Kate had presciently dreaded the first game because she recognized that bad luck was overdue: the Sox were on an eight-game winning streak and pitcher Jose Contreras was on a nine-game winning streak, each too long to sustain.

The Sox acted immediately to deal with this shift in fortune. Guillen went back to the standard black Sox warm-up jacket from the fashionable new vanilla-sleeved letterman's jackets he and his coaches had sported for game one. Mark Buehrle, who as the starting pitcher got to choose the uniform of the day, chose the short-sleeved pinstripe jersey after Contreras had gone sleeveless the night before. (Buehrle had followed the victorious Contreras in going sleeveless against the Boston Red Sox a week earlier.)

Leadoff man Scott Podsednik switched from high socks to low pants pulled down to his shoe tops. No doubt the fans had their own various mojos going as well, from inside-out rally caps to lucky shirts and underwear. I believe it was I who triggered the Sox' winning rally in the fifth game by removing the 1917 Sox cap I hadn't previously worn while watching games on TV, thus returning proper balance to the baseball universe.

But even if it's better to be lucky than good, best of all is to be both, and the great tend to make their own luck. So do the not-so-great. No one would have remembered the Merkle boner if the Cubs hadn't run the Giants down the last weekend of the season and won the replayed game. On the other hand, consider the Billy Goat curse placed on the Cubs at the 1945 World Series, which was followed by the collapses of 1969, 1984, and, of course, 2003. The public would have never known who Steve Bartman was (you knew it was coming, didn't you, Cubs fans?) if Mark Prior hadn't followed his interference play two years ago by walking Luis Castillo with a wild pitch, Alex Gonzalez hadn't booted a potential inning-ending double-play ball, and Ivan Rodriguez, Derrek Lee, and several other Florida Marlins hadn't come up with key hits. Not to mention if Kerry Wood hadn't given up the lead in the seventh game of the series the following night.

This is not apocryphal. It's a fact: pitcher Mark Redman turned to the others in the Marlins' dugout after Bartman's blunder and said, "All right, now let's make that kid famous." And they did.

And so I wrote to various other Sox fans the day after Paul's gaffe (he really should have given Pierzynski a tag just to remove any doubt) comparing the incident to the Merkle boner and finishing, "Now let's hope the Sox make Paul immortal." And they did.

They went to Anaheim, where Jon Garland, after a two-week layoff, followed in Buehrle's footsteps by pitching a complete-game victory. Freddy Garcia did the same the following night. And all along the Angels were victimized by bad calls and worse luck. In game four, for instance, Paul Konerko got the call on a borderline checked swing on a 2–2 count and hit Ervin Santana's next pitch, a hanging slider, out of the park for a three-run homer. Podsednik got picked off but was ruled safe, and came around to score. Pierzynski got away with undetected catcher interference on what turned into an inning-ending double play. (Steve Finley was already arguing as he ran down the line and got nailed by an eyelash, costing the Angels a run.)

At the same time, the free-swinging Angels were putty in the hands of the crafty Sox pitchers. At one point in the third game, Vladimir Guerrero had seen a total of eight pitches in five at-bats against Buehrle and Garland, going hitless and hitting into two double plays (he ended the series one for nineteen).

In the eighth inning of the fifth game, with the score tied at three, Pierzynski again got on base undeservedly with two out when Escobar tagged him with his mitt while holding the ball in his bare hand, and Crede again made the Angels pay by driving in the go-ahead run with a trickler up the middle.

Great teams find ways to make other teams feel cursed, in the process sometimes removing long-standing curses of their own. Poor Josh Paul— the longer the Angels go without another championship, the darker his lapse will loom. In Chicago let's agree to call it A. J. Pierzynski's stealing first, the play that sent the White Sox to the city's first World Series in forty-six years.

Destiny, Ability, and Camaraderie

November 3, 2005

ALL SPORTS, like all politics, is local. We can enjoy the skills of a Michael Jordan wherever we live, but it means something entirely different when Jordan plays in your town for your team. And in Chicago baseball is not merely local, in the sense of the hazy boundary line between the North and South sides, but tribal. It's something at once deeply personal and intensely public, and I heard that something erupt as I never had before—no, not even during the Bulls' six championships—with the final out of the World Series in the packed Bridgeport bar Cobblestones.

This was a sound unlike the roar one out earlier, when White Sox shortstop Juan Uribe went into the stands to steal a pop fly from the Houston crowd (an excruciating moment for Cubs fans haunted by the Steve Bartman incident two years earlier). That roar was guttural and appreciative: the championship so close yet not in hand, the Astros' tying run standing at second base in a 1–0 game. But when the last batter chopped a curveball over pitcher Bobby Jenks's glove and Uribe swooped in to nab it and throw a bullet on the run to first, the response was higher in pitch and sustained. It was the sound of a long-suffering tribe freed and triumphant. It was the joyful sound of catharsis. That sound, my friend, is what sports is about, and if you didn't know that joy when Uribe's throw beat the batter to first by an eyelash, I can only hope someday you do.

Less than a week before, on the day before the World Series began, elder statesman Paul Konerko explained the Sox' growing appeal by saying, "I think winning—people relate to that more than anything." But although the team attracted its share of bandwagon jumpers as it neared the championship, success wasn't exactly what made this year's Sox so captivating. That is, it wasn't just that winning created fans—the fans gave the championship its full significance. This World Series at last atoned for the Black Sox scandal, and for the Go-Go Sox teams of the '50s and '60s that could never get past the New York Yankees (and the one time they did, they couldn't get past the Los Angeles Dodg-ers). This series wiped away the frustration of the 1983 playoffs, when the Winnin' Ugly team was enchanted by the Baltimore Orioles' Mike Boddicker and the Dybber's fuckhead catastrophe spoiled Britt Burns's courageous pitching performance. In the end, at the ticker-tape rally when Konerko presented Sox chairman Jerry Reinsdorf with the ball from the final out, this series even rehabilitated Reinsdorf, who held the Sox hostage to get a publicly funded stadium fifteen years ago and played a big role in cutting short the 1994 season, when the Sox had what looked like their best chance in years to win a title.

"This team has done a good job of not worrying about the history of this organization," Konerko said. "I think the Red Sox did the same thing last year." But if the players had to put all of that history out of their minds, the fans clung to it and measured this year's achievement against it.

Fans who looked past the hype about curses saw a skilled and beauti-ful team—with the emphasis on team, on talents fitting together. To a man, the Sox players spoke of how much they enjoyed one another's company. "I think that it's destiny," said Jenks, a rookie who joined the team in July, "or a bunch of good guys who make a great team."

Chemistry is obvious on the basketball court, but it's intangible in baseball, which is such an individual sport, especially in the confronta-tion between pitcher and hitter. The bonding of baseball players, who spend so much time together, is vital to the team, but it needs to be ex-perienced firsthand, inside the locker room. Otherwise it's too subtle for the fan to see, except as it manifests itself in winning. "Winning makes winning like money makes money," in the immortal words of Henry "Author" Wiggen, the fictional pitcher of Bang the Drum Slowly, and of course it helped that the Sox led their league's Central Division from start to finish. The playoffs were more of the same: their series sweep gave them an 11–1 playoff record, tying a mark that had been set by the Yankees.

No team becomes a champion without unexpected contributions, and one of the pleasures of following a championship season is watching key players develop. Third baseman Joe Crede finally flowered into the impact player he'd been predicted to become when he was in the minors.

He'd been frequently criticized for his placid, distracted demeanor, but it turned out that under pressure, ice water runs through his veins. Whenever the Sox needed a clutch hit he seemed to show up saying, "You rang?" He capped a season of heroics with the go-ahead homer in the opener, when he also stymied the Astros with a series of diving stops, and he triggered the Sox' rally from a 4–0 deficit in the critical third game with an opposite-field homer off Houston ace Roy Oswalt. I've written before about the contributions of Tadahito Iguchi and Aaron Rowand, and of my personal choice for the team's most valuable player, catcher A. J. Pierzynski. Uribe completed a group that was rock solid up the middle. Yet to my way of thinking the keyest key player was pitcher Jose Contreras, and the pivotal game in the Sox' championship season was the series finale against the Yankees in August.

On a beastly hot day in a high-pressure game against his former team, with the Sox trying to halt a seven-game losing streak, Contreras held the Yankees at bay until the Sox erupted for four homers and six runs in one inning off Randy Johnson. That victory began a streak of nine straight for Contreras that extended into the playoffs. The difference in Contreras made the difference between a merely good first-place team, which the Sox were in 2000, and a playoff powerhouse.

Again there was that mix of destiny, ability, and camaraderie. Manager Ozzie Guillen said Contreras fulfilled his potential "not because we speak the same language but because he knows he has a friend in the manager." Guillen's way was to show faith in his players and protect them at all costs, even if it meant acting the fool from time to time to distract the media. Everyone from Contreras to the lowest benchwarmer responded, including Geoff Blum, who hit the game-winning homer in the fourteenth inning of game three, and Willie Harris, who led off the eighth inning of game four with a pinch-hit single, went to second on Scott Podsednik's bunt, advanced to third on a grounder to the right side by pinch hitter Carl Everett, and scored the game's only run on a trickler up the middle by Jermaine Dye—vintage Guillen small ball. That hit clinched MVP honors for Dye, but the honor could have gone to any of several players.

Every seat was taken, and despite temperatures in the forties a feeling of warmth and unity filled Sox Park for Chicago's first World Series game in forty-six years. It was in the cheers for Contreras as he went out to warm up, in the roar when Crede's homer sailed just beyond the reach of the leaping Willy Taveras into the center-field seats, and in the cheers as Jenks emerged from the bullpen to fan Jeff Bagwell on a hundred-mile-per-hour fastball to end the eighth. An inning later, when Jenks ended the game with another strikeout, fans jumped up and down and high-fived and hugged, then thanked their stars that the rain had held off.

The crowd the following night wasn't so lucky. A downpour canceled batting practice and a cool, spiky mist fell through the middle innings. I was watching in the warmth of the auxiliary press box down the left-field line, but I felt for the fans below. They looked especially miserable after Mark Buehrle, curling his mitt with nervous energy, squandered a 2–1 lead and fell behind 4–2. His counterpart, Andy Pettitte, labored in the cold like a horse pulling a carriage down Michigan Avenue, emitting huge steamy puffs of warm breath. Pettitte turned the lead over to the bullpen in the seventh, and the tension began to mount with Uribe's one-out double. When Iguchi walked with two out, all fans were on their feet. Dye loaded the bases on a dubious hit-by-pitch call, and Konerko came up with the crowd on the verge of hysteria. He clubbed a first-pitch fastball from Chad Qualls into the left-field seats, and as he lifted his arms and pumped his right fist trotting to first base, there was pandemonium.

Jenks, suffering a letdown from his previous night's heroics, allowed the Astros to tie the game in the ninth and prolong the fans' misery, but the outcome redeemed every minute of it. Podsednik got ahead of Houston closer Brad Lidge 2–1 in the bottom of the ninth and looked for a fastball. That's what he got, and he hammered it into the center-field seats. The fans went mad. They stood in the cold savoring the experience, and I ran down the ramps to the media interview room—where Konerko would take a friendly jab at Podsednik as they sat side by side, saying the Sox always thought they'd win, but "I don't think we thought it would be that quick—or on a home run by him." I thought of my friends Mike and Steve, soaked but happy in their right-field seats; of Kate, who no doubt had applied a little lucky lipstick moments before, wherever she was watching; of Wuk, who grew up a Sox fan on the South Side and now kept the faith deep in the enemy territory of Lake Bluff; and of our friend and colleague Jim Pecora, dead of cancer and buried this summer, who could talk eloquently in a smoke-tinged voice about the frustration of watching the Sox in the '50s and '60s, when they struggled to get past the hated Yankees.

I certainly wasn't alone in my reverie. It seems that all Sox fans were thinking of others near and dear, whether they could share in the moment or could not.

Mike Mulligan, a good friend and fine gentleman (in the words of former Sox announcer Bob Elson), had been in the stands, and he summed up the experience the following day on his WSCR show when he said, "If you were at that game, you deserved what happened." But it wasn't just that game. If you were a fan of the Sox for any stretch of the previous eighty-eight years you deserved this season every bit as much as the Sox themselves did. After all that time, it was full return on everything a fan invests in sports, a return all the more precious for how we never expected to see it.

Denying Our Own Eyes

July 20, 2006

I SUSPECTED Barry Bonds was using steroids as he hit his record seventy-three home runs in 2001; I felt sure of it by the start of the 2005 season. That's when the BALCO scandal was breaking, a year before the release of Mark Fainaru-Wada and Lance Williams's book *Game of Shadows*. But Bonds's leaked grand-jury testimony, the seed of the book, had little to do with my certainty. Rather, it was a table I saw comparing Bonds's seasons from his mid- to late-thirties with those of other baseball greats.

Babe Ruth at thirty-five: forty-nine homers and a .359 batting average; at thirty-six: forty-six and .373; at thirty-seven: forty-one and .341; at thirty-eight: thirty-four and .301; at thirty-nine: twenty-two and .288.

Ted Williams at thirty-five: twenty-nine and .345; at thirty-six: twenty-eight and .356; at thirty-seven: twenty-four and .345; at thirty-eight: thirty-eight and .388; at thirty-nine: twenty-six and .328.

Stan Musial at thirty-five: twenty-seven and .310; at thirty-six: twenty-nine and .351; at thirty-seven: seventeen and .337; at thirty-eight: fourteen and .255; at thirty-nine: seventeen and .275.

Hank Aaron at thirty-five: forty-four and .300; at thirty-six: thirty-eight and .298; at thirty-seven: forty-seven and .327; at thirty-eight: thirty-four and .265; at thirty-nine: forty and .301.

Willie Mays at thirty-five: thirty-seven and .288; at thirty-six: twenty-two and .263; at thirty-seven: twenty-three and .289; at thirty-eight: thirteen and .283; at thirty-nine: twenty-eight and .291.

Time afflicts us all, even baseball's immortals, and the table captures the ebbing skills of past greats as they aged from thirty-five to forty. But here's Bonds at thirty-five: forty-nine and .306; at thirty-six: seventy-three and .328; at thirty-seven: forty-six and .370; at thirty-eight: forty-five and .341; at thirty-nine: forty-five and .362.

Bonds produced not just a record seventy-three homers at age thirty-six but after that two of the greatest hitting seasons ever. His batting average when he was thirty-seven led the National League, and his 2004 season, when he was thirty-nine, featured a record .609 on-base percentage and an .812 slugging percentage, one of the highest of all time.

Much was written in those years marveling at how today's athletes keep themselves so much more fit than their predecessors. But the table offers stats of earlier players known for their conditioning, such as Hank Aaron, who maintained his statistical excellence but did not improve, and Stan Musial, who declined with injuries. Babe Ruth lived a life of excess and declined precipitously after a few last hurrahs (including his legendary called shot at thirty-seven at Wrigley Field). Ted Williams battled injuries triumphantly before fading.

Yet Bonds didn't merely fight off decay: he enormously improved. Meanwhile, I noticed that his skull looked bigger, a phenomenon linked anecdotally with human growth hormone. So in time I knew. Something too good to be true, I concluded, isn't.

But I didn't say so in print. I didn't even express doubt. I was like most in the media—from time to time considering the possibility that players were juiced, sometimes even mentioning it, but for the most part turning a blind eye. Mark McGwire and Sammy Sosa were asked about steroids during their 1998 home-run chase, and both denied using them, which was good enough for me and most writers. Of course, their sudden declines and abrupt retirements—Sosa's coinciding with baseball's tougher testing policy this year—said otherwise. Yet as late as the spring of 2005, the eminent *Baseball Prospectus*, my guide of choice, was writing in this vein on Bonds: "For all the hand-wringing, moralizing, and high-horsing the issue has triggered, the net effect of steroids on baseball players remains unknown. . . . We'll leave the moral outrage to someone else."

In the season and a half since, more than enough morally outraged reporters have taken up the slack. With anguish has come troubling self-examination. Steroids are illegal and, by most medical accounts, dangerous, and although a little cheating is actively encouraged in baseball—and amphetamines, or "greenies," have been part of the game for decades (going back to Jim Bouton's 1970 book *Ball Four* and beyond)—steroids offer too great an edge and exact too high a price to be permitted. How could we have let those players using them get away with it, even though we sensed—even though we knew—what they were doing? I found the answer to that question in history, in a new book about what remains baseball's darkest scandal.

The central point of Gene Carney's meticulously researched *Burying the Black Sox: How Baseball's Cover-Up of the 1919 World Series Fix Almost Succeeded* is that the attempt to conceal the fix—particularly by White Sox owner Charles Comiskey, who wanted to protect his roster, his fan base, and his profits—was potentially an even greater crime than the fix itself. Although talk of the fix was widespread before and during the Series, only sportswriter Hugh Fullerton pursued the subject after the season ended: for his pains he was derided by lapdog papers such as *The Sporting News*. Just like with steroids, for all the talk a grand jury investigation was needed to expose the scandal.

Then as now, the sports media didn't want to believe what they knew. Press-box crank Westbrook Pegler wrote in 1932: "The fake Series of 1919 produced some of the worst newspaper reporting that the American press ever has been guilty of and why all of us who were detailed to cover the show were not fired for missing the greatest sports story in 20 years is something I have never understood. We were terrible."

Eliot Asinof wrote, not in his *Eight Men Out* but in *1919: America's Loss of Innocence*, that "mostly the secrecy was maintained by the power of the owners themselves. Whatever they knew, or suspected, they concealed, terrified at losing the public faith in the game." Press skeptics were pooh-poohed, whistle-blowing players thanked and dismissed. "The official, if unspoken policy preferred to let the rottenness grow rather than risk the dangers of exposure, for all the pious phrases about the nobility of the game and its inspirational value to youth. In fact, that too was part of the business."

Retired boxing champion Abe Attell, who helped fix the Series, said this in 1944: "What I never could understand is why the blow-off took as long coming as it did. People knew it in Peoria and knew it six weeks before the Series. But I guess the answer is that baseball is such a great and decent game that they wouldn't believe their own eyes and ears."

Just so with steroids. The players didn't dupe us as much as we duped ourselves. I believe knowing this fuels our anger today.

2

Running with
the Bulls

Basketball in Black and White

November 23, 1984

In basketball, more so than in any other sport, a rookie can come in and utterly alter not merely the way a team plays but—in extreme circumstances—the way the game is played by every other team in the league. Only in football, at the running back and—less frequently—at the quarterback positions, can a first-year player dominate a team's temperament from the start the way a player like Michael Jordan will dominate the Bulls this year.

In baseball, a player like Vida Blue or Fernando Valenzuela may erupt upon the game and change the balance of the sport for one season, but more often than not he later finds himself chasing—or being chased by—the glories of that brilliant first year, so that rookie phenoms like Joe Charboncau descend quickly back into the obscurity of the lower minors, the subject now of two-inch fillers in sport magazines, and those like Ron Kittle labor under the pressure of equaling the years when the league did not know how to play them.

In hockey, rookies are so young they rarely set the league aflame in their first seasons, and a player like Wayne Gretzky is so great now precisely because he was plucked from Canada's junior leagues prematurely, to ripen amid the major league pressure of the now-expired World Hockey Association, a process the Blackhawks' Eddie Olczyk can repeat here in the NHL. Yet Bill Walton, Kareem Abdul-Jabbar, Larry Bird—these players carried their teams from last place to contention in their very first seasons; they were and are (aside from the as-ever unique case of Walton) the franchise, as is Michael Jordan with the Chicago Bulls.

Jordan is the franchise, first of all, because he will put the fans back in the stands. How well he plays, the first half of the season, is secondary to how he plays, with jams and razzle-dazzle, a fact of life prominently displayed in the Bulls' recent television advertisement, in which shots of the Bulls from last year are crosscut with Jordan, alone on a basketball court, in his purple high-tops and striped shoe laces, going in for a reverse slam dunk. He guarantees the Bulls a respectable house for each game because he's the player people want to see, a star of last summer's U.S. Olympic team and an extremely well-trained product of North Carolina, where he was coached by Dean Smith. Jordan is a player the common basketball fan recognizes, and the common basketball fan is what the Bulls need to attract to make it as a sports franchise playing to the divided demographics of Chicago's sports community. Jordan is the best player the Bulls could have drafted last spring. He appeals equally to the Vrdolyak types, who like to win if it doesn't cost too much in lost pride, and the Washington types, who rely on pride in the face of losing. Quintin Dailey was not ever that sort of player, and not solely because he is not as good.

Because, as Mike Royko says, Chicago is not known as a hotbed of liberalism. The concepts of black and white have little to do with the football world of Walter Payton and Dan Hampton (although they may have something to do with Vince Evans), but they certainly have plenty to do with the basketball world of Jordan and Larry Bird, the Great White Hope of the Boston Celtics, whom we saw play the Bulls last Thursday night. Basketball, for better or worse, is a game where race is noticed and commented on, from both sides. I saw last year's DePaul-Georgetown game in a bar in Cleveland, and aside from myself the only persons interested in the game were three black guys. We shared a respect for Patrick Ewing and Georgetown coach John Thompson, but these three, in their jokes and comments on the game—unmalicious but still pointed, making fun of racism by affecting it—portrayed DePaul as little more than a group of Uncle Toms playing under the old white master Ray Meyer. In Chicago, meanwhile, I can't mention the Bulls without someone remarking on the prevailing race of the Bulls' clientele or the quality of the neighborhood around the Chicago Stadium, followed by the same sort of chuckles and knowing glances of persons who laugh as they assume behavior lower than their own. Michael Jordan, believe me, has got his work cut out for him.

So, to tell the truth, I felt sort of ashamed to be making the Boston Celtics my first Bulls game of the season, because although the Celtics are, on one level, a very good basketball team, they are, on another—

especially in Chicago—the bastion of white basketball fans, and every satiny green Celtic jacket was to my mind a badge of white supremacy. Yet it was, after all, just a basketball game—there were, of course, no racial remarks hurled in one way or the other, no race riot, only the cheering of the Stadium's SRO crowd—and we settled in to watch how the Bulls would play. At the time, they were flying high, with a four-game winning streak, tied for first place in their Central Division with the mighty Milwaukee Bucks, considered one of the best teams in the league at 7–2. Admittedly, this is very early in the basketball season, but that the Bulls had a winning record at all was remarkable, and they had looked very good in their previous games on the road, including one forty-five-point performance by Jordan. The Celtics were to be their acid test.

They were burned badly. In this game and in the one that followed on Saturday, the Bulls' primary weakness was uncovered. We sat in the very back of the mezzanine, deep in the shelter of the first balcony, so that the scoreboard was unavailable and we had to keep a running count in our heads (if you went for beer or popcorn, you had to bring back the score). If we stood, the floor disappeared beyond the balcony, and our shouts resounded off the low ceiling and bounced right back in our laps. Larry Bird was, as usual, the whitest guy on the court. His every movement displays an awkward, stupid grace, like that of an Irish setter, and he does the most incredible things apparently without thought—the sort of player who has already spent a lifetime in the NBA by the time he is fifteen, playing by himself against the best he can imagine on his backyard court. "Hey, Bird, didja sharpen your elbows?" one guy yelled down the row early in the game, and we laughed, but the remark proved prophetic. Bird is a great player because, like Magic Johnson or the early Bill Walton, he can beat you any of three ways: with his scoring, with his teammates' scoring, or with his defense and rebounding. On this evening, he did it with rebounding; the Bulls held him to fourteen points, but he pulled down an amazing seventeen rebounds, and the Celtics as a team pounded the offensive boards at will. The final tally was 56–42 Celtics in rebounds, and that told the story.

Jordan had twenty-seven points, and Orlando Woolridge, the old Notre Dame power forward, had his usual nineteen, but it took him an unusual number of shots to get there, and Dailey, coming off the bench, was impressively erratic, with a soft touch one time down the court and a stiff dribble the next (he led the team in turnovers while playing only half the game). These three are the nucleus of the new, young Bulls (they have one of the youngest teams in the league), but aside from Jordan it is an uncertain nucleus: Dailey continues to have problems off the court (he was AWOL for a game earlier this year), and Woolridge is not yet the muscle man the Bulls need. Newly returned David Greenwood led the Bulls in rebounds last year, but he is not the type of player who can clear out the area under the boards, which is what the Bulls require, especially as long as they try to get by with two backup centers trying to combine to become one full-time center. Neither Caldwell Jones nor Dave Corzine is known for his muscle (Corzine was called a "sniveling fag" by the guy who yelled at Bird, but the issue for today is implicit racism, not homophobia). In other words, the Bulls will be interesting as long as Jordan plays in Chicago, but they will never be good until they get an enforcer under the boards, a point that was clear to all who saw the Celtics game, but was pounded home by Moses Malone, the big, tough center of the Philadelphia 76ers, when he scored thirty-nine points and cleared nineteen rebounds against the Bulls on Saturday night, turning an otherwise close game into a convincing 109–100 Bulls defeat.

So it does, in the end, come down to how well the Bulls play, and this is where Jordan is convincing. Many players have come into the league with Jordan's talent, but few with his skill, which is to say that Jordan plays with the flair of a person with the future of a sports franchise on his shoulders, but with the knowledge and responsibility of one who knows what's best for the team—any team—that he plays on. In one of the first few games the Bulls played, Jordan took the last shot of the game and missed, and the Bulls lost by one point, but the next game he again took a shot in the same situation and the Bulls won, a very fine showing of leadership and responsibility in a rookie. Jordan is going to be playing and playing well in Chicago for a very long time. How he alters the Chicago environment is something more uncertain at this point, but is not to be overlooked. Like another Michael, he appeals across the spectrum to a wide range of people. The Bulls are introduced, before the game, as "Thriller"—a song with an audience of white and black, unlike George

Clinton's "Atomic Dog" or P-Funk's "Pumpin' It Up" or Cameo's "Talkin' Out the Side of Your Neck"—plays on the public-address system, and although there are those of us who wish it didn't have to be that way, certainly worse things have happened and will continue to happen in Chicago. At least they're not playing "Benny and the Jets."

The Shot

May 11, 1989

THE PROBLEM with basketball is that the games too often come down to not merely one but a series of "last shots"; that, and the professional season lasts too long. The sport nevertheless is enjoying a well-deserved resurgence. Attendance is higher than ever in the National Basketball Association because the games no longer consist of forty-six minutes of trudging up and down the court and then two minutes of basketball on the way to a final shot, but rather forty-six minutes of one team trying to blow the other out and vice versa, and then two minutes of basketball on the way to a last shot. Still, this overabundance of tension and clutch plays causes the separate games to be lost, as some new splendid contest and last-second basket comes along every week. Basketball will never produce anything on the level of Bill Mazeroski's home run to end the 1960 World Series or Carlton Fisk's blast in game six of the 1975 Series, for the simple reason that it's producing events like that all the time. Already Nick Anderson's last-second thirty-footer to lift Illinois over Indiana at the end of the Big Ten season is diminished, and how was it, exactly, that Michigan beat, who was it, Seton Hall in the NCAA Tournament final? And Michael Jordan's next-to-last-second shot to beat the Milwaukee Bucks only a couple of months ago: who remembers that?

Nobody, not even Jordan, probably, because his basket to win the game last Sunday, which sent the Bulls past the Cleveland Cavaliers into the NBA Eastern Conference semifinals, was one of the baskets of the season and, he later stated, the basket of his career. In this, he may be a little overwhelmed at the present. We remember his hoop to win the national championship for North Carolina in 1982, when he was a freshman, and while he says he was just a kid at the time and unable to appreciate the gravity of the occasion (we assume that's how he was able to make the shot in the first place), we were a few years older than Jordan at the time and recall that game as one of the greatest sporting events of the decade, making his shot last Sunday ever so slightly less important in our eyes.

Still, there's no denying it was a great shot, preceded by another great shot by Jordan himself only six game seconds before, and if the Bulls manage to advance any further in the playoffs it will grow in importance; but now we're moving too rapidly from behind our event to ahead of our event, and perhaps it would be best to establish what made Jordan's shot so great.

We skipped out of the White Sox game last Sunday after attending the ground breaking for the "new" Comiskey Park (surely a name that can't last, but what are they to call it—"Comiskey Park II," "Son of Comiskey Park," "That New Ballyard with the Extra Box Seats So the Owners Can Make More Money"?), and we did so with the full intention of doing a season-ending postmortem on the Bulls. We joined the rest of Western civilization in picking the Cavs in their five-game series. We were surprised but not shocked by the Bulls' victory in the first game, in Cleveland. The Cavs were without star guard Mark Price in that game, the Bulls were rested and well prepared, and they simply beat them off the ball to win the game. Price was back for the next game, and the Cavs won.

We joined the Bulls for game three by running out to our neighborhood tap, a SportsChannel client. There we saw the Bulls win the game and take the lead in the series, but we also developed our theory on the series: it was that tired old saw, "the Bulls are a better basketball team, but the Cavs have better athletes," and familiar as that refrain is, it nonetheless appeared to be true.

We joined the Bulls as they opened a twenty-two-point lead, then watched them proceed to blow it as the Cavs closed to within three in the fourth quarter. It was a tremendous game, and watching the Bulls stave off the charging Cavs was like watching a well-coached team of a previous generation somehow brought into the present and cast against a group of today's superathletes. This was an impression anyone would get from watching the two teams play, and it was emphasized by the Bulls' lucky all-black sneakers. Bill Cartwright has a very old-generation appearance on the court to begin with. He is not the natural athlete that Brad Daugherty, his Cleveland counterpart, is, and he knows this. In his

antiquated black sneakers and trudging, hardworking aspect, he appears
in every way to have just stepped out of an old black-and-white highlight
film, where he had been playing with John Havlicek. Jordan, too, has
classic looks. When he wears black sneakers, his greatness is somehow
emphasized—he looks like one of the all-timers, with his characteristic
low gait in which his shoes barely seem to leave the floor except when
he's leaping. Cartwright appears to have stepped out of a highlight film,
but with Jordan it's like watching a highlight film from bygone days as
it's being recorded.

Delightful as this fantasy is, it doesn't win basketball games. How
the Bulls won this one a week ago Wednesday—and how they won
last Sunday—is still something of a mystery. The Cavs would bring it
down and pass it in to Larry Nance or John "Hot Rod" Williams—their
two monster forwards—and they would blow past our slight forwards,
Horace Grant or Scottie Pippen or Brad Sellers, with Cartwright or Dave
Corzine standing helplessly nearby, and then jam the ball through the
hoop; anyone watching the game had to wonder why they weren't capable of doing that every time down the court. (The answer is fine defense
the rest of the time by those same players.) Price was having an off night
in game three, but he was joined by Ron Harper in the Cleveland backcourt, and he's a great player, too. The Cavs had the edge at every position except one, and they turned up the pace of the game in the second
half as the two teams went racing from end to end like hockey players
in the Stanley Cup final. (The best thing about SportsChannel—aside
from forcing cheapskates like ourselves to their local pubs—is that, as a
cable channel, it doesn't have to pressure the league to insert television
time-outs into the action, and when two teams get to racing one another
to test who has the better athletes, that race can go on for a while.) It
was a pace that prohibited note taking, but I paused to cite a terrific
scoop layup by Jordan off an errant alley-oop pass, then wrote, as the
fourth quarter began: "We're tired, out-manned, out-athleted—can we
hold on?"

Yes, they could, with Grant and Pippen out-muscling and -hustling
their Cleveland opponents for an amazing twenty-eight rebounds between them, and with Cartwright—even more amazingly—stripping
the ball from Harper on the dribble in the closing moments to send

Jordan on the way to a jam that gave the Bulls a seven-point lead they held at the end of the game.

Yet the game had the flavor of autumn in it—that last gasp of a team overextended and about to collapse. Our thinking was that coach Doug Collins (newly and poorly recoiffed with a haircut that makes him look like a second-grader ready for the class picture) was doing a great job preparing the Bulls, from a purely strategic standpoint, and they therefore were playing better as a team, but that the Cavs—with their superior athletic skills—would recover faster, and that skill and not teamwork would tell in the last two games, both of which would be played with only one day's rest, and the second after a plane trip.

We were quite plainly too anxious to watch Friday's game, which the Cavs won when Jordan missed a free throw that would have put the Bulls three points up in the closing seconds. The Cavs exploited the opportunity, made the final basket in regulation, and sent the game into overtime. There the Bulls lost—leaving the court one by one with foul trouble as if it were an epidemic—sending them back to Cleveland.

"Hot Rod" Williams started his second straight game in game five, as the Cavs continued to try to exploit their greater size. The Cavs, however, did not try to blow the Bulls out at the beginning. Both teams appeared to be holding something in reserve throughout the first half, as if neither believed it could gain and hold a big lead against the other and was simply biding time until later. Yet the Cavs led after each quarter, and when Nance stripped Brad Sellers on a dunk attempt in the third frame we wrote down that it was the symbol of the series.

For the fourth quarter, we turned off the sound on the television and turned up the radio for the play-by-play by hometown pair Jim Durham and Johnny "Red" Kerr. The Cavs, here, were armed with two players we designated as "Bull killers": Craig Ehlo (does he score against anyone else in the league but the Bulls?) and Price, a well-known and historical antagonist who led Georgia Tech over Illinois in a regional final in 1985. Here the Cavs came out strong, but twice Horace Grant slipped through their rebounding defenses to tip in stray shots—one of which saved a miserable, tired attempt by Jordan that completely missed the rim. Cartwright, meanwhile, was playing one of his best games of the year, and he took Daugherty down low on one play and went strong to the hoop. Daugherty fell, trying to draw the charge, but the referees slapped him with a foul instead, and the shot went down to tie the score. Cartwright, however, missed the free throw.

As did Jordan—time and again. His weariness was on display at the free throw line, where he couldn't pull himself together enough to go through the precise motions required to get the ball up and through the hoop. Once in action, however, he was amazing, a body in motion—even a tired body—tending to stay in motion. He had an outstanding second half.

With three minutes left, Cartwright suddenly left his man open to double-team the ball on defense, and the gamble paid off, as we got the ball and scored to stay tied. Then he gave us the lead at 94–93 with a remarkable acrobatic tip-in—most unlike him. The Cavs came back and scored, but then we took a two-point lead as Jordan, double-teamed, found Pippen open for a three-pointer. Ehlo the Bull killer came back with a three of his own, however, to put the Cavs up 98–97, and after a couple tense sequences we had the ball with the same score and 19 seconds left.

Jordan took the shot, of course, and of course he made it, with six seconds left, but then the Cavs called a time-out and ran a heart-wrenching play. The Bulls were set up in a solid man-on-man defense, but the Cavs beat it with the oldest play in the book, the give-and-go. Ehlo passed in and ran straight for the hoop, catching a return pass on the way and laying the ball in.

Three seconds left. The Cavs did not guard Pippen, who was passing the ball inbounds, and instead put two men on Jordan. The shot we never grew tired of watching, through the postgame, the late-night news shows, the sports extras; but what was really rewarding, time and again, was watching Jordan get open while being guarded by two men. He cut out, toward center court, then back in, between the two, where Pippen delivered the ball, then a few quick dribbles to the free-throw line and the shot. Ehlo was one of the men on him, and the confrontation was a classic. As the ball went up and toward the hoop he went spinning out of the play, like Darth Vader at the end of *Star Wars*, and the ball went in.

There's no doubt a temptation to make too much of this shot. Jordan saved himself and the Bulls after almost costing them game four (almost costing them the game while scoring fifty points, that is), and losing this series would have meant the team would have fallen well short of its achievements of last year. Jordan—who expects excellence of himself and his teammates and who appears to, as such, have a tendency toward disillusionment—might have reacted poorly to early retirement in the playoffs. That's overdramatizing the situation, however, and besides, the point is now moot. The Bulls have already gone as far as they went last year. They did so against dramatically improved competition, because they themselves are improved. All fans of the Bulls must now grant—as they should have granted all along—that the Bulls have a fine coach, a good center, two rising young forwards, and the best player in the league. But that sounds too much like the postmortem we were expecting to write.

As for the series with the New York Knicks, Cartwright plays well against Patrick Ewing, Charles Oakley comes home for a final test of last spring's trade, and Jordan—well, Jordan will have to provide more last-second shots like the one of last Sunday.

Rising Bulls

December 13, 1990

THE BULLS returned home late last month from a seven-game road trip that saw them go eighteen days between dates at Chicago Stadium. That's not quite forty days in the wilderness, and only James Worthy knows what temptations they were faced with and overcame on the road, but there was no denying that something happened out there that transformed the Bulls, quite suddenly, into the real thing. They departed in confusion and returned with a unity of purpose, and in their next two home games, as it's written, there went out a fame of them through all the region round about, making believers of us all.

Not to get bogged down in messianic delusions, but the Bulls left us thinking—after their 155–127 thrashing of the Phoenix Suns, a team that, like the Bulls, reached the league semifinals last season—that they are truly a championship-caliber team, that when they're on their game no one is a match for them. They've been brought down a notch since then, but—if we dare mix Testaments—they've been to the mountaintop. The rest of the season, right down to the playoffs, will be spent trying to recapture, harness, and perhaps even improve upon their play of late November and early December.

Leading the way for the Bulls were, once again, Michael Jordan and Scottie Pippen. Last season, when Pippen blossomed into an all-star, he began to complement Jordan in a way that was continually amazing. Ever since he joined the Bulls, Jordan has had streaks where he elevates his game and carries the team for five or ten or even twenty minutes at a stretch. Pippen, last year, began to try to raise his game to keep pace with Jordan during those stretches, and the two took control of the team. They dictated the Bulls' style: tough defense, always on the alert for the steal, and opportunistic basketball, always hoping to trigger the fast break and the easy—or startling—hoop. It seemed sometimes they knew each other's thoughts, or that some basketball muse was whispering the same orders to both. Basketball played at the level Jordan and Pippen were playing it last season cannot be dropped and then picked up after a three-month vacation; even for players of their skill, it takes time and practice. And Pippen, in the first few games of the season, found himself in frequent foul trouble. When they arrived home from the road trip, however, they were beginning to show flashes of their midseason form.

In their homecoming, against the Washington Bullets, the Bulls opened going straight to Jordan. They posted him down low, under the hoop, against the smaller Darrell Walker. "We wanted to get him going," said coach Phil Jackson afterward, "because he actually has an advantage in the post area with Walker, and Walker's always been a threat to us. We like to put him on the defense right away and keep him back on his heels." With Jordan scoring fifteen in the first quarter, the Bulls opened a 39–26 lead.

Even so, Jackson's strategy had little to do with the intricate play of Jordan and Pippen. They displayed their mastery early and often. Jordan hung out a long, wide, tantalizing sideline pass to Pippen, enticing Washington's Bernard King to lunge for the steal. Pippen pulled the pass in as King dove out of bounds, and he drove for an uncontested dunk. Later, Jordan got the ball in the backcourt on the transition and, while seemingly issuing orders to John Paxson, passed long to Pippen under the basket on the fast break for another dunk. Then, early in the second half, in their most amazing sequence of the game, Pippen stole the ball under the Bulls' defensive basket and, falling out of bounds, lofted a saving pass to Jordan. He dribbled the ball up court on the double, with Pippen returning to play and circling wide down the sideline. Jordan cut quickly into heavy traffic in the middle of the court at the Bulls' free throw line, sacrificing himself to the play, and—with a blank look in his eyes, glancing at nothing and everything—dished blind to Pippen cutting to the hoop to give the Bulls an 80–58 lead. They led another fast break moments later, with Jordan again dealing Pippen a wonderful pass. The Bullets blocked the dunk with a frustration foul, which only left Jordan and Pippen smiling at one another as they met at the free-throw line for a high five.

In the following game, against the Suns, Jordan and Pippen were at it again, to the point where, when Pippen was slightly errant with an alley-oop pass on the fast break—the most exciting play in basketball when it's performed correctly—it only gave Jordan the opportunity for a one-handed leaping slam dunk on the run. It was the play of the game in a very well-played game. By this time, they were working so well together that Jordan—who found that the Suns' double team was coming at a specific spot near the free throw line—drove to that spot while signaling with a shimmy of his eyes for Pippen to circle under the basket along the baseline. When Pippen's man abandoned him to double on Jordan, Jordan passed to a wide-open Pippen for the jump shot, which he sank effortlessly.

Yet the Bulls were playing too well across the board to allow Jordan and Pippen all the credit. The bench came to life and began to punish the opponents, just at the moments when—because Jordan and Pippen were sitting down—they thought they could get back in the game. Because of the physical demands on the Bulls' starting point guard, John Paxson, his understudy B. J. Armstrong was usually first off the bench, and he soon established himself as the team's most improved player. He pushed the ball assertively up court on the fast break, drove and dealt out assists in the Bulls' half-court offense, and—most important—when he got an open shot as a result of a double team, he hit it. Last season, Armstrong's defender could double-team the ball without worrying about Armstrong's shooting; not so this season. And with Jackson showing a preference to let the entire second string play at once, so that it could develop its own chemistry, it was Armstrong who set the pace. "It's just confidence more so than anything," he explained. "Last year was my first time playing in the league, with these guys, and running the offense, and I just feel more confident. I know where my shots are going to come from, and I feel more familiar with Michael and with the rest of the guys. It's a matter of confidence and relaxing."

That placed him in a unique position to help the newly acquired Dennis Hopson, who has already emerged as one of the team's critical players, both as Jordan's caddy and as the second unit's main scoring threat. By the game with the Bullets, Armstrong and Hopson were beginning to develop some chemistry of their own—nothing like Jordan and Pippen, but effective nonetheless. Armstrong explained his teamwork with Hopson, saying, "I'm very conscious of where he is on the floor, because he's a scorer, and with a scorer you've got to get the guy the ball to get him off early."

Given that sort of consideration, Hopson began to shake off the jitters, the desire to impress, that marred his play in the team's first few games at home, before the road trip. "Yeah," Hopson said, "you want to do well, and you're hesitant. And basketball is just—you just go out and play. It's just a matter of me wanting to do the right things, to get a feel for the offense and get a feel for what's going on. Because when you're on the court, you don't want to do anything wrong and you get to thinking," and he shook his shoulders back and forth in an exaggerated fashion to emphasize the point, "and you're hesitant—hey," which he punctuated with a shrug. "So now I'm just playing and if I make a mistake—so what. It's coming naturally like the game should."

What was most impressive about the Bulls, however, was that while they aimed to play "naturally" as individuals, as a team they played according to a clear set of tactics. That was the remarkable thing about the 155–127 victory over the Suns. The Suns, like most teams from the Western Conference, prefer an up-tempo pace, a running game of rebounds and fast breaks. "They continually tried to push the ball at us," Jackson said afterward, "to see if they couldn't get us in a running game, because they feel comfortable in that and they wondered if we feel comfortable in that—and we do. There's no doubt about the fact that we want to run, we want to push the ball. We wanted to run with them if they wanted to run."

The first two quarters were played at a feverish pace, with Jordan and Pippen excelling. The Bulls led 40–38 at the quarter and 69–67 at the half. The diminished second-quarter scoring reflected not a slower pace but simply more missed shots. The Bulls' cheerleaders, in fact, changed outfits for a special routine in the second quarter, but the lack of pauses in the play kept them off the floor until after halftime.

Shortly after the intermission the Suns showed signs of tiring, even as they tied the game at 75. Their center, Mark West, picked up two quick fouls, giving him four for the game and sending him to the bench in favor of backup Andrew Lang. The Bulls, sensing a weakness, abruptly shifted gears, bringing Bill Cartwright to the fore. "When Bill got foul trouble on West," Jackson said, "they had to make some adjustments. Their adjustments were such that Bill continued to hurt Lang when he came in off the bench." The Bulls, at one point, went to Cartwright three straight trips down the floor, and suddenly they had a twelve-point lead. Stacey King came in to give Cartwright a blow, and he scored on two trips. Horace Grant, meanwhile, also hurt the Suns inside, leading the Bulls with nine points in the quarter. (After discovering vision problems during the off-season, he's finally found a pair of corrective goggles he seems comfortable with. They make him look as if he's stepped out into the lobby during a lull in a 3-D movie, but they seem to be working.)

The Bulls administered the coup de grace by bringing Armstrong back in for Paxson and resuming the game's former fast pace. Armstrong pushed the ball up court relentlessly until the final buzzer, at one point scoring on a magnificent bounce pass from Hopson in a tangle of players on the fast break.

It was a telling display by the Bulls, the perfect execution of a game plan in which they ran with the Suns, waited for them to tire, then went at their weakness, and finally used their deep bench to chase them off the floor. The 155 points set a regular-season record for the Bulls.

At one point in the fourth quarter, the Bulls' blimp broke free and, lifted by the updrafts from the overheated crowd, wafted up to rattle around in the rafters of the Stadium. When the crowd began to disperse it drifted down to the second balcony, where an usher pulled it in by the ring of its nose, but for most of the final period it was up there, bouncing back and forth, a symbol of the Bulls' season. The Bulls can rise to amazing heights. They may drift from time to time, but no team in the league can stay with them when they're right.

The Transformation

June 20, 1991

AT FIRST, I thought the shot was no more astounding than, oh, a dozen or so other astounding shots Michael Jordan has pulled off in his seven seasons in Chicago. On seeing the replay, I granted that, no, this one was right up there—top three or five. Of course, Jordan does this sort of thing so regularly that there is no real ranking of his greatest shots; one sees one and, after one begins breathing again, one says, "Yes, that's one of the great ones, right up there."

Yet as it was replayed again and again—and it was the highlight of choice during the week from when it was originally performed until the Bulls won the National Basketball Association title a week ago Wednesday; and the Disney World people have picked it up for their ad, so it's going to remain the number-one sports replay on television for a while—it took on more and more importance.

Here was Jordan transforming himself before the fan's very eyes. He went up strong, looking to dunk the ball, then utterly changed his bearing as he changed his grip from right hand to left, stretching himself out horizontal and scooping the ball delicately up, off the backboard, and through the hoop. The shot expressed, in a single moment, the changes Jordan has undergone over the years—especially the recent years—his transformation from an extraordinarily talented basketball player into a champion. Where once he would have driven on straight to the basket, willing to accept the foul if he missed the slam dunk—the same decision almost every player in the league would make—here he was suddenly willing to soften his approach, alter his aim in midair, in order to get off a clean shot, not just take the foul. The season just past saw Jordan give his teammates—his "supporting cast," he often called them—a previously unheard amount of say in how each game went, in whether the Bulls would win or lose. Coach Phil Jackson used the word *trust* for what developed between Jordan and his teammates and said, "Michael was willing to share some of the spotlight." Jordan altered

95

his approach to make his game softer, more egalitarian, team-oriented, which is a much more difficult style of play. Michael Jordan made himself, at long last, complete. And when it was all over, Jordan and the Bulls were champions.

The shot wasn't the turning point in the Los Angeles series—we didn't then know it, but that point had already been turned—yet it did come in the midst of the run in which the Bulls first proved they were the superior team. After holding a 48–43 halftime lead and padding that to 58–51 early in the third quarter, the Bulls ran off a 39–20 extended spurt, beginning with a pair of Scottie Pippen free throws resulting from a flagrant-foul call that Lakers coach Mike Dunleavy labeled "the big play in the game." I'd seen the Bulls play at this level around last Thanksgiving and again in January and February, before their slight slump, but this was the NBA final, against the Western Conference champions, the Lakers, and they just ran them off the court. The Lakers never really recovered.

In the second game, the Bulls were simply playing good basketball and expanding their lead until John Paxson wrestled the Lakers' center Vlade Divac to a jump ball in the third quarter. Divac deflected the toss to Earvin "Magic" Johnson, just as he was supposed to, but Pippen leapt and tipped the ball into the air from behind Johnson, then beat the Lakers' Terry Teagle to the ball, batting it down the center of the court, then beat Johnson to the ball near the Bulls' free throw circle, grabbed it, and jammed it left-handed over Johnson. Jordan, who had picked up two quick fouls early guarding Johnson, returned to action with four fouls, Jackson later explaining, "He wanted back in. I really didn't want to put him in, but he wanted back in. He wanted to be part of it."

From then on, the second game was a highlight film.

Early in the fourth quarter, Jordan, on the dribble, took the Lakers' James Worthy one-on-one. He pulled up at twenty-one feet and swished a shot through the hoop—88–71. Jordan and Pippen then forced a fast-break alley-oop. Their timing was slightly off, the pass was slightly errant, but everyone in the stadium could see it coming, and when Pippen pulled it off—jamming it like a father closing a closet door before his mountain of sweaters falls off the top shelf—we all went "OooOoooOOOH!" 93–71. Then, of course, came the shot.

"It was a feed to Cliff" Levingston, Jordan said afterward, "and Cliff threw it back to me. I saw a clear lane to the basket, so I was going to dunk it. But then I saw long-armed Sam Perkins there, and I exposed the ball, and I felt he was going to go up and try to block it, and it was just instinct to change it. I changed it to my left hand and managed to get it off.

"It was one of those creative things. Creativity—you just don't know what's going to happen."

Or, as Johnson saw it, cracking up the hundred-plus members of the media with his humor: "When Michael has it going like that, that's where all his creativity goes as well. He had his jumper game going and that's when he's dangerous, because he gets the feeling of being unstoppable, invincible.

"When he came down the lane he went up, went one way, put it in one hand, threw it up, about five more yards, said, 'I don't know,' put it in the other hand, and banked it off the glass. He's that type of guy. He can do the impossible, the unbelievable. It was his game tonight. He really took it over in the second half. He smelled the win."

The turning point in the series—after the Bulls lost the first game—came eight minutes into the second game, when Jordan committed his second foul guarding Johnson. Jackson then brought in Levingston for Paxson, put Pippen on Johnson, and had Jordan take Divac, the Lakers' tall, ungainly, European import center. "We anticipated going to that" alignment, Jackson said, "but not quite as early as we had to go to it with Michael in foul trouble."

Combined with the effective double-team scheme the Bulls' coaching staff had devised after the first game, Pippen's tenacious defense of Johnson stifled the Lakers. Los Angeles had burned the Bulls down under the basket in the first game. Now Johnson had to fight like a mountain climber going up a difficult slope just to get the ball across center court, and when he did get the ball in low, the Bulls player defending the ball overplayed to the outside and another Bulls player ran to the baseline, shutting off the drive in either direction. Playing safety, under the basket, usually guarding two Lakers players, was Jordan, threatening to pick off any hasty pass and take it ninety feet for the slam dunk, a threat he carried out more than once. The Lakers solved this defense from time to time in the three games out in Los Angeles, but never with any consistency. Jordan returned to guarding Johnson most of the time, but the option to switch Pippen onto Johnson was always there, and it clearly inhibited the Lakers' play.

After the second game Los Angeles coach Mike Dunleavy said, "We did what we had to do"—win one in Chicago. "Now we're going home with the home-court advantage." Already, however, he looked—and sounded—confounded. "They did a nice job. That's all I can really say."

The Lakers got the benefit of most of the calls in all three games in Los Angeles, but the NBA's notorious "home cooking" didn't bother the Bulls any more than it had at any other time this season. They believed themselves a good road team, and they were composed right up until they won it all. In a tight third game, Pippen fouled out in the final moments on a very questionable call in which Divac ran over him, put the ball up, and made it, sending him dancing down the lane kissing his fingers. (Divac later clarified that he was not blowing kisses to the fans but was simply thanking his hands for doing such fine work.) With the Lakers two points up and only seconds to play, the Bulls inbounded it to Jordan, who went the length of the court, pulled up just right of the free throw circle, and popped the shot off the back rim and through the hoop; it couldn't have been done in a more forthright fashion, especially in light of his game-losing miss in the first game. Jordan then carried the Bulls through the overtime, driving again and again past the wearied Lakers. The Bulls, then, had done what they wanted to: the series would definitely be coming back to Chicago.

Or would it? The fourth game was a rout, controlled by the Bulls from tip to final horn, in every aspect of the game. Johnson tried to rally the Lakers in the third quarter, making a truly magical three-point play in which he was fouled while double-teamed by Jordan and Pippen, but the Bulls weathered the run and coasted home.

I had tickets to games six and seven, and at this point—there's no denying—I was growing concerned. It was awful to see the Cubs lose three in a row in the playoffs out on the West Coast in 1989, ending their season, but if anything could be worse this was it: watching the Bulls win three in a row out there to end their season. This sort of thinking was clearly selfish, however, and by the start of the fifth game I had altered my perspective, softening to the point where I felt either way I couldn't lose. The Bulls, however, were not going to lose either, barring some Los Angeles miracle. The Lakers were more inspired—they had to be, with starters Worthy and Byron Scott both out with injuries—but the Bulls were just trying to stay close. There was a confident nonchalance to their play; the game had the feel that if the Bulls had a chance to win in the last five minutes, they would.

Pippen carried the Bulls through a slow sequence in the third quarter, getting them into an 80–80 tie going into the final frame. It was tied at 93 with five minutes to go, but the Bulls hadn't made a shot from the field in three minutes. Then, however, Jordan drove, hit traffic, and pitched back out to Paxson, who sank the shot. The Bulls came down on the break moments later, and a pass again went out wide to Paxson, who hit the shot. He made ten of the Bulls' twelve points at one stretch in the final quarter of the season.

He had also made all eight shots he took in the second game—this after scoring just six points in the series opener. As Jordan had said after the second game, "I told John personally, if we're going to go down, we're going to go down with no bullets in our holsters. You've got to keep shooting. You've got to get it going. The shots are there for you. You've got to make Magic work. You've got to make him pay for helping out on the defensive end."

He did.

Anyone who questioned how much or how sincerely Jordan wanted to win the championship—anyone who thought he'd again be satisfied with the league MVP award—was answered by Jordan's emotional response to winning it all. Clearly in tears before he even left the court, he hid between the shoulders of his teammates on the way out and shied from the television cameras in the locker room. Bob Costas finally tracked him down, finding Jordan sitting between his wife and his parents, with his forehead resting against the championship trophy.

Michael Jordan is one of the great players in NBA history, and at this point he probably is the greatest basketball player on the planet, but going into the playoffs after seven seasons in Chicago his career still lacked a championship. Johnson, his main competitor for the title of greatest player of all time, had won five titles with the Lakers in the eighties. Jordan was looking at a future in which he'd be called a player who was

great at the expense of his teammates, or in which, perhaps, like his
clearest predecessor as a basketball artist, Julius Erving, he'd win a title
after he could no longer say it was really his. This championship made
Michael Jordan complete, and I think that's the release he experienced
after the final game.

Jordan can play out the rest of his career simply trying to put new
shots in his personal all-time top ten—the fans are ready to accept that
now; I know I am. He'll always have this one, his title, the one he—
and Scottie Pippen and John Paxson and Horace Grant and, yes, Bill
Cartwright and Cliff Levingston and Craig Hodges and Will Perdue and
Scott Williams and B. J. Armstrong—brought home, with a little help
from a couple of other guys and some guidance from the coaching staff
of Jackson and Tex Winter and John Bach and Jim Cleamons. The best
thing about it was that this was a truly great team, which played basketball at its highest level. The qualities that won them the championship—
imagination, ingenuity, creativity, courage—were the qualities all of us
should draw from; the Bulls were pleasing to watch viscerally, intellectu-
ally, and aesthetically.

I watched the seconds tick down, and the city erupted. I remembered a night when the White Sox clinched first place and I went out on
the field of Comiskey Park and then drove home up Lake Shore Drive,
honking the horn all the way. A week ago Wednesday, after the interviews and the highlight replays and the local news reports were over,
I went outside and sat on the stoop and listened to the sounds of cars
honking and fireworks exploding, and, in that way, I shared my Bulls
with the city of Chicago.

The Zen Triangle

February 6, 1992

TEX WINTER first developed his triangle offense decades ago, but it went nowhere until he got the Bulls to adopt it, after Phil Jackson became head coach. It's an unorthodox approach to offensive basketball, to be sure, but it's not like the wishbone or the veer or the run-and-shoot in football—grand schemes that dramatically alter the offense and that demand to be taken on their own terms by the defense. The triangle is more a philosophy than a strategy, more an outline than a scheme; it replaces set plays with patterns and tendencies, diagrams with positions on the floor. It may not work for any other basketball team in the world, but it has certainly been the trick for the Bulls.

The triangle allows Michael Jordan and Scottie Pippen maximum freedom while keeping them within a pattern that averts chaos. It suits Jordan and Pippen's improvising the same way set chord changes and an agreed-upon chorus cycle (say, sixteen bars) suit a jazz musician. Sonny Rollins, for instance, can howl away with the knowledge that with the slightest of hints he can signal those in his band when to return to the refrain; likewise, Jordan can drive through traffic knowing that John Paxson is on the wing, Pippen at the top of the circle, and Horace Grant at the corner of the lane. It's been the key to making Jordan and Pippen function as team players.

The triangle is so named because, in its most basic form, Bill Cartwright posts up low on the right-hand side of the lane, Paxson sets up on the right wing, and Jordan dribbles near the free throw circle, creating a triangle formation. Pippen and Grant set up on the left so that if the defense is too firmly entrenched on the right Jordan can pass to Pippen, who passes in to Grant while Jordan moves without the ball into the left-hand baseline corner, establishing another triangle. In actual practice, it works as follows: Against Houston two weeks ago, Pippen drove on a midtempo fast break and ran right into the Rockets' intimidating center, Hakeem Olajuwon. Pippen backed out on the dribble, into the right-hand corner, drawing Olajuwon and another defender. Pippen then swung the ball swiftly to Paxson high on the right wing, who then passed to Jordan high on the left wing, who took an open three-point shot and hit it, giving the Bulls a 57–41 lead on the way to a twenty-point first-half advantage that would all but put the game away. The triangle gives Jordan and Pippen the ability to probe the defense for weakness and sets them within a framework that makes it easiest to exploit that weakness with an open shot.

Complex as this is—and backup guard Bobby Hansen, acquired in the first month of the season, says he's still picking it up—it's simple enough for a fan to understand and recognize on the floor. Yet the Bulls—even they themselves insist—won last season and have won this season more with defense than with offense. Since the Bulls are a quick, improvisational team, they rely on their defense to get the offense moving, to set Jordan and Pippen free in the open court, and to score points in spurts. The Bulls' defensive scheme, however, is not so easily grasped.

Defense is by nature, well, defensive; there's no better way to put it. The defense reacts to the offense and attempts to counter its strengths and strategies. The Bulls win with a defensive intensity as keen as any in the league. They learned much from the Detroit Pistons in the last few years (as has much of the league—especially those in the Eastern Conference). The National Basketball Association doesn't allow zone defenses—the scheme of preference in college—placing instead an emphasis on offense and one-on-one driving. Oddly enough, this emphasis on offense made the pro game not more interesting but less. Before Earvin "Magic" Johnson and Larry Bird arrived in the league over a decade ago—and even, for a while, after—it was commonly said that an NBA game was forty-six minutes of guys running up and down and then two minutes of basketball. The players were simply too skilled offensively; in most cases, twenty-four seconds was ample time for someone to find an open shot and make it. The Pistons changed that. They allowed no uncontested shot. If Paxson had an open twenty-footer from the wing, John Salley was out running with a hand in the air as he put the shot up. That's what separated the Pistons from the rest, and that's still what separates the contenders from the pretenders in the NBA, where much of the Western

Conference continues to play as if defense were just the way to spend time until a team gets the ball back.

It wasn't just a matter of wanting to play defense, however. The Pistons also adapted defensive schemes to counter opponents' trends and emphasize their own strengths. The celebrated "Jordan rules" were a simple application of strategy. Jordan likes to drive right, so force him left, into the lane, where help—in the form of Bill Laimbeer, Rick Mahorn, etc.— would be forthcoming.

The Bulls also allow no uncontested shots. "We're going out there with the attitude that we're going to play at least forty-five minutes of tough defense," says Grant. "Once we hit teams with that strong defensive effort, that really takes them out of their ball game." Even when badly fooled, Grant or Pippen or someone is running out to stick a hand in the face of whoever is shooting. (The Bulls also foul as judiciously and with as much determination as any team in basketball; when they decide to take a foul, they try to make sure the ball will not go in the hoop. Put the opponents on the line for two shots, but deny them the three-point play.) Yet the Bulls have also adopted some schemes that make the Pistons' work look like kids moving bottle caps on a playground, because, again, their schemes are based not on diagrams but on improvisation.

In Jordan and Pippen, the Bulls have two of the best defensive players in the league. They are also very similar in size and ability, however, and they poach relentlessly on each other's territory—with the other's complicity, of course. Against the San Antonio Spurs at home last month, Jordan and Pippen were matched with Willie Anderson and Sean Elliott—likewise two players of similar size and ability. The Spurs ran Anderson and Elliott back and forth along baseline screens, but Jordan and Pippen would simply switch men, effectively negating the screen. "It's something that's happened naturally over time," Pippen says. "We're the same type of player, and we feel confident with whoever we're out there guarding on the court. Basically, I feel I can guard whoever Michael's guarding."

As on offense, the Bulls try to allow Jordan and Pippen maximum freedom. When a team has players of their abilities, it pays to find ways to let them display those abilities. Yet Pippen takes issue with notions that the defense is tailored just to Jordan and him. "I think the defense is tailored to everyone's strengths," he says. "I think we've got enough quickness out on the court between me, Michael, Horace, and John that we can cover for one another and gamble."

Gambling is key: it's what separates the Bulls from most other NBA teams; it's what makes their defense so important to their offense. Again, however, the key word is *judicious*, as in judicious gambling—risks Jordan and Pippen know the rest can cover for. Jordan and Pippen are cat quick, but in Grant they have a player large enough to be an enforcer and quick enough to make up for their mistakes. "Whenever Michael or Scottie goes for a steal," Grant says, "it's up to the other guys on the court to make sure their guy doesn't get to the basket."

The Bulls have been accused of playing a zone, but what they really play is a rapid-rotation man-to-man. On defense, they don't move to locations, they move to players. It's comparable to the military defense of the village in *The Seven Samurai*, where the samurai are always leading the villagers quickly to weak spots in their perimeter. There's a willingness to concentrate resources where they're needed from instant to instant. That results in other weak points, but by the time the enemy adjusts, the resources can be shifted back. The Bulls rotate toward the ball either to double-team or to cover for Jordan or Pippen when they're caught out of position, but the idea is to leave the other team's open man as far from the ball as possible. Most other teams in the league don't have the perimeter-passing framework the Bulls have in the triangle.

In short, the Bulls' offense and defense are mirror images of each other (their time spent in practice shows). On offense, the players move to locations; on defense, they move to the nearest opponent. The offense tries to create a weakness in the defense (an uncovered man) and exploit it through rapid passing; the defense tries to patch each weakness as it emerges, counting on Jordan and Pippen to seal the passing lanes.

The key to both offense and defense, however, is energy. The offense went through a rough patch about a quarter of the way through the season when the improvisers weren't improvising. A jazz band with the best horn charts in the world will nevertheless sound lame when there's no energy in the musicianship. Likewise, the Bulls went on a road trip last week and looked flat in the first two games, in San Antonio and Houston. The offense lacked energy in the first half in both games and put the Bulls in a hole. The defense tried to make it up in the second half, but in the end couldn't keep the opponents from scoring. This crisis produced two of the most exciting games of the season for the Bulls, but they were both excruciating losses. Against the Spurs, the Bulls clawed their way back to where Jordan put them within three points with a slam dunk off a free throw Pippen missed and a steal and slam on a fast break, but that was as close as they got. The Spurs' forwards, Elliott and Terry Cummings, just kept rolling to the hoop.

Was this a crisis? No. The Bulls were simply discovering the boundaries of their athletic ability. Their offensive and defensive schemes attempt to exploit their almost across-the-league edge in athletic ability, but they can easily become overreliant on that edge. It carried them through last Friday against the Dallas Mavericks, allowing them to regain their balance for the game last Sunday in Los Angeles against the Lakers—an impressive win on national television in which, at crunch time, the Bulls turned up the pressure on defense and set Jordan and Pippen loose on offense. Theory merged with execution, and the Bulls were winning against the league's best once again.

Bringing It All Back Home

June 18, 1992

THE IMAGE was immediately recognizable: Michael Jordan leaping, legs akimbo, and pumping his fist in the air.

It was his response to the Shot, three years ago, when he lifted the Bulls toward the top of the National Basketball Association with the last-second jumper that defeated the Cleveland Cavaliers, and it was how he commemorated the Bulls' second straight championship last Sunday night.

It was the first championship won by a Chicago team in a home game since the Bears won the National Football League title at Wrigley Field in 1963. A crowd of 18,676 fans came to the Stadium to savor something that occurs only a handful of times in a lifetime—if one lives in Chicago, and one lives a long life—and when the game was over they refused to leave. They shouted at the end as much as they'd shouted at the beginning of the evening, when they aped fans of the Blackhawks by screaming all the way through the national anthem. Finally, after every standard in the Bulls' crowd repertoire had been played over and again, the Alan Parsons Project introduction music came on the public address system, the crowd (only slightly diminished) roared to a crescendo, and the Bulls came up from the basement locker room.

Jordan was the last on the floor, but the first to leap up onto the scorer's table, where he pumped his fist and held two fingers high in the air. Soon all the Bulls were up there, passing the championship trophy back and forth along with bottles of champagne, and the public address system just kept playing the same tape loop of Gary Glitter's "Rock 'n' Roll, Part 2," with the crowd stomping and clapping and screaming in unison—"Hey!"—and we were seeing it and feeling it and experiencing it for the first time (well, in my life, anyway). We were dancing at courtside and in the highest reaches of the second balcony and everywhere in between.

Only eleven days before, the Portland Trail Blazers arrived the very picture of confidence. Their physical fitness, manifest in the sculpted

106

appearance of their bodies, rivaled the Bulls'; these were clearly two of the best-conditioned teams in the league (only the New York Knicks can compare). What's more, the unique cut of their uniforms—especially their dark road colors—emphasized their physiques; with BLAZERS in block letters on the front, and with both jerseys and shorts tapered to the waist, and with the shorts boxy and baggy, they looked like a professional beach volleyball team—played basketball like one, too, at times.

Pictures are two-dimensional; when the Blazers burst into three-dimensional motion, they dispersed all appearance of confidence. The team moved tentatively throughout the series. The times the Blazers dished to guys cutting down the lane for slam dunks, or out wide on the fast break, were few and far between. The image they brought into the series was of being out on the run, executing what looked like a complex warplane bombing pattern, separating and then all closing on the same target. They showed bursts of that game, but were never able to sustain it for more than a few minutes at a time.

Even Clyde "the Glide" Drexler seemed atypically cautious. "Glide" might be the most fitting nickname in basketball, certainly more so than the too-vague-for-my-tastes "Air" Jordan. Drexler is six foot seven, with broad shoulders and a thin waist, and he moves with an erect, formal carriage. His shoulders, even when he's out in the middle of a fast break, always seem square to the basket. He runs with long, low strides, so that he really seems to be gliding along the way one of those big, late-sixties Thunderbirds used to cruise the highway. Yet Jordan took him utterly out of his game. Coming into the series, Drexler was being called the second-best player in the league, and his teammates kept repeating—although he himself wouldn't admit it—that he wanted the thing Jordan had, the championship, which would—like a tap of the shoulder by the queen's scepter—admit him to the basketball pantheon of Jordan, Larry Bird, and Earvin "Magic" Johnson. With Johnson retired and Bird hot on his heels, Jordan is the sole owner and proprietor of the pantheon right now. From the first minutes of the final series, he was not about to move over for Drexler.

Jordan's first-game performance was truly Ruthian. It was the game's greatest player rising to new heights under the greatest of challenges. Asked beforehand to sum up the differences between himself and Drexler,

Jordan admitted that Drexler was a great player, but granted him only one advantage, and this begrudgingly: "Clyde's a better three-point shooter than I choose to be." So he went out and made six three-point field goals in the first half of game one, punctuated by his bashful shrug to Magic Johnson himself, seated courtside as one of the night's television commentators. The six treys set a playoff record for a half, as did his thirty-five points. "The shots started falling from everywhere," he said afterward, "and I started running for that three-point line. I felt in a great rhythm. It felt like a free throw, really, from that distance."

It was not a set part of the Bulls' strategy. How does anyone plan a called-shot home run? "It was not premeditated," said Bulls coach Phil Jackson, "although I know that he's aware of the three-point shooting of the Portland Trail Blazers because we have emphasized it recently."

The Blazers had actually seemed to control the first few minutes, something that would be the case in the first and final games of the series and in none of the games in between. They went up 17–9. By the half, however, Jordan had led the Bulls to a fifteen-point advantage. For Jordan to play their game, their style, and to thrash them so completely at it was something that really crushed the Blazers' confidence, which is just what Jordan intended to do. They never really recovered.

Scottie Pippen took over in the third quarter, scoring sixteen points, but even then Jordan stole the spotlight—with Pippen's help—when Pippen fed him with an inbounds alley-oop pass that Jordan rose for, caught fully outstretched, and then slammed through the hoop.

After the game, in the Bulls locker room, on the board where the team usually has its game plan written down in outline form, all that stuff had been wiped off and instead someone had drawn a large ace of spades, with the number 23 in the middle.

There were Portland victories in the second and fourth games, but both were comebacks in which the Bulls seemed to simply lose track of what they were doing—the same sort of collapses that cost them games against the Knicks and the Cleveland Cavaliers. After leading his team from ten points down with four and a half minutes to play in game two to an overtime win going away, the Blazers' Danny Ainge said: "Momentum is a pretty fickle thing. You know, they had the momentum with two or three minutes to go in the game. We'll probably have the momentum going into game three, but the momentum can change with one three or a dunk or a big play."

Throughout the series the Blazers seemed content to wait for the momentum to come their way, while the Bulls seemed intent on robbing the game of any sort of momentum—until the final game. That's why the games had that ugly, rough-hewn appearance of fits and starts. Jordan put the Bulls' game plan as pithily as it could be put after the first game: "I liked the pace because we controlled it. As long as we can control it, it's a great pace for us. But our main objective is to try to control the tempo—run when we have to run, set up when we have to set up, and try to keep them off balance."

That was certainly the case in the third game, played in Portland after only one day's rest to make the trip across half the continent. The Bulls got an early grip on the game and simply outlasted the Blazers. The second Portland comeback gave the Blazers the fourth game, but the Bulls again seized control early in the fifth game, opening 10–2 and holding on the rest of the way. Drexler had the most awe-inspiring play of the night, a tip jam to pull the Blazers within fifteen (cough) in the third quarter, but that came after Pippen again fed Jordan on an alley-oop, this one a set play out of the Bulls' half-court offense. The Blazers had tried guarding the six-foot, seven-inch Pippen with six-three guard Terry Porter early on, but Pippen chewed Porter up, finishing with twenty-four points, eleven rebounds, and nine assists; he also removed Drexler from the game by drawing an offensive foul late in the fourth quarter. It was Pippen's headiest and best game of the series—until the sixth and final game, that is.

Pippen was the Bulls' touchstone throughout the playoffs: when he decreed they were golden, they were, and when he said the Bulls were counterfeit, they looked it. In the sixth game he played all twenty-four minutes of the first half; although he scored thirteen points, he played erratically, and the Bulls struggled. His opposite number on the Blazers, Jerome Kersey, scored fourteen points in the half, and Portland led at intermission 50–44. And that was after a 16–7 run by the Bulls to end the second quarter.

This game, like the third, was played with only a day's rest to make the trip—only now with the time change costing the athletes an additional two hours. The Bulls looked listless, the Blazers gutty. The Bulls seemed to have taken the Blazers' best punch in the second quarter, but they fell behind even more in the third. The Blazers went fourteen points up before Pippen took a much-needed rest, increased the lead to seventeen points, and led 79–64 going into the final frame. The Stadium hustle board, keeping track of rebounds, steals, and blocked shots, showed an amazing 45–26 advantage for the Blazers, including 33–22 on the boards and 8–2 in steals.

Pippen replaced Jordan in a patchwork lineup with the second team—Scott Williams, B. J. Armstrong, Bobby Hansen, and Stacey King—and led them on a 14–2 run to open the quarter. Kersey was hit with his second flagrant foul of the series. The first, oddly enough, turned to the Blazers' advantage in the fourth game, but this one swung that fickle momentum to the Bulls. King made one of his two foul shots, then Pippen scored over Drexler on the ensuing possession, cutting the lead to single digits at 79–70. Pippen scored again over Drexler to make it 81–74. Then Armstrong, after losing the handle on the ball in the lane on a backdoor play, dribbled outside and sank the jumper. On the Blazers' next possession, Buck Williams committed an offensive foul, and back on the Bulls' end he fell down trying to draw an offensive foul, allowing King an open shot that he hit, making it 81–78. Eight and a half minutes were left, the crowd was as loud as I'd ever heard it, and—after an extended rest—Jordan was ready.

Jordan was rested, Pippen was playing with the confidence that had been so inconstant in his game, and everyone in the Stadium felt, suddenly, the game belonged to the Bulls—even the Blazers. For Jordan, who had opened the series with such an amazing performance, this game offered a new sort of challenge. "That's probably the most that I've cheered," Jordan said afterward about his stint on the bench, and, while his answer trailed off, it seemed to be the most that he had openly cheered about anything in his entire life. "I felt like Cliff Levingston for a moment there.

"When I came back in the ball game, I just wanted to blend," he added. "Everybody else was already on the go. Everybody else was already in rhythm. I just wanted to catch up."

And so it was that the Bulls won their second straight championship with the greatest player in basketball striving to elevate his game to the level of Scottie Pippen and a bunch of scrubeenies. After Jordan's return, the Bulls finished by outscoring the Blazers 19–12, with Jordan scoring twelve of the Bulls' points and Pippen the other seven. It was Pippen who, with the twenty-four-second clock running out, sank a desperation three-pointer to tie the game at 85. It was Jordan who, after a bad pass by King, stole the ball from Buck Williams right under the basket and slammed it home to put the Bulls ahead, 89–87, for the first time since the score was 4–2. It was Pippen who, with just over two minutes to play, hit a pull-up jumper to give the Bulls the lead for good at 91–89. Jordan made it a comfortable four-point lead with one hundred seconds to play on a turnaround jumper over Drexler. And he returned the lead to four, 95–91, with an acrobatic drive, knifing between two Blazers for a lay-in with thirty-three seconds to play. The final, after two Jordan free throws, was 97–93.

The Bulls were erratic through the playoffs, winning one game impressively and losing the next miserably. Yet they always won the games they really needed to, and toward the end they won them even when they didn't need to (both the semifinals against the Cavaliers and the finals against the Blazers ended in six games). This last game was the Bulls' playoff run in miniature: the team looked befuddled, weary, and then pulled itself together almost in the blink of an eye. Last year they were a beautiful, intelligent, smooth-functioning team. This season they were a courageous team, battling no opponent so much as they battled themselves. And they won it here at the Chicago Stadium.

Outside the Stadium, where Madison and Monroe had been blocked off to traffic, cars circled the blocks just to the east and west; people were blowing their horns, and hanging out the windows, and yelling and screaming and cheering. Driving home up Damen, I saw none of the violence that struck areas both rich and poor in the city. Fireworks exploded, three-way intersections drew huge crowds—especially the one at Damen, North, and Milwaukee—and at Armitage I slowed to let a procession of kids carrying an immense Bulls banner cross the street. I drove through African American neighborhoods and Hispanic neighborhoods and white ethnic neighborhoods, and in all of them there were people milling on the corners, yelling for drivers to blow their horns, almost as if to seek confirmation. Those of us lucky enough to have been there were overjoyed to honk in response. Yes, it really did happen. No, it wasn't just some mass-media chimera. The Bulls really did it.

We saw it with our own eyes.

Three-peat: The Jordan Is Mighty and Shall Prevail

July 1, 1993

BILL JAMES, a longtime source of information for this column, sometimes refers to what he calls athletic intelligence. Like any form of intelligence, it is the ability to process information, only with the added physical dimension of sport. Exceptional athletic intelligence is what separates Frank Thomas from other young sluggers and Greg Maddux from pitchers with sharper curves or better fastballs. Applied to basketball and the Chicago Bulls, it is what separates repeat champions from teams that peak and are then played out. The Bulls' three-peat—put a nickel in Pat Riley's cup—was above all, I believe, an achievement of athletic intelligence and sheer will. It is probably the highest point this city's sports teams will attain for, oh, at least a year.

After the rough-and-tumble primal competition of the series with the New York Knicks, the Bulls found themselves on a very different plane in the National Basketball Association finals, against the Phoenix Suns. Not only were the Suns a typical—if exceptional—Western Conference team, stressing finesse over brawn, they thought a good game, and they talked an even better game than that. This was a high-minded series in every sense of the phrase, and it left a very serene and satisfying feeling in its wake—and not only because the Bulls won, although of course it would have been quite a different feeling otherwise. There was Charles Barkley displaying his peculiar—and affecting—sense of sportsmanship, while analyzing the relationship between the players, the media, and the fans. There were the Suns nursing their flighty point guard, Kevin Johnson, back to confidence and challenging for a series that almost got away from them at the outset. There was Michael Jordan, like Barkley, pondering his relations with the media after ending his self-imposed silence, and there was Jordan—and almost everyone on the Bulls' side—

talking about history, while the Suns spoke of destiny, replete with religious significance.

In the harsh spotlight of national television and hundreds of accredited members of the media, these two teams were forced to devote as much attention to themselves as to their opponents. At that level, basketball—like any sport—becomes a mental game, a contest of resolve, discipline, and self-knowledge, and the Bulls once again proved themselves unequaled in that regard. It takes talent but more than that, great mental toughness to win a title, and the demands increase exponentially year by year.

Comparing teams from different eras is a meaningless pursuit. What matters is whether a team defeats all competition, and how long it can claim that it did so. In three years the Bulls have eliminated twelve teams that wanted either to halt their pursuit of the title or to knock off the champions. In that time the Bulls have faced elimination themselves only once, for one game. They are a team of talent and tactics but also of strong will; they find a way to beat people, and they play well enough to do it. They have never really been challenged. How good are they? I don't think they themselves know yet.

The Bulls' strength in this area belongs in large part to Jordan, an immensely talented but, above all, competitive athlete who simply refuses to be beaten. But I think a great deal of the credit also belongs to head coach Phil Jackson.

Up until the finals, this playoff season was really Jackson's vindication. He outcoached the NBA's winningest active coach, Lenny Wilkens, in the conference semifinals against the Cleveland Cavaliers; he found ways to take the ball out of the hands of guard Mark Price and center Brad Daugherty, the Cavs' two best players, and the Cavs never solved that defense. Jackson also outcoached New York's Riley, the man considered by most hoop pundits the game's top tactician and motivator. While Riley counted on an improved squad using last year's game plan, which took the Bulls to seven games in the playoffs, the Bulls came up with new wrinkles and ended the series in six. Both John Paxson and B. J. Armstrong, after the series, credited Jackson and defensive assistant Johnny Bach with a scheme that stressed taking the ball out of point guard Doc Rivers's hands. Now, the Knicks, like the Cavs, have a two-man offense, based on center Patrick Ewing and guard John Starks, the team's assist leader. Why would Rivers deserve the defensive attention? Because he was the lone skilled ball handler on the team. Where Ewing and Starks played great two-man basketball, it took Rivers to get the ball to Starks. For the most part, the Bulls shorted out the New York offense before it could come close to making a connection.

Jackson, meanwhile, credited the players. In an appearance on his *Know Bull* television show after the Knicks' series, he said the Bulls were exceptionally intelligent as a group of athletes, that they could visualize tactics off the court and deploy them—with relatively little practice time—on the court, an invaluable quality come the playoffs and the steady schedule of game–day off–game.

It is Jackson who has brought out the intelligence of this team and found ways to inspire it. "He likes to challenge you mentally," said Paxson during the finals. "He's very good at understanding the long-range picture of things. And he deals with players very fairly—in his criticism and his praise he's very fair.

"I know that I'll look back, after having played for him, as a guy that stimulated me a little more than just with a basketball game, made me aware of some things outside the game. They make you aware of what's going on outside the game but they all were brought back to the game."

"He's a very articulate man who finds all ways of focusing the team," said Bach during the finals. "I think Phil has asked them to do a lot of things. We're not a team that stands out there and does it by rote. He leaves some things up to the team, their decision. He might say, 'Michael, you and Scottie figure out how you want to handle him.' I've seen him in time-outs ask the team how they want to handle it. He puts the game where it belongs—in the hands of the players."

This democratic attitude could only work with a team as talented and as heady as the Bulls. Jordan seems to have an innate sense of the game's strategy, and for basketball savvy he is matched by Scottie Pippen. (After last year's Olympics, Larry Bird said his appreciation for Pippen's play had increased tremendously; he called Pippen one of the most intelligent players in the game.) Jackson's democracy—and his vocabulary of Eastern mysticism, drawing on concepts like "energy" and "surges"—has led sportswriters to habitually underestimate his abilities. But in an age of self-satisfied athletes, he has found ways to keep his team hungry and focused, and there's also no denying that the Bulls' solid sense of the fundamentals Jackson and his coaches have instilled—the triangle offense and the rapid-rotation defense—is what allows them to improvise so well.

"It makes our defense more flexible, and certainly we're playing against a team that is flexible," added Bach. "I think we have a good handle on them now. That's the great part of our series—you get better and better handles, better and better adjustments, and the team that can make the best adjustments out there—not major ones, but minor ones—generally is the team that will pull it off and win it."

Bach spoke these words before the fourth game of the finals, after the Bulls' tough defense in the third game had failed to keep the Suns back from a triple-overtime victory in Chicago Stadium after two losses at home. I think Bach was overstating the case, in part to bluster his way through the team's defensive struggles. As Jackson himself said after the series was over, "We never could get a hold of this team. They always found a way to squiggle out whenever we got the lead."

The Suns, indeed, were a frighteningly talented team on offense, and the Bulls' defense could never quite contain them. When they were on, the Suns flowed to the basket like water, or like a herd of gazelles, and like such natural forces they seemed immune to most man-made obstructions. Aside from giving Johnson as hard a time as possible bringing the ball up, the Bulls could never quite identify any pinch points in the Suns' offense. In fact, after Jordan carried the Bulls almost single-handedly to a 3–1 series lead with his fifty-five-point performance in the fourth game, the way the Suns exploited the Bulls' usual poaching defense in game five was dispiriting, for both the Bulls' players and fans. With Pippen cheating on Barkley, Suns rookie Richard Dumas surged to the basket for twenty-five points. It seemed the Suns were the team making the fine adjustments, while showing a defensive intensity they aped from the Bulls. After the fifth game, Johnson explained, "I just think, when you play a team enough, pretty soon you start finding things that you can do against them."

In the fifth game, won by the Suns 108–98, the Bulls seemed to be laboring under the onus of the history they sought to make. They couldn't make a shot early on, and then they wasted their energy just getting back in the game. Yet in this loss Jackson made his final discovery: that the Bulls' best short-term lineup against the Suns might just be one with Paxson and Armstrong on the floor at once.

With the Suns concentrating on shutting Jordan down, the Bulls' outside shooters were left alone on the perimeter. Pippen's shot was off consistently after the first two games of the series, and so was Armstrong's in game five—they combined to make only eleven of twenty-eight attempts—but Paxson hit four of five, all from three-point range. That, in drama, is what is known as foreshadowing.

Off the court, Barkley reigned over the series; he emerged as not merely a great player but one of the great figures in sports. The night of that fifth game he was in his element. Before the game he sat in his locker stall and commented, somewhat bitterly, about all the riot-prevention measures the city was taking in the event of a three-peat. "You should never divide up the will before the person's dead," he said.

After the game, he did his comedy routine. Describing his pregame day, he said, "I'm walking down Michigan Avenue and I don't see anything in the stores. I started to get worried there for a second. I thought I was back in the neighborhood."

He also engaged in a little repartee with WLS radio's Les Grobstein. "I guess you all can take that damn plywood off the windows now," he said. Grobstein asked if they'd be putting it up in Phoenix. "We're civilized, we won't riot," he said. But there are ex-Chicagoans there, Grobstein added. "Just the rich Chicagoans who moved there," answered Barkley.

Barkley always seemed to have a fresh perspective on the import of the series; at one point or another he found a way to violate every sports cliché in the book. He especially took no jock-talk guff from TV commentator Earvin "Magic" Johnson, who suggested these two teams—led by close friends Barkley and Jordan—were too chummy and needed to hate one another more. "I think that's bogus, you know," Barkley said. "Come on. You shouldn't hate anybody." Meet the new role model; if I had a son, I couldn't think of anyone I'd more want him to emulate.

Except, perhaps, Jordan—and that's a big perhaps there. Who woulda thunk, before the finals, that if Leo Durocher's adage "Nice guys finish last" held up, it would be the ruthless Jordan winning out over nice guy

Barkley? Yet that, indeed, was the case. Pursued by increasing findings that he is obsessively competitive off the court, he only became more competitive on the court. His three-point shooting in the first game of last year's finals was a Ruthian feat, but this year Jordan established himself—once and for all—as a Ruthian figure of Ruthian appetites.

Hanging in my office is that famous photo of Babe Ruth in which he looks, dead on, at the camera. He has a somber expression on his face. The backdrop is one-half mottled white, one-half a most ominous black, and the bat over his left shoulder points to the black. I'd like to see Jordan shot in such an aspect. Like Ruth, Jordan epitomizes something about what's exceptional and what's warped in our culture, and, as with Ruth, it's a wonder that he can translate these opposing forces into such majesty on the field of play.

The Jordan is mighty and shall prevail. After much was made of Johnson's defense and Jordan's poor shooting down the stretch in the third game, everyone knew Jordan would explode in the fourth game. (In the pregame layup drills he was firing the ball through the hoop with slam dunks.) Everyone knew, the Suns most of all—yet still he was unstoppable. He drove to the hoop with long and lovely finger rolls in the lane; he pulled up and fired the ball off the back of the rim so that it ricocheted straight to the floor without so much as a ripple of the net; he hit high, arcing turnaround jumpers. And after that performance he sat scowling in front of the assembled members of the media and asserted that his job was not complete.

Jackson made it clear Jordan's shots had been based on the team's fundamental concepts, but he also granted him dominance with a strong military metaphor. "The dribble penetration was open to Michael all night long," he said. "Once we got in our basic offense, Michael just found that space open and took it and captured it and commanded it."

That, I believe, is why basketball has replaced baseball as the sport of choice—especially among the young. Whereas the serendipity of the lineup lends itself as much to Francisco Cabrera being the big-game hero as Ruth or Reggie Jackson—an "utterly unpredictable" element of the game, as Harry Caray says, which baseball fans treasure—basketball, the sport for today's impatience, has the go-to guy, and there has never been anyone who fills that role as well as Jordan. He finished that fourth game, after the Suns had closed to within two in the final minute, with a drive that followed the path of a cyclone, across center court, down the sideline, and into the lane, where he ran into Barkley, bounced off his chest, hovered in the air while palming the basketball in one hand, and then sank the shot. Followed with the free throw, too.

The media got a brief glimpse of Jordan's motivational methods after the fifth game. Horace Grant had played miserably, scoring only one point while his counterpart, Barkley, romped for twenty-four. Grant slipped out with Pippen, trying to avoid the reporters, but as the two skirted the fringe of the crowd in the interview room, Jordan picked that time to speak up, through the loudspeakers, saying in response to a question, "I know Horace Grant is probably feeling the worst of all of us and I know that he wanted to win as bad as all of us. He did not play the way he wanted to play." Comfort, empathy, and the lash.

In the sixth game, back in Phoenix, the Bulls recovered right away. They led 37–28 at the quarter on—get this for foreshadowing—a Paxson buzzer beater. They led 56–51 at the half and 87–79 through three quarters. Then, however, both teams turned up the defensive intensity, man to man, no stunts, and it was left to Jordan to carry the Bulls. He scored all nine of their points—as everyone knows—right up through his coast-to-coast rebound and lay-in in the final minute, which pulled the Bulls back within two. And then, of course, surprise of surprises, a couple of Francisco Cabreras came to the fore.

Jackson, ever consistent in his coaching style, asked the team what they wanted to do after they got the ball back and called time-out with fourteen seconds left, trailing 98–96. Go for three, they decided. Jordan, of course, would take the shot. He got the ball on the inbounds, passed to Pippen, and moved up toward the three-point line, but Johnson was right with him. Pippen drove toward the lane, was halted by Suns center Mark West, and, with Jordan covered, passed to Grant in the area West had vacated. Grant was confronted by Danny Ainge, providing help, and passed into the area Ainge had vacated—to Paxson at the three-point line. There were no Suns left to shift over. Paxson hit the open shot with 3.9 seconds to play. He later described it as the championship-winning shot everyone—he included—has taken on the driveway, hundreds if not thousands if not hundreds of thousands of times. What a glorious mixture of dream and reality. Jackson might well call it the ultimate visualization.

My desk, right now, is surrounded by short stacks of stat sheets, note- and quote-filled notebooks, and newspapers. I'm taking a break to look one more time at a wonderful Associated Press photo of Grant swatting away Kevin Johnson's last-second shot in game six. Johnson is in midair, his eyes are closed, and his fingers are sticking up in the shooting position like the bare limbs of a tree that has had its topmost branches lopped off. Grant, chasing Johnson from behind, got all ball, making the Bulls champions for the third straight season. Tomorrow it all goes into a box and into the basement. It's history, and it deserves to be preserved.

Those trying to diminish the Bulls' stature have pointed out how poorly they played, especially down the stretch, against the Suns. After winning the first two games in Phoenix, the Bulls really were outplayed as a team in each of the next four games. Their poor performances, I think, were a product of how acutely they felt the importance of what they were doing. Reports coming out of the Bulls locker room after the finale had Armstrong collapsed on the floor, in tears, as were several of his teammates, while Pippen asked a national TV audience if this was really happening.

After the Bulls won, we went out on the street and watched the cars go honking by and listened to the fireworks erupt near and far. After a while, we came back in and caught, on SportsChannel, raw, unedited footage taken in the Bulls' locker room. They came through the door and gathered, one by one, in a corner of the room, hooting and hollering, and after Jordan—the last, of course, and still clutching the ball he had chased down at the end of the game—made his way in and over, they knelt and prayed. When the prayer was done, Jackson and Jordan sought each other out and hugged long and hard. I'd like to think they both realized how much they owed each other.

The Comeback

March 30, 1995

WE THOUGHT we had seen the last of them, these images of Michael Jordan at play: palming the ball and faking a pass over an opponent's head, teasing him as if he were a kitten; ball in hand, facing away from the basket, arching his back as if he wanted it scratched; leaping, hanging in the air to get a shot off, his legs splayed yet asymmetrically balanced, like the pieces of a Calder mobile; prowling pantherlike on defense; shifting with a stutter step from a calm, erect dribble into a drive down the lane, tongue wagging all the while; and of course dunking, arm out front, ball in hand, and some unfortunate running along below like a boy trying to chase a rain cloud.

Oh sure, we'll be seeing those images forever on videotape, but it's something different and infinitely better to see them in person or live on television in real time, to share the moment with thousands, if not millions, of like-minded fans. Michael Jordan's abrupt retirement, and then his equally abrupt return a week ago last Sunday, cast in relief the very reasons we watch sports. A great athlete enhances our lives, in his grace and beauty, his flair for the dramatic, and his very demeanor on and off the court. (It's an ontological point to be made, but if he didn't enhance our lives in all those ways, he wouldn't be great.) That athlete's retirement, then, diminishes us all, whether at the end of a slow and graceful decline or, as was the case with Jordan, as an unexpected turning away from the game that was his greatest means of expression.

What is lost, in cases like Jordan's, is a feeling of closure—of fullness and satisfaction, one hopes—of an athlete getting the utmost out of his abilities and moving on. (My father took me to see Stan Musial in his last go-round in Pittsburgh's Forbes Field in 1963, and while I remember nothing of the day—and, in fact, Musial made only a pinch-hitting appearance—it's something I cite with pride, an emblem of the precious things passed from one generation to another, truly great athletes being among the most precious of all.) Jordan's retirement had much the

121

same effect on sports fans as his father's death must have had on him. Not to compare the events in magnitude, but in each there was a sense of irremediable loss, of not duly savoring what had turned out to be so fleeting and evanescent.

So of course the city was giddy—bordering on hysteria—when the rumors of a Jordan comeback were floated for the umpteenth time and—oh happy day—there were no denials forthcoming. And when he confirmed it, with a simple, two-word message, "I'm back," well, if the much-abused *second coming* bordered on blasphemy then perhaps another biblical reference was more appropriate: The city was enraptured.

Jordan himself later said he felt embarrassed to be treated like a god, but he had to have expected it in some measure. Coach Phil Jackson had tried to dissuade Jordan in his initial retirement by citing his great gifts and the public's great appreciation of them. Yet that was not something Jordan wanted to hear, as anyone who remembers the 1993 playoff season knows. The masses and their media had been in one of their periodic "let's see how much pressure he can take" modes, and while Jordan's exploits on the court were up to the test, his behavior off the court—petulance alternating with silence—oftentimes was not.

It was unpleasant to see him struggling so with the outside demands of the game, because that had always been one of Jordan's exceptional qualities: his ability to withstand the public scrutiny, to analyze himself, to be—if not always eloquent in the manner of a Bobby Jones—at least forthcoming, to an extent uncommon for an athlete in this era. If his basketball abilities atrophied, a little bit, during his eighteen months away from the major league spotlight, his forthrightness returned. After his first game, in Indiana against the Pacers, he sat through a thirty-minute media conference and stated that he came back because he loved the game. The following day after practice he did another thirty minutes with reporters. He said his time spent in baseball's minor leagues had both humbled him and refreshed his work ethic. "I guess I had to go see the guru," he said.

So while Jordan was treated like a god on his return, his play and his self-image were noticeably more mortal. He missed his first six shots in Indiana. While he helped rally the Bulls from a double-digit deficit in the fourth quarter with a series of drives and no-look passes, it was

Scottie Pippen who led the way, tying the game with a last-minute basket and sending it into overtime, where the Pacers—a hot team playing in sync—at last prevailed. Jordan looked much better a week ago Wednesday in the more familiar confines of the Boston Garden, where he shot well, played well overall, and at one point teamed up with Pippen on a pretty back-door play (Jordan's palmed-ball fake pass, on that occasion, was no fake). Yet over and above his performance in those games, there were the familiar idiosyncrasies we had missed for so long: his backpedaling after a successful shot, the way he walks quickly into a diagrammed play before lowering his shoulders and lurching into full speed to cut around a screen and accept a pass.

These were the things many of us had forgotten to treasure the first time through, and so we were overjoyed at the opportunity to etch them into the mind's eye. Just as Jordan was back, he said, for the love of the game, the fans were back at the United Center last Friday—24,247 strong—for the love of the player. A tape loop of Jordan highlights ran on the stadium TV screens from the moment we arrived, about 5 P.M., until the 7:30 start, and it was hard not to get caught up in the feeling of instant nostalgia when those highlights fell into sync with Louis Armstrong's "What a Wonderful World" on the public-address system. Later, during a break in the first quarter, more highlights ran while the Jackson 5's "Never Can Say Goodbye" played in the background. The attitude of this time preserving what we'd squandered was best expressed in one fan's sign, which read, "We're the luckiest people on [a painting of the earth]," punctuated by a small, script "thank you" in the corner. The United Center may not be the echo chamber the Chicago Stadium was, but Jordan's name still couldn't be heard during the introductions.

It didn't matter, for the moment, that the TV camera angles hadn't lied from Indiana and Boston, that Jordan's basketball skills clearly had slackened during the layoff. In the second quarter he pushed a fast break, sliced between two defenders, went up—and found himself a little short of the hoop, so that he had to roll the ball in over the front rim, much as he had in one play in Indiana. In the third quarter Jordan again came up shorter than he expected on a leap off a fast break, this time bouncing the ball off the front rim. The rebound wound up in his hands, but then he badly missed a bank shot. At one point Brian Shaw stuffed him on his fadeaway turnaround jumper. Jordan is thirty-two, but much of his lost lift is probably due to upper body weight he added to play baseball. Early reports before spring training claimed he had put on twenty pounds in his chest and arms, and his triceps are obviously more developed than they were when he left basketball. The lift should be back when there's less to lift, or when Jordan grows accustomed to his new aerodynamics.

Overall, the Bulls were out of sync against the Orlando Magic in Jordan's United Center debut, and prone to uncharacteristically stupid errors. Toni Kukoc committed a foul with a half-second left in the first quarter, and turncoat Horace Grant (booed with gusto) converted the two free throws to tie the game at thirty-two at the break. With the Bulls down 93–90 in the fourth quarter, Larry Krystkowiak picked up two technical fouls. He was ejected from his spot on the bench, but much more costly were the two free throws Anfernee "Penny" Hardaway converted to send the Magic on their way to a 106–99 victory. Jackson kept Jordan in the game even late, when he appeared gassed, explaining later, "I wanted him to have an opportunity to really play this game. And, you know, people came to see him."

That is a refreshing attitude. Jackson's love of competition is almost as great as Jordan's, but he also has a sense of the players as human beings as well as a wider perspective of what the Jordan comeback means, not only for the Bulls but for Jordan and the fans. With Grant gone, the Bulls lack a ferocious rebounder. Yet that seems secondary to the immediate problem of getting Jordan comfortable with the new Bulls and vice versa—especially in light of all the hoopla—and if any coach can handle that, it's Jackson.

Jordan came off the court late in last Saturday's game in Atlanta after committing a minor muff, and he was smiling, shaking his head. Jackson looked stern, but then as Jordan said something in passing he started smiling too, as did the players on the bench. With all of us trying to re-preserve memories of Jordan, this stood out as something we hadn't seen in a while; certainly it was an unfamiliar sight in that last championship season. Jordan smiling without pitching a product: what a concept.

Jordan had not been so lighthearted after the Magic game. He explained that Jackson was playing him so much as a sort of crash course in team chemistry and in Jordan's own conditioning. And to be sure, there were moments of sudden clarity. Early on, Kukoc led a three-on-two fast break, passed to Pippen at the edge of the lane, and Pippen returned a touch pass to Jordan trailing in Kukoc's wake for a dunk. Just before halftime, Jordan led Pippen with a classic two-on-one alley-oop pass for a jam. And in the third quarter came the moment everyone had been waiting for, a Jordan steal in the open court leading to a dunk—not poster material, but cathartic nevertheless.

In a way, it really doesn't matter what heights Jordan attains on his return to basketball. With three straight championships, an unrivaled renown for athletic creativity, and a fiery reputation as a competitor, his position as a great is secure. But what his comeback does, above all, is put a great athlete in a position for additional greatness—right where he belongs. He may not succeed; he may fail. But either way, triumph or tragedy, there is sure to be great drama for as long as Jordan plays.

On the day he went out to play the U.S. Amateur golf final last summer, eighteen-year-old Tiger Woods was given a simple piece of advice by his very driven and ambitious father: "Let the legend grow." A quote like that is priceless, but only if Woods comes from six down to win, claiming the lead on the penultimate hole by hitting a wedge into a narrow strip of grass between flagstick and water on a par three. How many other athletes, given the same advice, go out and butcher the day? The world will never know.

Last Saturday Jordan completed his first week back with that away game in Atlanta, not twenty-four hours after the loss to the Magic. Once again there were moments of brilliance mixed with moments of ragged play. In the third quarter, however, Jordan took over like the Jordan of old, hitting a lovely array of jumpers and drives to score eighteen points and lead the Bulls ahead of the Hawks. Then, however, he staggered toward the end. With the Bulls up three points in the last minute and a half, Steve Smith blocked a Jordan jump shot, and the Hawks scored on the breakaway. Then they scored again to take the lead. They had a chance to score yet again, but missed a shot as the twenty-four-second clock ran down and Jordan rebounded the ball with six seconds to play. After a time-out, the Bulls inbounded the ball at the far end of the court to Jordan. He trotted the ball up, businesslike but unhurried, against Smith. Then he lowered his shoulders, picked up speed, faked left, jimmied right, leapt, and shot over Smith's outstretched hand. And it rattled in, with no time on the clock.

Let the legend grow.

Head Games

May 30, 1996

LEAVE IT to Dennis Rodman—who else?—to put the Bulls' entire season in pithy perspective. "No one gives us any credit for being an intelligent team," Rodman was quoted as saying after the Bulls had taken a 3–0 lead over the Orlando Magic in the NBA Eastern Conference finals. "They have a lot of enthusiastic-type players, but that doesn't win ball games. You have to win up here, in your mind," he said, and although we read it in the paper we could almost see him tapping his long fingers against his temple. "If you don't have your mind set to go to war, you're not going to win."

The Bulls have spoiled us. We are now at a point where watching any basketball game that doesn't involve them is unsatisfying. Every other team in the league, every college or high school team, has the things it likes to do and the ways it likes to do them. It's a matter of which team can run up and down the court doing the things it likes to do more often. Other coaches talk about intensity, and when they lose they insist—as the Magic's Brian Hill did against the Bulls, or as Jerry Sloan of the Utah Jazz did in the Western Conference finals against the Seattle SuperSonics—that the tactics are sound but the players' concentration was lacking.

The Bulls play fundamentally sound basketball. Their triangle offense and their versatile defense—in which they can switch assignments every time down the court—combine to give them an unpredictable array of tactics they can adapt to almost any situation. No other team in the league can handle their best game. But that's something that can be said of several teams. The difference with the Bulls is that they find a way to win when they're not playing their best game, when they don't have the energy or the intensity, and they find a way to keep their opponent from playing its best game. If the Bulls can't beat a team with beautiful basketball, as they did in the first game against the Magic, they'll drag that team into the mud and whip them in the trenches, winning ugly by frustrating the other team mentally, as they did in the third game. If they can't match the other team's emotional intensity, as was the case in the second game, they'll change their tactics to reinvigorate themselves. Of course, every once in a while Michael Jordan is going to go off like a rocket, as in Monday's finale when he scored forty-five points. As coach Phil Jackson put it, the Bulls found a different way to win every game.

When the Bulls stomped the Magic by thirty-eight points in the opener at the United Center, NBC analyst Bill Walton said the outcome wasn't about *Xs* or *Os*—that is, the tactics on the floor. He couldn't have been more wrong. What Jackson realizes is that tactics dictate temperament: when a team is prepared mentally for a game, its players are apt to play with more confidence. To cite a basic example, Jackson has talked and written at length about how good defense tends to instill a unified team approach, while good offense—as in the case of Jordan—can sometimes separate a single player from the rest of the team. Tactics dictate temperament: it's an elementary concept that is lost on most other coaches and TV analysts. Walton is typical in seeing the game as two sets of guys running up and down, with the game going to the quicker and more aggressive bunch. Walton was a great player at UCLA and in the NBA, renowned for his intelligence. Yet having recently seen a game involving Walton and the Portland Trail Blazers on the Classic Sports Network—a typically sloppy contest dating from the '70s—we now regard Walton as a smart player in a dumb era, and a dumb analyst in a smarter era.

Let's return for a moment to the Bulls' win over the Knicks in the fourth game of the conference semifinals at Madison Square Garden. In the closing moments of a close game, with the Knicks overplaying the passing lanes and manhandling the Bulls' smaller, quicker players in their attempts to cut to the hoop, Jackson put the ball in Rodman's hands and asked him to act like a point guard. Think about that one for a second. A good coach never asks a player to do something he can't do. A great coach knows his players' abilities—even those the players haven't recognized in themselves—and challenges them to fulfill those abilities. In the playoffs, under heavy pressure, Jackson asked his power forward to play like a point guard, and Rodman twice drove the lane and both times found Bill Wennington for open baskets, the second of which put the Bulls in the lead for good in the final minute.

Nevertheless, the Magic's Brian Hill pegged Rodman as the Bulls' offensive weak link. He came up with a defensive scheme that assigned center Shaquille O'Neal to guard Rodman whenever possible. This, he thought, would allow O'Neal to roam far and wide, poach on his teammates' turf, and control the lane by double-teaming the Bulls on their drives to the basket. What he ignored was that his scheme would free Rodman to sweep the boards. What's more, left alone near the hoop, Rodman began to look to score (no doubt at Jackson's urging). The Bulls played an all-around good game in the series opener, winning 121–83, but the key statistic was that the Bulls out-rebounded the Magic by an astounding 62–28. Rodman had twenty-one rebounds—the only player on either team to reach double figures in the category—he hit six of ten shots from the field for thirteen points (a season high), and he had one lovely assist, a touch pass off an offensive rebound under the hoop to Luc Longley, who laid the ball up and in with the ease of someone tossing a hat onto the top shelf of a hall closet.

Afterward, Hill was contemptuous of his team's effort. "Rebounding is nothing but effort and attitude," he said. When lumbering Jon Koncak replaced Horace Grant—who came into the series hurt and left it after a gruesome three-car collision with O'Neal and Scottie Pippen in the first game—in the starting lineup for the second game, Hill persisted in assigning Rodman to O'Neal on defense, with Koncak covering Longley. The Magic had plenty of effort and plenty of attitude in this game, opening a fifteen-point lead at the half. Yet Rodman kept the Bulls in the game almost single-handedly, scoring ten points and pulling down eight rebounds. In the second half, Jackson called for the Bulls to crank up the defensive pressure and play a trapping full-court press. They still couldn't buy a basket, and fell eighteen points down with just over six minutes to play. Then, as if wheels spinning in mud suddenly struck pavement, they held the Magic without a field goal for five minutes and closed within two points by the end of the quarter. Pippen actually could have tied it with a couple of last-second free throws that he missed.

The Magic by now was a rattled team, from the last scrubeenie on the bench right up through coach Hill. With Pippen hounding the Magic's talented point guard, Anfernee "Penny" Hardaway, Hill shifted him into the role of shooting guard and put the ball in backup Brian Shaw's hands, a move that couldn't have pleased the Bulls more. Hardaway had been the Magic's best player in the first game, scoring 38 points, but shifted to off guard he played without confidence and faded into the background. He wound up making only 6 of 15 shots from the floor as the Bulls won 93–88. Rodman, by the way, finished with 12 rebounds and a new season high of 15 points. Tactics dictate temperament.

Given three full days to prepare for the third game in Orlando, Hill offered nothing new. What sort of confidence did that instill in his team? After they'd been beaten twice, what good did it do to tell them to go out and play the same way, only this time at home? None what-soever. The same flaws apparent in the Magic a year ago, when they were swept by the Houston Rockets in the NBA finals, were once again glaring. Orlando general manager Pat Williams had put together an ex-cellent six-man team, with O'Neal inside, shooters Shaw, Dennis Scott, and Nick Anderson outside, and Hardaway commuting between them, plus Grant as the inside rebounding strength and emotional cement. But Hardaway aside, this was not a team of prodigious offensive abili-ties—none of the three shooters was capable of consistently putting the ball on the floor and going to the hoop—and in the end they were left with limited options. During the regular season the Magic fed O'Neal in the post, waited for the double team to come, then passed outside to an open shooter. But with the Bulls playing Longley (if not Rodman) straight up on O'Neal, Orlando's shooters dried up like cut flowers left out in the sun.

With an injured Anderson joining Grant and Brian Shaw on the bench for the fourth game—a stiff neck sidelined Shaw for both games last weekend—the Magic tried to get more offense by sending Donald Royal and Anthony Bowie cutting to the hoop. The Magic seized the initiative and led by nine at the half. Pippen had carried the Bulls in the third game with twenty-seven points, while Jordan scored only seven-teen. So Jordan was due. He hit his first seven shots and kept the Bulls within striking distance. In the second half the Bulls again swarmed unpredictably on defense, forcing a turnover on the Magic's inbounds pass to start the third quarter. When Steve Kerr nailed a three to put the Bulls ahead 74–73 at the end of the quarter the Magic was done.

Jordan cut around a screen and hit an open jumper to give the Bulls a 92–82 lead. Soon he sank the dagger, a three out of a fast break to reassert a ten-point lead, 95–85, in the closing minutes. The series was summed up with sixty-five seconds to play and the Bulls ahead by seven. Scott went to the free throw line and missed both shots. Rodman rebounded the ball, was fouled instantly, and, erratic free throw shooter that he is, swished both foul shots to put the Bulls up nine. The sweep was complete.

Unless the Sonics are in the process of pulling off one of their classic chokes, the Bulls await a team of truly prodigious talents, a younger team that matches up well with them offensively. Yet the Sonics, like the Blazers of four years ago (like the Walton Blazers of almost twenty years ago, for that matter), are a stupid team that has grown fat on the thoughtless pantywaist basketball played out West. They took a 3–1 lead on the Jazz, a truly one-dimensional squad, by running two guys at John Stockton to short-circuit Utah's trademark pick-and-roll between Stockton and Karl Malone. Without that play the Jazz would be helpless. (The Bulls would beat Utah four straight.) The Bulls, however, are a team of many more offensive facets. They might even go to Longley as an offensive threat, as Seattle is even weaker at center than the Bulls are. Defensively, the Bulls will put Pippen on Gary Payton, get the ball out of his hands, and generally muddle the Sonics' offense. When the Sonics bring out their best lineup, with Sam Perkins coming off the bench to play center, roam the perimeter, and shoot the three-pointer, the Bulls probably will counter with Toni Kukoc, whose minimal defensive abilities are well suited to guarding a spot-up shooter like Perkins, and whose versatile offensive game should give Perkins fits on the other end of the court.

The Bulls are a mentally strong team that has spent the entire season in the media spotlight. The Sonics are a team with a recent history of choking in the playoffs. The franchise hasn't been to the finals since 1979. Look for Jackson to throw one of his trademark mind fucks at them, the way in 1992 he leaked the Bulls' scouting report that said the Blazers would choke if given the chance, thus siccing five hundred reporters on them just as the series was about to begin. Turn up the pressure on the Sonics, take them out of their game, above all make them think—a weak spot of almost all NBA teams—and let the Bulls' skill at managing tight contests prevail.

The Sonics have the players to give the Bulls problems, but not the brains. Call in the cats and dogs, Chicagoans, and prepare for more riotous good fun: Bulls winning at the UC in six games.

Father's Day, Bloomsday, Championship Day

June 27, 1996

STATELY, PLUMP Jerry Krause—well, who knew or cared how he spent the morning of Bloomsday, Father's Day, June 16? His work was long since done. He had put together a team of eleven players to fit defined roles around Michael Jordan—thirteen, actually, counting Dickey Simpkins and Jason Caffey, fourteen if one granted the wide-ranging role of pacifier, cheerleader, and good-luck charm to Jack Haley—and they proved to be the greatest basketball team of all time.

Yet it was coach Phil Jackson, not general manager Krause, who made it all work, who fused these personalities into an entity, a team that came to epitomize almost everything he wrote about in his book *Sacred Hoops*, released oh so long ago, at the beginning of the season last fall. Many general managers in many sports have put together teams that looked dominant on paper; but because the general manager—or, more accurately, the coach the general manager put in charge of the team—had no feel for the way colossal egos needed to be fused for a group to function as one, these teams usually did not work. There are two teams to every team—the team that could be and the team that is—just as there are two people to every person: the potential and the actuality. This potential was the mystical element to the Bulls' season, and it more than fulfilled the greatest expectations: a 72–10 regular-season record and a 15–3 playoff mark in seizing the championship. What was most stunning about the 1995–96 Bulls, however, was the way this team projected mutual respect, compassion, and, yes, that word known to all men.

The most curious thing about *Sacred Hoops* was the difficulty a reader had in recognizing any of the Bulls' three championship teams in its pages. "Compassion is where Zen and Christianity intersect," Jackson wrote, then quoted B. J. Armstrong's line that the untold story of those teams was "the respect each individual has for everybody else." He also

133

discussed how the team had to learn to control its anger and its hatred
of the Detroit Pistons before it could defeat them. Yet the Bulls' first
three championship teams were hardly collections of pacifists brandish-
ing love as their mighty sword. It's true, the team in general and Michael
Jordan in particular had to learn trust, and this trust made everything
possible. But what the Bulls learned best from the Pistons was a ruthless attitude that set out to destroy an opponent not only physically but
mentally. There was not much compassion to Jackson and the Bulls before the 1992 NBA finals, when they leaked their scouting report saying
the Portland Trail Blazers would choke, just as there was little respect
granted the New York Knicks in any of their playoff meetings with
the Bulls. Those three championship teams were mentally cruel to the
verge of sadism; they recalled the Bobby Fischer line, "I like to see 'em
squirm." What was most amazing about the 1995–96 Bulls was the way
they really did come to embody Jackson's avowed philosophy of love and
compassion.

These are flowery concepts for sports to project, so perhaps it's best to
fall back on the words of one Leopold Bloom: "Force, hatred, history, all
that. That's not life for men and women, insult and hatred. And everybody knows that it's the very opposite of that that is really life. Love. I
mean the opposite of hatred."

Led by a Jordan who had been humbled in his eighteen-month so-
journ through the wilderness of baseball, and who had rededicated
himself to the preparation it took off the court to play well on it, the
Bulls showed a newfound respect both for one another and for their
opponents. It was Jordan who displayed the team's fierce will to win,
night in and night out. He carried the team almost single-handedly to
an early-season win in Vancouver that was meaningless in a practical
sense but critical to the pursuit of seventy victories, and later, with a little
help from Toni Kukoc, through Dennis Rodman's six-game suspension.
While Jordan continued to talk trash here and there on the court, off the
court he was diplomatic at all times. Jackson showed a similar restraint.
Rodman played mind games through the first three games of the finals,
but Jackson showed none of the old media gamesmanship; the worst it
got was when he complained about the Sonics' "zone" defense before the
first game of the series.

When asked who was the most valuable player of the finals, Jackson responded, "Michael Jordan was the MVP of this final," and the Sonics' Shawn Kemp, who made his own bid for that honor, echoed, "No doubt, number 23." Yet it's worth noting that the team had to carry Jordan both in the seventieth win, in Milwaukee, and in the clinching sixth game against the Sonics, when he made only five of nineteen shots from the floor and admitted to feeling somewhat paralyzed about playing on Father's Day, with thoughts of his murdered father on his mind.

Later, holding the NBA championship trophy in his hands, Jordan was asked what he saw in its reflection. Looking directly into his face, he said he saw his sons and his father, and then he kissed it. "I had a lot of things on my heart and on my mind," he said in the media interview session, after breaking down in the locker room immediately after the game. "I had the good fortune to be on a team that came in and played extremely well. . . . I'm just happy that the team kind of pulled me through it, 'cause it was a tough time."

There were many elements to the team victory. The last game saw the outside shooting of Steve Kerr and Toni Kukoc, both of whom emerged from slumps to hit key three-pointers, the gritty play of Scottie Pippen, who shook off ankle injuries to drive to the hoop for the game's first basket, which gave him space later on to hit shots from outside, the return of Ron Harper, whom we'll get to later, and the inside play of center Luc Longley, who scored in double figures in five of the six games. There was the quiet efficiency off the bench of Bill Wennington, Jud Buechler, and Randy Brown, all of whom won games at various times of the year, and the service of former Pistons James Edwards and John Salley. But the person who really carried the Bulls whenever they weren't playing well was Dennis Rodman.

"He won two games," Seattle coach George Karl said when the series was over, referring to the second and sixth, both of which saw Rodman tie the finals record for offensive rebounds in a single game with eleven. He won considerably more games than that during the season, and he was also the one who off the court embodied the full range of what the Bulls were trying to accomplish. Looking back at our copy of *Sacred Hoops*, we noticed that on first reading it last fall we'd underlined that Armstrong line about respect and had then written at the bottom of the page, "Dennis Rodman?" The Bulls and their fans proved themselves ready to grant Rodman respect as a rebounder and defender, a heady player and a specialist willing to accept his role (in that, he was emblematic of the entire team). What caught everyone by surprise was what Jackson called the "heart space" Rodman was granted, by both his teammates and the fans.

Much has been written and said about the nature of Rodman's appeal, and it's been surprising how little of it has referred to the traditional Christian myths of the prodigal, the sinner repentant and redeemed. Sure, as a cross-dressing free spirit Rodman is a sports figure who engenders tolerance—think of what the response to his book-signing ensemble would have been twenty or even ten years ago—but that doesn't really capture what makes him unique. Rodman was one of the baddest of the Detroit Bad Boys, surpassed for evil only by Bill Laimbeer (and even that's debatable). Yet he came to Chicago and people embraced him. Why? It wasn't just that he made the Bulls champions again, although that certainly played a part in it. Rather, his popularity—especially with children—was almost certainly due to the example he provided as someone who had once been bad and was now out to atone for it. In the end, he apologized to Pippen for "what I did five years ago"—when he pushed Pippen into a battery of photographers and his chin was lacerated by a camera—in front of 250,000 people at the Grant Park championship rally and, of course, millions more on television. His presence on the team, with that of Edwards and Salley, was the single greatest symbol of the Bulls' unity, of their ability to reconcile good and evil, competition and respect, victory and compassion. A quarter of the Bulls' playoff roster consisted of former members of the hated Pistons. What better illustration of what Jackson called "the practice of acceptance" could there be?

Rodman, however, was not in himself the single largest difference between the Bulls' three great championship teams and the 1995–96 team that established itself, in our opinion, as the greatest of all time. Rodman is more of a role player, a specialist, than Horace Grant, but he is not a better player overall. Longley, while solid, is not the all-around player Bill Cartwright was. Kerr simply fills the role of John Paxson. And while Pippen and Jordan are both smarter than ever, and Jordan is now armed with a turnaround jump shot that makes him less defensible than ever, neither is as talented now as three years ago. No, this team won on its unity. If there was a single greatest difference between these Bulls and the rest, it was Harper. It was instructive that the Bulls lost two of the three games in Seattle, where a knee injury held Harper to a total of fifteen minutes on the court. Yes, the Bulls won without him in the third game, but that was while playing their best. The Bulls needed Harper—needed his defense—when they weren't at their best, and in the end that defense was the difference between winning sixty-seven games, as they did in 1991–92, and a record seventy-two.

Look at the 1996 Bulls and the other three champions, and the two differences that jump out are Kukoc's ability as an offensive force off the bench and Harper's defense. Kukoc, however, was too erratic to explain a seventy-win season in himself. But Harper's defense was there every game, something amazing to Karl. "I think you should give Ron Harper his due," he said, "because he's a guy who came here and turned himself into a very good defensive player, when I don't remember him being a defensive player at Los Angeles" with the Clippers.

When Jackson was asked if Harper was the single greatest difference between this team and the other champions, he said, "I think it's the defensive aspect of this team and the size of the guards." The series with the Sonics was proof. Harper not only played strong defense on Seattle point guard Gary Payton, he gave the Bulls the option to switch either Jordan or Pippen onto Payton without creating a mismatch elsewhere. At six feet six inches tall, Harper is big enough to guard a small forward, something that couldn't be said of either Armstrong or Paxson, who had trouble enough with point guards. The defining aspect of the Bulls is that the league's leading offensive team prided itself on its defense. As Jackson wrote of his coaching mentor, Red Holzman, "Red believed that hard-nosed defense not only won big games, but also, and more importantly, forced players to develop solidarity as a team."

Shawn Kemp was noble in defeat, in the angular grace he projected and that distinctive backpedaling swagger he had following a basket. Sitting in the media interview room after the sixth game, he spoke as Jordan entered to low-grade hysteria behind the curtain set up as a background for the podium. "At this point," Kemp said, "you realize it doesn't come from your physical ability on the court. A lot of it's mental, and as a young player I think that I'm going to take that home with me." Then he went behind the curtain and gave Jordan a long hug before Jordan came out.

The Grant Park ceremony was a love fest, of course, but it was Jackson again who put the prevailing sentiment into words. This was a team, he said, that formed "a community of people who enjoyed and loved each other. The thing that was great about it is that Chicago loved them back."

For the second time in five years, the Bulls won a championship at home. This one was a little less spontaneous—in '92 the Bulls emerged suddenly from their basement locker room to dance atop the scorer's table, whereas this time a platform was set up in front of the scorer's table for the players to celebrate on—but it was also a little more delicious. Jordan's eighteen-month retirement had changed everything. It granted perspective both to his achievements and to the team's. He came off the floor near the end of the game and gave Jackson a tremendous hug. Then as time ran out he seized the ball from Kukoc's hands and fell to the floor, where Rodman, of all people, fell on top of him. After a few overwrought minutes in the locker room, Jordan emerged to chants of "Michael! Michael! Michael!"

Who knew a year ago that he stood on the brink of his greatest championship, the one, not coincidentally, he would most share with his teammates? We were all of us older, wiser, more appreciative than we had been five years before. And all of us, on that platform and in the stands, at the United Center and at home, on the streets and in our cars, tried to savor and preserve it in the moment as best we could. Yes we said yes we will yes. Oh yes.

Tanned by the Spotlight

February 27, 1997

WHEN THE Bulls' pregame introductions begin and the lights go down, the entire United Center is ringed with tiers of Roger Brown silhouettes in the skyboxes. Then, from the darkness of the seats the flashbulbs start popping, first only a few, then in bunches, and finally one glittering crescendo as Michael Jordan is introduced. After the game, reporters queue up and down the corridor outside the Bulls locker room along a line taped to the floor; once allowed in they encircle Jordan's locker ten feet deep, with the TV camera operators in the back standing on chairs. Between those two events, while the actual game rages, Dennis Rodman is apt to steal the spotlight at any time, by falling into a courtside cameramen and patting him comfortingly on the chest or by stretching out fully horizontal while diving out of bounds for a loose ball in a game the Bulls already lead by twenty points.

The media frenzy surrounding the Bulls is part of the show—has been for several years now. It's testimony to the quality of the Bulls' play that, nevertheless, they usually manage to make basketball the primary attraction. Indeed, almost every day some new distraction comes along to make us recall something Miami Heat coach Pat Riley said during the 1993 Eastern Conference finals, when he was running the New York Knicks. Riley was asked if he expected the turbulence around the Bulls— back then it was the issue of Jordan's gambling—to distract them. Riley said that to the Bulls it might not be a distraction; it might be the atmosphere they were most comfortable with. Tanned by a full decade in the spotlight, the Bulls seem as comfortable in the media glare as a starlet at Cannes. Look at bench players like Steve Kerr and Toni Kukoc as they watch from the sidelines. Both slouch during the game and stand during time-outs with the posture of '50s juvenile delinquents, as if the opponents haven't shown them anything they hadn't seen before. Kukoc typically adds the touch of a towel draped around his neck and tucked under the collar of his warmup jacket, giving him the look of a European man of leisure, at ease as the center of attention.

Rodman returned to action from his eleven-game suspension for kicking a cameraman against the up-and-coming Charlotte Hornets. It was the Bulls' first game after the all-star break, and the occasion brought three hundred members of the media to the United Center—not counting the TV tabloid *Extra!*, which had escorted Rodman's estranged father Philander to the game but had been denied formal credentials. Somehow, however, basketball proved paramount in the end.

Rodman returned unrepentant. The only thing, at first, that passed as a gesture of atonement was his change of hair color from multihued splashes (he'd looked as if he should have been playing bass with the Muppets in Dr. Teeth's band) to a uniform greenish-yellow tinge the color of late spring wheat. Early on, when the Bulls were assigned the ball out of bounds, he flicked the ball to the nearest referee with an insouciant flip of the wrist, then slapped the ref's bounce pass inbounds to Scottie Pippen. Later came the moment when he patted the cameraman.

In the meantime he played some solid basketball, pulling down one of his patented five-tip offensive rebounds and passing outside to Ron Harper, who hit a three to give the Bulls a 14–11 lead. The scrappy Hornets kept the Bulls focused. Rodman battled the Hornets' Anthony Mason, another of the Bulls' old transplanted nemeses from the Knicks, and Jordan was in a scoring duel with Glen Rice, fresh from an MVP performance in the all-star game. Jordan finished the first quarter with twelve points but Rice had fourteen, and Rice also led at halftime 21–19. Jordan killed the clock and sank a jumper only a couple of seconds before intermission, but the Hornets' Vlade Divac quickly took the ball and fired a court-length inbounds pass to Mason, who drove for a layup over a scrambling Jordan. The score was 55–53 Bulls.

The Hornets took the lead briefly in the third quarter before the Bulls pulled even at 69. Then Rodman fed Jordan with a beautiful bounce pass on a baseline drive, and Jordan went up under the hoop and did one of his round-the-clock reverse lay-ins for a 71–69 lead. Kerr tried to get involved in showtime with a between-the-legs trailer pass to Jordan on a three-on-one fast break. Truth is, Kerr looked like a flamingo laying an egg while attempting a running takeoff—the pass so startled Jordan he hesitated and was fouled on the dunk. The Bulls were playing confidently, however, and entered the final frame up 84–75 with the game apparently in hand.

Pippen was having an awful night, and the Hornets rallied. But when Pippen in the closing minutes hit one of his floating, flatfooted jumpers from the free throw line, the Bulls led 96–91. Mason hit a prayer of a three with the twenty-four-second clock running down, and then—the unthinkable—Jordan missed two free throws with two minutes to play. A Charlotte turnover later, Jordan got a chance to redeem himself and made both free throws, but then Pippen fouled Rice and was whistled for a technical arguing the call. Rice made all three free throws to pull the Hornets within one at 98–97 with thirty-six seconds to go. Jordan, taking the ball to the hoop, drew a foul and made both free throws, but after a Charlotte time-out he inexplicably left Mugsy Bogues alone outside and double-teamed Mason down low, even though the Hornets needed a three to tie. Mason passed out to Bogues, who launched one of his five-foot-three mortar shots right through the hoop to tie it at 100 with nine seconds left.

Coach Phil Jackson "doesn't like to call time-outs in that situation because it gives the defense a chance to set up," Kerr said afterward. He was explaining the final play to just a few reporters, as most were packed around Jordan's locker waiting for him to emerge from the trainer's room. "So I saw Scottie with the ball, we all spread the floor, and he decided to give it to the Messiah, and it was a good decision."

Jordan, out beyond the three-point line, shimmied left, shimmied right, leaped, and rattled the shot off the back of the rim and through the hoop—automatic.

"Ho hum," we said to *Daily Herald* beat writer Kent McDill after the game. "Who hasn't written this one up a hundred times before?"

"I just punched up A4 on my laptop," McDill said.

From there the Bulls ran roughshod. In their next game, in Atlanta, the Hawks' Christian Laettner tried to mimic Jordan's heroics but missed a last-second three-pointer, giving the Bulls an 89–88 win. Then they whipped the Orlando Magic 110–89 in front of a national TV audience. The Denver Nuggets came to town playing thoughtless Western Conference basketball and the Bulls outran them 134–123, the highest score in the league in this season of defense. Pippen had a career-high forty-seven points. Next, Pippen poured in seventeen in the first quarter against the Bullets; Jordan, on the other side of the teeter-totter, scored eighteen of the Bulls' twenty-four fourth-quarter points (including fifteen in a row) in the 103–99 victory on the road.

The Bulls came home the following night, last Saturday, to play the Golden State Warriors. If ever there was a game likely to be overwhelmed by the sheer pandemonium surrounding the Bulls, this mismatch was it. Yet the Bulls played stunning basketball. Kukoc, who passed for more yardage in this one game than the Bears' Dave Krieg did all season, completed four lovely, long, arcing passes for fast breaks: two to Jason Caffey and two to Pippen.

The two to Pippen were both glorious. The first came off a Kukoc steal in the backcourt. He dribbled out and down the sideline to just beyond the half-court line, then hung out a long, lead alley-oop pass. The ball was up there, lingering, lingering—for whom?—when Pippen came leaping out of a crowd like the lead dancer in a ballet company, grabbed it, and was fouled as his shot bounced hard off the back rim. He made just one of two foul shots, but that made the score 90–69. Moments later, Kukoc sent a long pass over Pippen's far shoulder as he ran down the right side of the court. Pippen snared the ball one-handed, dribbled once in stride, and leaped for an easy lay-in.

The whole game was show time. Jordan still had the laser going from outside after warming it up late the night before against Washington. He scored fifteen in the first quarter and fourteen more in the third on the way to a game-high thirty-four on thirteen-of-nineteen shooting. Pippen, Jordan, and Kukoc came down on a three-on-none break, and Pippen took it all the way, finishing with a reverse dunk. Harper left a fast-break trailer pass for Caffey and a ripping jam. This one was over early, and it ended 120–87.

The only distraction was a Rodman tiff with the refs. After not drawing a single foul in the first half, Rodman was whistled for three quick ones in the third quarter, with a doubtful technical thrown in for good measure, then was called on a double foul with the Warriors' Andrew DeClerq. He was noticeably upset, and on the verge of a blowout—more likely always when the Bulls are up twenty points and he knows he can take the rest of the night off with a (relatively) clear conscience. Any other coach would have sat Rodman on the bench, where no doubt he would have stewed before exploding when he returned to the floor. Instead, Jackson replaced center Luc Longley with Kukoc, meaning that Rodman had to switch to guard Golden State center Felton Spencer, who had six inches and at least forty-five pounds on him. The message was clear: if you have trouble concentrating on the task at hand, here's a bigger challenge to keep you occupied. It wasn't until Rodman picked up his fifth foul that Jackson replaced him.

Now is the time of the season when the competitive teams separate themselves from those with nowhere to go, and blowouts become commonplace. Jordan was asked if it was difficult to play out the string, if maybe it wouldn't be better to start the playoffs now.

"I don't think we want to start looking ahead to things," he said. "I think we just want to keep constantly challenging ourselves, no matter who we're playing against. If we have that approach, it makes us a better team when we have to dial it up."

After months of lingering a game or two behind the seventy-two-win pace of last year's team, the Bulls' sixth straight victory allowed them to catch the 1995–96 team at 48–6 after fifty-four games. "Probably, it's more impressive this year because it's been a lot more of a grind," Kerr said. "Last year was fresh and exciting. This year everybody's expecting it, and teams are coming after us harder. It's not as exciting as it was but we're still right there, so it's probably a bigger accomplishment this year."

Kerr said that putting together back-to-back seventy-win championship seasons would establish the Bulls as the greatest team in NBA history. The Bulls' pursuit of that goal will bring heightened scrutiny (as if it could get any higher). And, of course, there is the lingering specter of Rodman.

Yet as Kerr said after the Golden State game, "It's not going to bother us. It hasn't in the last two years [since Jordan's return from baseball] and it's not going to start now. I don't really pay much attention to it."

That's the Bulls: shooting coolly from outside in the middle of a media cyclone.

Doo-Doo and Shit

June 5, 1997

"I PLAYED like doo-doo," Michael Jordan said.

He was talking about his four-of-fifteen shooting performance in the second game of the Eastern Conference finals between the Bulls and the Miami Heat. Yet his playful, childish choice of words did not come off the top of his head, as Scottie Pippen would soon reveal. Pippen sat down alongside Jordan in the media interview room following that second game, an ugly 75–68 victory that set an NBA playoff record for the lowest score since the arrival of the twenty-four-second clock. After Jordan answered a couple more questions, the *Sun-Times*'s Lacy Banks asked one of Pippen.

"Y'all done with me?" Jordan said, getting up from his chair.

"No, no!" Banks said.

"No, we can't let Doo-Doo leave," Pippen said, his face breaking into a huge smile. Jordan smiled too as he sagged back into his seat. "We've already given ourselves names in the locker room," Pippen soon explained.

"I'm Doo-Doo," Jordan interrupted. "He's Shit." The media room cracked into hysterics.

There have been moments on the court when Jordan and Pippen displayed a Babe Ruth–Lou Gehrig dynamic, an ability to drive each other to great heights and pick each other up after great pratfalls—most recently in the final game of the Bulls' opening playoff series against the Washington Bullets, when with the clock ticking down and the Bulls one point behind Jordan lost the ball, only to see Pippen snatch it and drive for a game-winning slam dunk. Their smiling, wisecracking ways on the bench at the end of a rout are the very image of the giddy confidence Ruth and Gehrig projected in the early Murderers' Row years of the New York Yankees' dynasty. As Jordan put it after that second game, in denying that the Bulls' flat performance had been intentional: "We'd rather have a blowout so that he and I could ice our knees down and joke about the people in the stands." Yet rarely had the Ruth-and-Gehrig jocularity

144

been as visible as it was now. Following a most humbling night of play on the court Jordan and Pippen managed to strike the pose of greatness off it, and never had the separation between them and other players been quite so glaring.

The Heat, from coach Pat Riley on down, had been morose about losing both of the opening two games in Chicago. "They have given us so many opportunities to win it's ridiculous," said Miami center Alonzo Mourning. Riley added that this brutal second loss—a defensive tussle in which both teams looked inept on offense—was even more aggravating than the opening defeat, in which the Heat blew an early fifteen-point lead and an eleven-point halftime advantage to lose 84–77.

Yet here were Jordan and Pippen laughing about the game. "You never want to look Ugly in the face," Jordan said philosophically, again cracking up his audience of reporters. Yes, it's easier to laugh as the victor than as the vanquished. "If we're playing ugly because of their defense, they're playing uglier because of our defense," Jordan said. "As long as they're playing uglier than we are, you won't hear me complaining." Yet not even this explained the elevated spirits Jordan and Pippen found themselves in. Having finished a final question, Jordan got up out of his seat saying, "C'mon, Shit, let's go." Their comfort under intense pressure and media scrutiny—not any mere *X*s and *O*s on a locker room blackboard—is what the Utah Jazz had trouble matching up with as the NBA finals got under way Sunday at the United Center.

Actually, the Jazz looked remarkably composed from the opening tip. They had never been to the finals before but they are an experienced team, very set and secure in their ways. Coach Jerry Sloan has taken the pressure-release plays he learned from Bulls coach Dick Motta in the early '70s—the picks Chet Walker and Bob Love and Norm Van Lier and Sloan himself used to set for each other—and refined them to the point where they are now almost baroque in their complexity. The Jazz are a very regimented team but thoroughly unpredictable, and the Bulls had a difficult time in the opening game getting the defensive stops they'd achieved so routinely against the Heat, the Atlanta Hawks, and the Bullets.

The Jazz led 42–38 at the half on the strength of plays like the final possession: a crisp pick-and-roll run by point guard John Stockton and power forward Karl Malone, followed by a surprising Stockton pass—not to Malone cutting to the hoop, but crosscourt to small forward Bryon Russell for an open three. He hit it to halt a six-point run by the Bulls and turn a one-point game into a four-point game.

Yet the unique pressure of the finals eventually got to the Jazz in the form of eight third-quarter turnovers—three by Malone and two by Stockton—and then two more by Stockton on consecutive possessions at a critical juncture of the fourth quarter. There were also Malone's three missed free throws in the fourth quarter, including, of course, his twin misses with nine seconds to play in a tie game (this from the 1996–97 "most valuable player," who had shot 82 percent from the line in the playoffs coming into the game).

Jordan and Pippen finished with thirty-one and twenty-seven points—the only Bulls in double figures—and they were involved in most of the critical plays in the second half, including, of course, the last one. Jordan drove the baseline late in the third quarter and passed out to Pippen at the top of the circle for an open three and a 57–56 lead, the Bulls' first since the middle of the second quarter. The Jazz regained a five-point advantage early in the final frame, but Jordan made a crosscourt pass that allowed Ron Harper to step into an open three. That made it 70–68 Jazz. Utah got another five-point lead, but then Stockton committed his two straight turnovers, allowing the Bulls to go ahead 76–75 when Jordan drove the lane and passed out wide to Luc Longley for an open shot. Jordan, Harper, and Pippen—the Bulls' three most effective players throughout the playoffs—all touched the ball on a crucial basket, with Jordan missing but Harper rebounding and passing out to Pippen for a three that put the Bulls up 81–79. Stockton responded in kind to put Utah back in front, then Jordan made only one of two free throws to tie it at 82 in the final minute. But Malone missed both of his and Jordan came down with the rebound. After a time-out, Toni Kukoc relayed the inbounds pass to Jordan, who lured Russell into an attempt at a steal, then leaped while Russell lunged. The ball banged off the back rim and through the hoop. Jordan calmly turned and pumped his fist once.

So while the Jazz survived the finals pressure to play a good game, they lost in a particularly excruciating fashion. Malone said afterward that he didn't want to hear any excuses about the team with finals experience being able to pull the game out, but even Stockton had to admit, "There's a lot of things different about this whole thing"—among them a reporter from the Philippines pointing out, very diplomatically, that Stockton had committed seven turnovers for the game ("Thank you," Stockton responded), and a litany of questions that began with phrases such as "How deflating . . . ?" "How helpless . . . ?" and "How agonizing. . . ?" Because of the playing schedule dictated by NBC, Utah had two off days here in Chicago to endure more questions like that before getting a chance to redeem itself. The Jazz were completely unlike the Heat in demeanor and savvy—in short, in class—but after losing a game they could well have won they faced the same fate as every other team that's faced the Bulls.

The Heat came in with chips on their shoulders, but instead of elevating their play that attitude only seemed to distract them. They were defensive, insecure, and ultimately inferior. Riley always appeared most concerned with how he was stacking up against Jackson and Jordan at the podium, but he lost that battle for good when he couldn't come up with a snappy comeback to a moronic question asked by WSCR-AM talk show host Mike North after the third game in Miami. "If God came down and said you could win the next four games but you'd have to shave your head, would you do it?" North said. A simple yes would have sufficed, but Riley glared at North as his eyes turned red and smoke began coming out of his ears, then muttered, "That's a hell of a question."

Mourning, meanwhile, let Dennis Rodman into his head early in the series and never got him out. "Y'all know Dennis," he said after the first game, addressing the media as if they were the members of a jury and this was his opening statement. "Y'all know his antics. It's unfortunate that we as players have to put up with that." Yet it was Mourning who raised a huge welt on Pippen's forehead with a nasty elbow in the fourth game, the only one Miami was able to salvage.

After Jordan used that incident to inspire himself, saying the series was now "personal," Mourning and the Heat wilted in the fifth game. Mourning had opened the series refusing to take part in the usual gentlemanly fist taps before the opening tip, but before the fifth game Jordan upped those stakes and refused to shake Mourning's hand when it was proffered at the even more diplomatic pregame meeting of captains and referees. Mourning was crushed—or at least played as if he were. He did not make a basket from the field until there were 2.5 seconds left in the game. "He did it himself," Jordan said afterward. "We didn't do nothing. He just talked himself out of the game."

The series was captured in miniature in one critical sequence early in the second game. Jordan hit Pippen with a lovely arcing lead pass on a fast break, and Pippen was fouled under the hoop. The refs, however, made no call, which was typical of the series and especially typical of that game, when more elbows than shots connected in the free throw lane. Pippen was irate, barking at the refs and then almost absentmind-edly turning his attention to the Heat's John Crotty, who now had the ball. Pippen slapped the ball to the floor. Both players dived for it but Pippen seized it and stood up. Crotty, still on the floor, tried to tangle his legs in Pippen's, but Pippen looked down at him with a mixture of disbelief and disdain and banked in the short jumper, with the refs at last calling a foul. Pippen then gave it to Crotty verbally in no uncertain terms, and when Miami's Willie Anderson jumped in as the third man in the fray the refs hit him with a technical foul. The Bulls' Steve Kerr made that foul shot. Pippen then missed his attempt to complete his own three-point play, but Brian Williams came down with the rebound and passed outside to Kerr, who faked a shot and passed to Pippen cutting to the hoop for a slam dunk. When the dust from this little sequence had cleared, the Bulls were up 29–16, and given the tempo of play—which Jackson later compared to a football game—it was like a lead of two touchdowns. The Heat scrambled back into the game in the second half, but the Bulls won with better execution down the stretch—the story of the series, and the story, really, of their four previous championships.

Aside from the fifth game, when Pippen went out early with a foot injury, Jordan and Pippen dictated the terms of the Heat series. After their poor performances in the second game they combined for thirty-six points in the first half of the third game, on the way to a win that all but sealed the series. Pippen brought the Bulls within one in the first game with a clutch three, then opened game two with a pair of threes and hit another that reinstated a ten-point lead with a minute to play. Jordan reigned in the third game and again early on in the fifth before the bench finally got involved.

Those two aside, it was Harper who played solid defense and time after time found himself in the right place at the right time on offense. It was his three, after Jordan drew a double team with a baseline drive, that put the Bulls in front for good, 75–73, in the first game. The same play worked again as Harper put the Bulls up 66–58 late in the second-game scrum. Harper would miss two free throws to put the lead in jeopardy, but he converted one of two in the final minute to seal the win by making it a three-possession game. (Pippen playfully put an arm around his neck and made as if to strangle him as they walked to the sideline after that.) He hit another critical three to make the score 91–78 with five minutes to play in the clinching fifth game. Along the way, he played a stifling defense against Miami point guard Tim Hardaway, just as he had against Mookie Blaylock of Atlanta in the second round. And quite unlike Jordan and Pippen, he was humble all the way.

"I can't guard Hardaway," Harper said after holding him to thirteen points on four-of-fourteen shooting in the opening game. "I got slow feet. My knees hurt. And I have a bad back. So I can't guard him." That was the full text of his remarks to the media that night. "Later," he said. Behind every Ruth and Gehrig, there's always a Bob Meusel.

Still, it was Jordan who led the way, never so much, oddly enough, as in the fourth game, when he missed his first fourteen shots from the field and at one point in the third quarter had made just two of twenty-four. But he got hot and almost single-handedly pulled off the comeback before the Bulls finally expired 87–80. There were times in that fourth game when he seemed as willful and instinctive as a salmon swimming upstream, as with his head down, on the dribble, he just kept leaping and shooting. In a mild media scandal, it was said after the game that Jordan had spent the day off between games three and four playing forty-six holes of golf. But when he scored fifteen in the first quarter of the clincher all was forgiven, and after that game Jordan was again in gleeful spirits—this time by himself at the podium, as Pippen had been injured.

Asked if he had a new nickname now, Jordan thought for a moment then said, "Golf Fanatic." Given his heroics in the first game of the finals, and his team's calm under pressure, it looked as if he would soon be able to exercise that fanaticism free of guilt.

A Sense of the Familiar

June 19, 1997

THE CONFETTI was a new touch, no doubt left over (if replenished) from last year's Democratic National Convention and fired off anew. Otherwise, the occasion of the Bulls' fifth NBA championship in seven years—and the third won here at home—was a familiar experience: the jubilation at the final buzzer, the playing of Queen's "We Are the Champions" and the tape loop of Gary Glitter's "Rock 'n' Roll, Part 2," the players dancing on the scorers' table and holding their children on lofty shoulders, the booing of NBA commissioner David Stern, Bulls owner Jerry Reinsdorf, and general manager Jerry Krause, followed by cheers for coach Phil Jackson, for each player, and especially for Michael Jordan, who was presented his fifth NBA finals MVP award. Even last year's question haunted the proceedings: Will Jackson, Jordan, and Dennis Rodman be back next year? This year there was a sense that the event was even more evanescent than it had been a year ago, and the confetti enhanced that impression. It spun and fluttered and hung in the air, giving the United Center the look of a fishbowl that players, spectators, and media were sharing, as other fans peered in from living rooms, dens, and bars across the city, across the nation, and around the world.

The feeling of instant nostalgia, of not merely preserving but guarding the moment as it happened, is something I and many others had fought during the second game of the series, when the Bulls took a commanding 2–0 lead against the Utah Jazz. They headed west for three games in Salt Lake City with no promise that they would return—not to play more basketball, anyway. Yet return they had, after losing twice and then saving the critical fifth game with one of Jordan's greatest performances. And so, with the most impressive sports dynasty of the '90s poised on the brink of dissolution amid celebration, I surrendered to the sentiment that this was a scene that should be impressed on the mind: the confetti fluttering, the fans stomping, Jordan waving his hand with five fingers outstretched (then mugging for the cameras by holding up his other hand and a sixth, a seventh, and an eighth finger), unlikely hero Steve Kerr hugging his wife and gleefully quoting "Yo, Adrian" from *Rocky*, and finally a giddy Brian Williams, the last piece of this season's puzzle, his dour, chubby-cheeked visage softened to reveal a Bacchus beneath the Buddha.

In many ways that transformation epitomized the differences between this year's Bulls and last year's. Last year's journey, mapped out by Jackson's book *Sacred Hoops*, was an almost mystical pursuit of transcendence. Could such disparate personalities—the humbled Jordan, the embittered Scottie Pippen, Croatian Toni Kukoc, Australian Luc Longley, Canadian Bill Wennington, various native scrubs, and, last but certainly not least, the converted villain Rodman—unite to play beautiful basketball? They could and did. This year's struggle was much less serene, much less a lesson in Zen. Defending the title turned out to be a classic tale of reclaiming what belongs to one, on the order of the *Iliad*.

"When you think about it, we've been playing together for eighteen of the last twenty-one months, with hardly a rest," Kerr said. "Last year was fun. I wouldn't consider this year as fun. It was more of a grind. But that makes it much more satisfying.

"I can understand why Michael retired after the third time. I can't even imagine what another run would be like, physically and mentally. It's so grueling. And this is just two for me."

The satisfaction of last year's championship seemed much more personal to the Bulls. They had wondered if they could do it, and they did; the struggle had largely been with themselves. This year's struggle seemed to be much more external, a proof to others to cement their place in history. As with many Greek heroes, the Bulls dwelled on their previous exploits—not in a bragging way but simply as statements of fact. Jackson compared Jordan's game-winning shot in the first game of the Jazz series to his miss in the first game of the 1991 finals against the Los Angeles Lakers, and Jordan admitted that he had thought of that game too, revealing that he always reviews his last-second misses before psyching himself up with memories of his successes when faced with the same opportunity. Jackson likewise compared Jordan's game-winning assist in the sixth game to the way he repeatedly gave up the ball to John Paxson in the fourth quarter of the clinching game in 1991. "Teams can finally find a way to play with a superstar in the crunch when he finds his teammates and they rely [on each other] and come through and play the team game," Jackson said. "That's what makes a championship. And Michael showed that championship level tonight by moving the ball to Steve." Even Kerr said that in the sixth game he had images of the bench players rallying the team to an inspired comeback, as they had in the final game in 1992 against the Portland Trail Blazers (a game he watched from home while a member of the Cleveland Cavaliers).

Comeback lightning struck repeatedly for the Bulls this season, especially in the playoffs. It became their modus operandi, and for good reason. The Bulls could no longer run down their prey with beautiful extended sequences of pursuit. They were older, some were injured, some sickly, and they won not with the energy of youth but with the pounce of experience. It wasn't until after the championship was won, and I looked down at the running account of the fourth quarter of the sixth game and saw that the Bulls had closed from nine points down with 11:24 left in the game to go one point up with 8:52 to play, that everything became clear. The Bulls had won time and again in that manner throughout the playoffs, by playing in bursts, and while fans and the media alike wondered where the beauty was, that was the way they'd had to play. They'd had to marshal their resources, keep the opponent within view, and then win with a crushing stroke. This style was deceptive. The Washington Bullets, the Atlanta Hawks, the Miami Heat—all kicked themselves for "giving away" games to the Bulls. The Jazz felt that way too after the first game. Yet, by the end, having learned by repetition, they had different thoughts.

"We didn't give anything away. They took it," Karl Malone said. "They did the things champions do."

The Bulls' pounce in the first game resulted in two straight turnovers by the normally dependable John Stockton. The second, a steal by Rodman, led to Jordan driving the lane and passing wide to Longley, who hit the open shot to put the Bulls up 76–75. From there the lead rattled back and forth until Jordan's decisive shot. It should be emphasized that nothing was animalistic about the Bulls' pounce. Everything they did in those moments was done with deliberation.

On the game-winning play Pippen inbounded the ball to Kukoc, then cut past a Jordan screen. This froze Jordan's defender, Bryon Russell, who had to make sure Pippen wasn't going to be open on a back-door play, and at that moment Jordan jumped out to take the pass from Kukoc. Let Jordan tell it from there.

"The double team never came," he said, "and I knew I was in a one-on-one situation. So I was dribbling, getting ready to cross over, and once I did cross over [Russell] went for the steal, lunged forward, which I thought was my opportunity to take one move to the left, pull up, and shoot the basket."

The Bulls pounced at the outset of the second game, scoring the first six points, and sealed the win with a 16–2 run at the end of the first half. Pippen drove the baseline and found Ron Harper open on the outside for a three, making it 36–29. After a defensive stop, Jordan got two free throws, missing the first and making the second; this was followed by the Bulls' full-court press and another Utah turnover, leading to a Harper lay-in—39–29. Harper hounded Stockton into another turnover, a steal by Jordan, who passed to Pippen for a slam dunk—43–29. The Bulls went to a small lineup in the closing moments. Jordan drove to the hoop, was fouled, and made both free throws for a 47–31 halftime advantage.

The Jazz, however, were not pushovers. Ahead by nineteen with six minutes to play, Jackson called a time-out but left a weary Jordan and Pippen in the game. The Jazz ran them down and made it close, and though the Bulls won 97–85 the Jazz drew on that momentum to rally themselves and win the third game in Utah. The Jazz also made one of the few key adjustments in the series, putting Russell instead of the smaller Jeff Hornacek on Jordan full time. Utah controlled the fourth game as well, until the Bulls pounced to take a 71–66 lead, the last two points coming on a long rebound to Pippen and an outlet pass to Jordan for a dunk. After Stockton hit a three-pointer from the general area of Montana, Jordan sank a dagger with a jump shot over a triple-team—73–69. But those were all the points the Bulls would score, and the Jazz slipped away. In the most beautiful play of the series, Jordan missed a jump shot, Malone ran out past him, and Stockton pulled down the rebound to the side of the lane and in one fluid motion fired a one-armed pass the length of the floor to hit Malone in stride over Jordan for a basket that put Utah up 74–73. The Jazz added four points for a 78–73 win to tie the series at two.

The fifth game offered the one unprecedented Jordan exploit of the series, a mythical, Ruthian performance—the Babe's "stomachache" and his called shot rolled into one. Jordan came down with a stomach virus and started throwing up in the early morning hours of game day. He stayed in bed throughout the day, missing the shoot-around practice, and emerged only for the game. He looked spent and miserable in the early going, and the Jazz took a sixteen-point lead early in the second quarter. Then, while Malone and Stockton sat on the bench, the Bulls made their first pounce. A lineup of Longley, Kukoc, Pippen, Jordan, and Harper whittled the margin while Malone was on the bench and even took a 45–44 lead before the Jazz struggled back to a 53–49 half-time advantage. The Bulls kept it tight at 72–67 after three quarters, and then again put on a push. It was ignited by an utterly uncontrived play, Kukoc coming down by himself on a fast break, no one under the hoop but a trio of backpedaling Utah players, and firing up a three to make it 77–74. Jordan followed moments later with another three to tie the game at 77.

From there the Bulls hung on like a boxer in a clinch. A two-minute scoring drought ended with the shot clock running down on the Jazz, the Bulls scrambling for a loose ball on the floor, and Stockton picking up the rolling ball and making another long three to put Utah up 84–81 with three minutes to go. Jordan kept the Bulls within reach of the lead with an answering basket, and then the teams exchanged free throws. In the final minute Jordan had a chance to put the Bulls ahead with two free throws, but he missed the second to leave the game tied at 85. Kukoc, however, kept the ball alive with a tap that landed at Jordan's feet at the free throw line. He dribbled out and passed to Pippen in the low post who, drawing Russell on the double team, passed out to an open Jordan. He launched a three, and no one knew how it got there— Jordan was almost staggering to the bench during breaks in play. But it did—88–85 Bulls. (That gave Jordan his final total of thirty-eight points, with the lion's share of those coming in the second and fourth quarters—talk about marshaling scant resources.) After a quick basket, the Jazz committed the critical mental mistake of the series. With less than twenty-four seconds to go, a single-possession game, they failed to foul on the inbounds pass. The Bulls broke the weak Utah press for a Longley dunk to seal what would turn out to be a 90–88 victory.

The Bulls came home with momentum, but the Jazz had the desperation and led the sixth game 23–17 after a quarter and 44–37 at the half. They controlled play in the third quarter as well, though the Bulls showed flourishes. Jordan drove through traffic for a layup and the first points of the second half, holding the ball aloft at the end like a waiter scurrying through a busy lunchroom with a tray of drinks. He later rebounded the ball and went coast to coast to make it 48–45 Jazz. But the Jazz regained the initiative and could have taken a commanding nine-point lead into the final frame but for a long Bulls rebound that bounced to Jud Buechler, who fired in a three-pointer at the end of the quarter to make it 70–64 Jazz. The Jazz did get their nine-point lead back early in the fourth, but then the Bulls pounced, with Pippen leading bench players Buechler, Kerr, Kukoc, and Williams. Kerr hit a shot over Stockton to make it 73–68. The Jazz isolated Malone and Stockton on the same side of the court, but the Bulls had become adept at countering that particular strategy. Williams pulled down a rebound and hit Pippen with an outlet pass. Pippen stopped and popped for a three-pointer to make it 73–71. Again the Jazz went to the two-man game. Again the Bulls stopped it, with Kukoc helping out along the baseline. That led to Kerr hitting a three on a crosscourt pass from Buechler to put the Bulls ahead 74–73.

Jordan came off the bench. The Jazz went back in front. Eschewing a pass to the open Kerr on the wing, Jordan hit a jumper in the lane over a double team to tie the game at 76. Hornacek hit a three; Jordan answered with a deuce. The Jazz hit Shandon Anderson cutting wide-open to the hoop on a back-door layup, but then the Bulls managed to isolate Kukoc on the shorter Hornacek in the low post and Kukoc turned and threw the ball into the hoop like a man tossing a hat onto a closet shelf. It was 81–80 Utah. The Jazz again ran the back-door play to Anderson, only this time he air-balled a layup over the hoop. Jordan hit to put the Bulls back on top 82–81. They maintained the lead until Russell hit a three to tie it at 86 with 1:44 to play. The game had reached a stalemate, both teams playing ferocious defense and the referees refusing to make a call. The Jazz's Chris Morris had a shot at a lay-in and, harassed by Pippen, missed it. Rodman came down with the rebound with twenty-eight seconds to go and immediately called a time-out.

Jackson drew up the play in the huddle, and everyone everywhere knew the ball would wind up in Jordan's hands. But from there what? Kerr later said that Jordan sat there quietly, visualizing the play, then turned to him. "You be ready," Jordan said. "Stockton's gonna come off you."

"I'll be ready," Kerr said. "I'll knock it down."

"And I was like, will I?" Kerr later added with a smile in the interview room.

Jordan got the ball on the left-hand side of the floor and, just as he had expected, was double-teamed by Stockton. Jordan leaped, faking the shot, and passed to Kerr, who had moved into the dead center of the free throw circle like a placekicker lining up a field goal. He threw the ball up, launching it from his heels, and it swished through the net.

After a Utah time-out, Pippen—who was everywhere all the time on defense, Stockton later said—deflected the inbounds pass, sprawled for the loose ball, and slapped it across the court to Kukoc for a breakaway slam dunk. Kukoc came down and immediately began to celebrate and the Bulls and the fans and the city with him.

This was the best of the Bulls' five finals appearances because it offered the most noble, poised, and intelligent opponent, and because the drama ebbed and flowed throughout. It had a lovely set of bookends in Jordan's game-winning shot and his game-winning assist, and in between was a great all-around team performance in the second game and Jordan's heroics in the fifth. If there were any doubt before, Jordan established himself here as the greatest athlete any of us are likely to see in our lifetimes. He stepped into the media interview room afterward with a magnum of champagne under his left arm and a cigar nestled comfortably in his right hand, and—unlike other members of his team—he was eager to talk about the future, especially given the speculation that Reinsdorf and Krause might opt to rebuild, booting Jackson and dealing Pippen before next season.

"We've done a lot for this organization," Jordan said, beginning a cost-benefit analysis that ought to be repeated in many a business school. He pointed out that the worth of the franchise has multiplied tenfold since his arrival. "So the profits have been made over the years. What we gain now—in trying to keep this team together and successful—we paid for over six, seven, eight, ten years. There has to be some sense of consideration, some sense of loyalty to myself, to Scottie, to Phil, even to those guys who have given of themselves the last two years, even Dennis.

"We are entitled to defend what we have until we lose it," he added, tapping his fingers on the table so that they would rap ominously—boom, boom, boom—from my tape recorder on playback. "If we lose it, then you could look at it and say, 'OK, let's change it, go through rebuilding.' No one's guaranteeing that rebuilding will be two, three, four, or five years. The Cubs have been rebuilding for forty-two years."

It's actually fifty-two years, but who's counting?

"You want to look at this as a business thing? Have a sense of respect for the people who have laid the groundwork so that you could be a profitable organization. I'd like to see us defend what we've attained," he added, "and Phil should be the coach, and I shouldn't have to be put in a position to have to play for another head coach other than Phil Jackson. Simple as that. Sad as it may be, I have choices. And I will not choose to play for another coach.

"For once, don't look at the bottom line. Look at the joy of this night."

That night, after I got home, having driven through a city where people were milling on almost every corner waving Bulls pennants and jerseys and homemade signs, I fixed myself a drink and sat on the front steps smoking a cigar. As I found myself studying the play of the corner streetlight as it filtered through the fingers of the locust tree next door, I remembered having preserved the same image in the mind's eye on four previous occasions. All around were the now-familiar sounds of a city celebrating its way into the wee hours: horns blaring and friends shouting to one another and a blast of fireworks now and then for punctuation. To think that an entire city should know such joy but five times. How precious are such occasions? How precious do they have to be?

The Last Shot

June 25, 1998

FOR ONE brief moment, my thoughts and Michael Jordan's were remarkably similar, though he later expressed them much more preciously than I ever would. There were 1.1 seconds to go in game five of the NBA finals at the United Center. The Utah Jazz were leading 83–81, but after a timeout the Bulls had the ball, and everyone knew it would be going to one of two persons: Jordan, who'd had an off shooting night but had made so many game-winning shots throughout his career, or Toni Kukoc, who had kept the Bulls in the game almost single-handedly by making eleven of thirteen shots from the field, four of six from three-point range, for thirty points. Jordan was later asked what he was thinking at that point.

"I have funny thoughts, actually," he said with a smile. "I was just joking with some of the guys . . . that for a split second, at 1.1 seconds, no one knew what was going to happen. Everybody was anticipating a big shot—on our side, on their side. Everyone thought I could make the shot. And that's the beauty of the game. That's part of the unexpected finishing of an NBA game. And I thought that was cute, just thinking about it."

Jordan had surprised the reporters covering the game by appearing in the interview room after missing that last-second shot not with a dour expression or in a downcast state of mind, but with a relaxed, pleasant, and easy demeanor. And his use of the word *cute* sent this jaded group around the bend. They burst into laughter, and the laughter caused the reporter with the next question to halt as he began it, which gave Jordan the slightest opening to elaborate. Even in defeat, he seized the moment.

"I mean, I was just sitting there thinking about the whole thing," he said. "At 1.1 I know I wanted the ball, but no one knew what was going to happen. Isn't that ironic? That's pretty much the way things have happened for me in my career, and I'm pretty sure everybody was hoping that would end that way—except for Utah people. At 1.1 seconds, everybody was holding their breath—which is kind of cute."

Oddly enough, I had felt that same sense of delighting in the moment as the Bulls called a time-out to set up their final shot. I had moved down from a press seat in the upper levels of the UC to a courtside spot vacated by a *New York Times* writer no doubt facing a deadline and at that moment slaving away in the relative calm of the media workroom. I looked at the Bulls in their huddle and at the writers typing ferociously all around me and at the fans all but bursting with tension, and I gloried in the moment. One nearby writer turned to another and said, "Don't worry, he makes the shot and we all go home," and I certainly felt the same. But I wasn't sure if Jordan would be taking the last shot or acting as a decoy for Kukoc (which is what coach Phil Jackson later said he had in mind, except that the inbounds play was a muddle, and after a second inbounds pass it was Jordan who hurled up a desperation shot that wasn't close). Not knowing was, as Jordan put it, what made everything so "cute," but what I knew with conviction was that if Jordan or Kukoc didn't make a game-winning shot in this moment, Jordan would in the next game or—and this is where Jordan's thoughts and mine diverged, because this last one was really my preference—in the seventh game. As everyone knows by now, Jordan made the game-winning, series-clinching, sixth-championship-sealing shot in game six in Utah, made it at the end of a sequence no less an authority than Jackson called "the best performance ever." Michael Jordan made the game-winning shot after a game-saving steal after a drive and a scoop lay-in through traffic that cut the Utah lead to one point after John Stockton had hit a three that seemed to give the Jazz the series-tying game. As one United Center placard had put it earlier in the series (at the risk of offending sensitive readers on racial grounds): "Babe Ruth is the Michael Jordan of baseball."

I knew the Bulls would win the sixth game or at worst/best the seventh because they had already won the series, had won it when they held on to win the fourth game to go up 3–1, after which, as Jackson acknowledged, everyone on the team knew it was "a matter of time." The fourth game was the one the Jazz really needed if they were to challenge the Bulls, yet they came out looking like whipped dogs after the forty-two-point thrashing the Bulls had administered in game three. They were clearly just hoping to hang around and maybe get lucky and steal a victory at the end, and if they had maybe it would have been a different series. Yet it wasn't to be, thanks to thirty-four points by Jordan, twenty-eight by Scottie Pippen—who at that point, with his lone-wolf defense and his reliable if second-fiddle offense, looked likely to end Jordan's string of five NBA finals most valuable player awards—and a fourteen-rebound, six-point performance by Dennis Rodman, all of his points coming at the free throw line, the last four on perfect foul shooting in the final three minutes of the game.

With just more than half of the fourth quarter to go and the Bulls up 68–66, Utah fouled Rodman to go into the penalty; every Jazz foul after that would send the Bulls to the line. But this seemed a mixed blessing with Rodman on the floor—he shoots foul shots the way a teenager takes out the trash. He made one of two, and the Jazz charged back to take the lead, 70–69. With less than three minutes to play and the score tied, Rodman rebounded a Pippen miss and was immediately fouled. "FUCK!" I wrote in my notebook. Rodman's first shot bounced five times on the rim before plopping through the net like a recalcitrant water droplet down a funnel. It was the pivotal point of the series; if that shot had bounced out, everything might have been different. As it was, Rodman made his next three free throws—the last two coming with forty-four seconds left to give the Bulls an 81–77 lead—and the Bulls claimed an 86–82 victory. It was over; the only detail in doubt was whether the Bulls would win it here or in Utah.

Rodman, of course, had called the ire of the sports-reporting world down on his head two days before the fourth game by deliberately missing practice and the media interview session in order to take part in a pro wrestling brouhaha in Detroit. The *Sun-Times*'s Jay Mariotti led the lynch party, calling Jackson spineless and saying Rodman had to go, as no title was worth the embarrassment he caused the game (though, to mete out the demerits in proper proportion, NBC play-by-play man Bob Costas chimed in with some similarly simpleminded sentiments on local radio).

I had been thinking a lot about the ultimate meaning of the story of Michael Jordan and the Bulls (thoughts I'm trying to hold on to until the story is finally over), and Rodman figured in. Rodman was a clue to what the Bulls' now six championships mean. That's because Jordan changed the way we think about sports in Chicago. Like Harold Washington only slightly before him, Jordan made a statement in every moment of his public life that it no longer was satisfactory to be a good loser, which is what Chicagoans had so often been up until the '90s. In politics, even more than in sports, good intentions don't mean shit; what's important is to win, preferably with ideals or honor intact.

Utah coach Jerry Sloan, himself a Chicago sports legend, seemed to speak for that old state of mind when he was asked if it would be worth winning if he had to tolerate Rodman. "First of all I wouldn't have him," Sloan said on the day before the fourth game. "That makes the question real simple. Winning has never been real important to me. Would I sacrifice everything for all the other guys on the team? It's never that important. I'd just as soon lose if I have to be put in that situation."

The old-school sports experts felt Rodman had to be put in his place. But Jackson's whole coaching process is about accepting individuals for who they are, yet getting them to meld themselves into a team on the court, a process that has never had much to do with arbitrary discipline. (He succeeded in melding the individualist Jordan into the team long before Rodman arrived in Chicago.) Furthermore, it takes a special person to play with Jordan and the Bulls, a person who can function in a media cyclone, who can ignore possible distractions and focus on team performance in the moment—and Rodman, since arriving here in the fall of 1995, has been that type of player. In fact, he apparently creates turmoil in order to make himself feel more comfortable within it, and that is what makes him an essential part of the Bulls—as a player and, more abstractly, as a clue to the team. The Bulls didn't cave in to Rodman— they didn't make a deal with the devil to win three more championships. Rather, their ability to embrace and incorporate Rodman is the quality that gave them the strength to win three more championships. That is perhaps Jackson's greatest legacy; he didn't make the individuals fit the team but vice versa. No other coach would have won six championships with these players, would have been able to keep things fresh, but the strain was great. He aged at the rate of a two-term president, and earlier this week he called it quits.

Jackson gloried in Rodman's fourth-game triumph as if it were his own—which, in a way, it was. "The much-maligned Dennis Rodman had a wonderful game for us tonight," he said. A makeshift poster displayed prominently in a restaurant reporters had to walk past on their way to the locker rooms stated it even better: "We want Rodman, not Mariotti," it said, adding at the bottom, "How many rings have you won, Jay?" Chicago sports fans, it seemed, would rather not go back to the attitude that preserving some Neanderthal sense of honor was better than winning.

The Jazz played the fifth game the way they should have played the fourth: with an air of desperation. They outshot the Bulls, making more than half of their field-goal attempts for the first time in the series, and, even more important, outrebounded them. Antoine Carr fed off the Bulls' and Pippen's double-teaming scheme to the tune of twelve points, and Karl Malone hit seemingly everything he threw up, finishing with thirty-nine points. Kukoc kept the Bulls in the game, scoring thirteen of their first fourteen points and finishing with thirty, but Pippen—beginning to suffer from back problems that would figure even more prominently in the next game—saw his MVP hopes go down the drain with a two-of-sixteen shooting performance. Jordan wasn't much better, making nine of twenty-six for twenty-eight points. Yet Jordan still had that final shot to win, and the Bulls didn't seem that worried about returning to Utah. Oh, they said all the right things about their concern at now having to win it on the Jazz's home court, but between the lines it wasn't hard to read their studied contempt. Jackson dismissed Carr's performance by saying, "They finally found someone off the bench who could give them a lift," and waved away the gathering hysteria by adding, "You guys have to remember, this is a two-point win by the Jazz, and you don't throw out the baby with the bathwater in that situation. We're fine." Winning in Utah would be difficult, yes, but Jackson and the Bulls felt they had a handle on the Jazz dating back even to their first-game loss, and the Sloan-coached Jazz didn't figure to come up with any new wrinkles any time soon, much less in the one day of travel between the fifth and sixth games.

Or, as Malone put it earlier, "I don't think they're taking us seriously at all." And the Bulls never really did. They had the Jazz outsmarted, and they knew it. It wasn't that the Utah players were stupid; it was that they were set in their ways and therefore dependable in their weakness.

"A loss like this can get your attention," Malone had said after the third game. "Our plays work, but we have to run them." Considering that the Jazz had just been beaten 96–54—a time to throw out baby, bathwater, and playbook if ever there was one—those were famous last words.

In all the commotion over Rodman early last week, in all the contempt that poured over his self-aggrandizement after he said he'd pay for the funeral of that fellow allegedly dragged to death behind a pickup truck in Texas, lost was this quote, as pithy an explanation for the Bulls' success as there is. Rodman was asked about how the Bulls bench had outplayed the ballyhooed Utah subs. "I think we have the smartest bench in the world," Rodman said. "As far as talent, we are probably at the bottom of the totem pole. But as far as smartness, awareness, knowledge of the game of basketball, we are the smartest twelve guys in the league. No one else in the league can understand why we win so much. If you look at us one through twelve, you see why we win so much."

So the Bulls had them beat tactically going into the sixth game; all they needed to pull together was their collective psyche. This Jordan seemed to understand when he made such a glib performance in the media room following the fifth game. "When we get on the plane tomorrow, I hope everybody's forgotten about this game," he said. "Sure, we blew an opportunity. It's happened to us before. My job as a leader is still to maintain the positive thought process it takes to go into a game, a road game, and come out with a win. Now how I do that I don't know yet. In '93, I got on the plane with a cigar and celebrated a little bit and got everybody else to enjoy themselves a little bit and relax a little bit and play the game. Tomorrow I don't know. I don't know how I'm going to do it, but somehow it's going to happen."

Jordan said in his recent interview with Henry Louis Gates Jr. in *The New Yorker* that the TV ad of his he liked most was the one in which he talked about how many times he had failed and how those failures had set him up for his greatest exploits. What can one add to what would prove to be the final game of the series except that it was perhaps the greatest display of that phoenixlike quality, not forty-eight hours after Jordan had missed what would have been the game-winning shot in Chicago? Pippen, who only later acknowledged that his back had limited him in the fifth game, had to leave with spasms in the first half after wrenching it on a dunk. The Jazz led 49–45 at the half and 66–61 after three quarters. No doubt haunted by memories of his seventh-game migraine against the Detroit Pistons eight years earlier, Pippen returned in the second half to give Jordan support and a much-needed rest, hitting a couple of important shots in the lane over the smaller Jeff Hornacek. After each of these, he gamely trotted up the court like an old man in need of a walker and somehow played courageous defense. Rodman, left alone by Malone, hit a big jumper to bring the Bulls within one at 68–67, punctuating the point with a Jordanesque shrug of the shoulders. Kukoc came off a Steve Kerr screen to hit a three and tie the game at 70, and after that the teams battled back and forth until, with the game tied at 83 in the final minute, Malone passed crosscourt out of a double team to John Stockton, who knocked down a three barely over the hand of the onrushing Ron Harper to make it 86–83 Utah with forty-one seconds to go. What happened then was the capping event of the Jordan legend—sixteen years and who knows how many game-winning shots after his season-ending, championship-winning jumper against Georgetown to give Dean Smith his first title in Jordan's fresh-man year, at North Carolina. If the parallel between alpha and omega is a little too tidy for reality then maybe that's a cause for optimism that this couldn't possibly be Jordan's last shot. And if it is? Well, it's just too great an ending to be real.

How did it rank? Let's go back to the authority, Jackson. Smoking a cigar, drinking from a plastic cup no doubt filled with some of the champagne that had somehow missed his shirt, he scratched pensively at his ear and said, "Last year, in the fifth game here, I didn't think he could top that, the performance he had in that ball game." That was the famous game in which Jordan carried the Bulls to victory and a 3–2 lead in the series by scoring thirty-eight points while suffering from stomach flu. "But I think he topped it tonight," Jackson said. "I think it's the best performance ever I've seen by Michael in a critical game in a critical situation to win the series."

What did he do? On taking the inbounds pass, he drove immediately around Bryon Russell and through traffic to scoop in a layup that gave the Bulls a two-for-one end-of-quarter possession advantage and closed the Utah lead to one at 86–85. After Malone used Jordan's man,

Hornacek, as a screen to get open for a pass at the other end of the floor, Jordan doubled back on Malone and, coming from behind, slapped the ball loose and beat Malone to the floor to pick it up. Then, with the clock ticking down, the Bulls, avoiding a time-out that would have given the Jazz the opportunity to set up the defense, automatically spread the floor to get Jordan one-on-one with Russell at the top of the circle. Jordan cut right—just as he had moments earlier—then stopped abruptly. Russell's feet went out from under him as he tried to reverse himself, and he fell, leaving Jordan wide open. No one ran at him. He stopped, leaped, shot, left his wrist flexed in the air, raised himself up ever so slightly on his toes as he landed—all the body English this shot required—and watched it swish through the hoop.

I have seen that basket dozens of times since then—who hasn't?—and what gets me every time, what brings tears to my eyes, is the way it goes through without even brushing the rim—not just game, series, match, and sixth title, but victory on style points as well.

How impossibly, extravagantly, eternally, appropriately cute.

3

Setting Free
the Bears

A Team as Great as Payton

November 15, 1985

AT LAST, at long last, Walter Payton is on a team as great as he is.

In a play during the second half of last Sunday's game against the Detroit Lions, Payton caught a pass over the middle. The ball was thrown slightly behind him, to his right, as he faced backup quarterback Steve Fuller, so that Payton had to give an unintentional but effective juke to the right as he caught the ball. He then turned back to his left, running at a diagonal across the field, but where the Payton of ten years ago had to make his own yardage, to fake each new defender until finally the pursuit of the defense on the whole overcame the time required to fake each defender singly, here Payton ran freely, easily, and with few obstacles. For there, out in the middle of the field, ten yards from the line of scrimmage, a series of Bears blockers appeared, and Payton ran across the field and set up each in turn, so that, like a night watchman, he seemed to be tripping a series of switches according to some schedule, and out went the Lions—one, two, three—like lights. The Lions did, finally, chase Payton down on that play, but that didn't lessen it in the least. Whether the play was planned that way is irrelevant; either Mike Ditka is some sort of coaching genius, setting up blocking assignments for his linemen ten yards downfield and beyond, or, at very least, the Bears linemen were humping it downfield to help Payton on his way, to make his job of eluding the Lions easier and, of course, to advance the ball. Either way, this is not the sort of thing the Bears have done in our lifetime, and it is not the sort of support that has ever been given to Walter Payton—not in Chicago, not in college, not in the peewee leagues.

We've always taken Payton for granted; he's been the best player on the Bears for a decade now. He made the Bears' offense good when it was good, and he made the Bears watchable when the whole rest of the team was awful. In order to see what a great player he is, we'd have to get some distance on him, to judge him as a player rather than as the Chicago football franchise. George Allen, a very wise football coach who made

his bones here under George Halas before going out on his own in Los
Angeles and Washington (we won't sully his good name with the USFL
cities), said Sunday at halftime, while sitting with Brent Musburger, that
Eric Dickerson, of the Rams, is a better running back. Allen was, however, wrong. He may have meant that Dickerson was, at this time, a better runner, the sort of back he could build a team around, and in this he
would be correct; but Payton is a far better running back, if we remember that running is only one thing an offensive back must do, and that he
should also be a fine blocker and pass receiver. Payton is all these things,
and he does them all equally well. Matt Suhey, who ran for over one hundred yards against the Lions, said in a television interview after the game
that Payton is a better blocker than he is a runner, and although Suhey's
eyes were shining with the glow of a player who does not often achieve
one hundred yards and who thinks that having him run the ball is a
pretty good idea after all, it did not belie the obvious respect Suhey holds
for Payton, the man who does everything correctly. If Dickerson is the
sort of one-dimensional back that a team is built around, then Payton is
fully realized, a great running back who will play equally well on any sort
of team and, in his ways both small and great, fill any deficiencies. That
sort of player is far more valuable, and if we can get the distance from
him to see him as a person doing a job, rather than as a player gaining
yards for our team, he is far more impressive to watch.

The Bears are having the same sort of effect on us these days. If we
can forget, for a moment, that these are the same Bears that have dis-
appointed us for decades, if we can watch them on television as if we
were watching one of the teams that are usually set in Dallas or Miami
or Los Angeles, we can see how great they are. Perhaps it was Fuller's
presence at quarterback that allowed us this distance last Sunday, but
for the first time this year it seemed that the Bears were a truly great
team in that they did all the small things correctly. The Bears, at this
point, are looking as if they deserve to be compared to the Pittsburgh
Steelers teams of the '70s. The Steelers were the best team we've ever
seen; they were a team for every football fan, for the aficionado and
the local rooter. Their defense was both nasty and complex: it consisted
of a great secondary, including Mel Blount and the still-active Donnie
Shell, it had a great front four, the Steel Curtain, including "Mean" Joe

Greene, and in between it had Jack Ham, the stereotypical Penn State linebacker, and Jack Lambert, the second-best middle linebacker the game has ever seen. On offense, Franco Harris and Rocky Bleier were made by the intricate blocking of the offensive line, and, of course, the Steelers were also capable of amazing plays in the air, with Lynn Swann at wide receiver and the rough-yet-elegant Terry Bradshaw at quarterback, a man who could fight a linebacker for a first down on one play and then arch a perfect spiral to Swann the next. This was a team that was amazing to watch—they typified all that is great about football—and it is the sort of teams the Bears are beginning to resemble, if we can forget, for a moment, about William "Refrigerator" Perry.

Not that Perry isn't a fine player; no, the Refrigerator backlash is not going to start here. It's just that Perry, like first-string quarterback Jim McMahon, has a tendency to distract by his mere presence. His performance in the Monday-night game against the Green Bay Packers, earlier this year, was one of the top moments of the football season so far, and it's what made him the celebrity he is. If his touchdown, his thundering spike of that football that made pigs squeal as far away as Iowa, and his comic attempts to lift his three hundred pounds off the ground for a leaping high five were guilty pleasures, his two blocks of linebacker George Cumby were pure football, regardless of how many times they were replayed. O. J. Simpson, in one of his brighter moments, said, before Payton's second score, "Get down low, George," and this joking advice, which seemed to be the very thought in Cumby's head at the moment, was nevertheless worthless, because the Refrigerator again blasted Cumby out of the way and Payton went into the end zone untouched.

McMahon, likewise, carries a presence as large as—if more ephemeral than—Perry's. His temperament seems to flavor a game. Watching the Bears when McMahon is playing well—or even when he is slightly off his game and is gutting it out—we are aware of his running the show, of his character in leading the team, and of his pure talent as a quarterback. He is a great player who is having a great year, and he is the player who makes the Bears' offense go, but watching last Sunday was instructive. Fuller is a quarterback of small talents, the stereotypical backup. He runs the team in a manner of someone who had been preparing for weeks without getting the chance: he relies on brains. The Bears, meanwhile, without McMahon's dogged leadership, seemed to be running themselves. We concentrated on the blocking last Sunday, and the intricacies of the Bears' line were remarkable. The Lions were running a three-man line, and the Bears muscled them at will all afternoon, allowing both Payton and Suhey their one-hundred-yard days. Lions nose guard Doug English, meanwhile, is a heady, aggressive player, and the Bears must have recognized this from the first, because they had English spinning with fakes and seemingly missed blocks that made him look like a commuter caught in a revolving door.

Of course, there is the defense, and as with all good defenses it is difficult, sometimes, to determine just what it is that makes it impenetrable. The Lions and the New England Patriots have both proved themselves as giant killers this year, yet both looked inept against the Bears. When the Bears win because a team just had a bad day, that's one thing, but when team after team seems to be having bad days against them, that's something else. Buddy Ryan's complicated and numerous defenses, of course, cause much of the problem. George Allen, meanwhile, pointed out that the Bears bunch their defensive line toward the middle, putting one man each on the guards and the center, which makes the difficult center position even more difficult, and which means that few teams—none this year—have been able to run between the tackles against the Bears. (The Lions' James Jones had a great day, yet gained only sixty-eight yards in nineteen carries.) Yet the defense, too, is establishing its personalities, with Dan Hampton and the yeoman Steve McMichael standing out, Wilber Marshall proving himself, and the great middle linebacker Mike Singletary getting greater. With his brainy-looking glasses, talking about the game on television and how disappointingly the defense played after yet another rout, Singletary looks like the man who runs the complicated Bears defense, and we love the way he squints toward the sideline looking for signals during the game, trying to make his eyes do the work usually done by those glasses. The secondary, meanwhile, is proving itself also; last Sunday, it made room for a rookie, Reggie Phillips, at cornerback, and we barely heard about him, which means he had a fine day, because cornerbacks are only noticed when they intercept a pass or when they let a touchdown get thrown over their heads.

Perhaps it's that the Bears are getting so good that they demand to be accepted on their own terms; it's no longer necessary to be a hometown fan, overlooking their deficiencies and loving Walter Payton. Perhaps it was, simply, that we took the Lions and their eleven points in the football pool last week that allowed us this clarity of vision. Eleven points allowed a large margin for rooting for both the Bears and the Lions, and when the Bears went up 21–3 we tried to root the Lions on to another score, yet there were the Bears, playing stern defense, forcing another field goal. When Tyrone Keys broke through the line and dumped the Lions' quarterback—scrubeenie sack time—we couldn't help but laugh. This week, we take the Bears in a pick 'em game against the Dallas Cowboys, and from then on we'll take them giving points to whomever they play, for as long as they play. They're just no fun to root against.

Super Bears

January 31, 1986

LIKE JIM MCMAHON, I felt strangely unmoved by the Bears' Super Bowl victory. Driving through town immediately after the game, we saw people running and yelling in the streets, and we heard the sounds of nearby firecrackers and saw the explosions of far-off bottle rockets, but these seemed merely confirmation that what we thought we had seen had indeed been true. The revelers were like the first robins of spring in that they supported what our senses had told us long before: the Bears are the best team in the National Football League. So what else is new?

Monday, in search of the real thing, I gathered with the throng of five hundred thousand at Daley Plaza to wait for the Bears. We were cold, and no matter how much we huddled it did little good. I covered my head with a Cubs baseball cap, complete with a line prepared for any photographer who might track me down ("You've got to remember the pain to enjoy the pleasure"). Teenagers usually dominate these sorts of affairs, and in the cold, especially, this was the case. They were excitable and antsy and moody; they didn't handle the wait well. A city employee kept trying to calm the crowd; although it was comfy but cozy where we were, about halfway down the plaza, people were evidently being crushed up front. "In consideration of you, your loved ones, and the Bears, please move back," he said, and one nearby kid responded, "No, you move back." They booed Harold Washington on his arrival, then aped his every cheer. Woodstock or Altamont? I thought.

I had never been to a ticker-tape parade, and from the looks of it neither had many of the other people, including those employed by the police and street departments. The city has, quite simply, forgotten how to throw a ticker-tape parade, like some old, bedraggled housewife who has watched the silver tarnish and the glasses dust over because her husband has long since lost interest in playing host. The streets weren't cordoned off, so that after Washington said the Bears' buses were only two blocks away and would be there in five minutes it was still thirty minutes before the buses got close enough for five Bears to walk to the stage without fearing for their lives. Yet that last thirty minutes was the best, and it won me over to the Bears and the teenagers and all the celebration.

The crowd at the plaza watched on the large outdoor television screen as the buses moved along by inches, and finally the Bears grew as anxious as the crowd and climbed up on the roofs of the buses. They were driving down Washington Street, and after a while I could monitor their progress because I could see the ticker tape falling out the windows of the buildings all down the street as if it were a waterfall of paper. Nearby, in the old State of Illinois Building, someone on one of the top floors pushed a huge, tangled mass of paper out the window, and in the cold wind it twisted and rose and fluttered; behind this building, plumes of white rose from the smokestack of another skyscraper, so that the fluttering of paper seemed to move in rhythm with the smoke. The Bears arrived like gladiators atop the buses, and the cheering increased. We endured a short speech by team president Michael McCaskey, booed a Marshall Field executive, and cheered them both off the stage when Willie Gault appeared. A handful of Bears followed, and when Steve McMichael, the anchor of the defensive line, got to the podium, the entire crowd seemed to deliver the "woof, woof, woof" cheer of the defense, so that it wasn't until later, on the news, that I heard what McMichael had said: "I just have one thing to say. We all have braggin' rights over the whole goddamn country."

Washington proclaimed the party over almost immediately after McMichael's pithy speech, and we booed and then moved for the exits. I followed a group toward the north end of the plaza, but everyone else seemed to be going south, and for a moment we were all lifted off our feet by one another, smiling and yelling, before the northbounders were pushed right and gave way to the southbound. The plaza, however, cleared quickly and smoothly, and as we walked away we saw fans climbing the light posts to take down the large, elegant Bears banners hanging there. When one fellow finally got one down—which took a good deal of effort—we cheered, and walked onward to wherever we were going, marching in the way of buses and taxis, knotting traffic for blocks in all directions. Is this paradise? I thought, is this it? and decided it was as close as we had been in some time.

It took me a while to enjoy the local Super Bowl hype—the endless photos and television tapes of every grade-school child doing the Super Bowl Shuffle—but the hype from New Orleans was something else entirely. I read everything, and I loved every small detail. What we must all remember is that we pick a Super Bowl champion the way we pick a president: we put people under far more pressure than any human being should be expected to endure, then we let them out saying, "Let the best man win." This was, easily, the most enjoyable Super Bowl hype since the Raiders and Al Davis showed up the entire league two years ago, but it was the most dramatic Super Bowl hype since the first big one, Super Bowl III, when Joe Namath "guaranteed" that the New York Jets, two-touchdown underdogs, would beat the Baltimore Colts. That, we must remember, was a brash, even revolutionary statement at the time, because athletes simply didn't predict they would win, not even when they had the better team. Modesty reigned. Nowadays, every player is guaranteeing victory, and some, like the Bears' Otis Wilson, were predicting slaughters, but this is what we've come to expect. It's the age of the braggart. Jim McMahon, however, found new ways to deal with the hype, and he took the pressure on his shoulders by denying it existed. His behavior before this Super Bowl was at least as revolutionary as Namath's before Super Bowl III, yet because he antagonized the press rather than playing to its excesses (as Namath did) he was denied an award he fully deserved, the Most Valuable Player.

McMahon took the pressure on himself. His teammates, therefore, received gentler treatment. Everyone was talking about what everyone else thought of McMahon and his acupuncture, McMahon and his mooning incident, McMahon and his opinion of New Orleans, McMahon and his headbands, and because of all these trivial distractions the Bears never had time to worry about anything else. Of course, all McMahon's pregame shenanigans make him merely foolish if he doesn't produce on Sunday, but he did. He ran the offense, he passed with precision, he took the ball on the run and he took some hits, and he scored two touchdowns. He seemed to overrule Ditka at the end of the first half and pushed the ball upfield when running out the clock was the more judicious tack. (Ditka's face, at these moments, looked like that of a Greek sailing hero tossed into a storm by the gods of the seas; he was waiting for disaster even as he trusted in his own good fortune and the luck of his quarterback.) Against the Patriots' vaunted turnover defense, McMahon threw no interceptions and committed no fumbles. Compare his statistics to Namath's, who was named MVP in a landslide: McMahon completed twelve of twenty passes, Namath seventeen of twenty-eight, for very similar percentages, but McMahon threw for 256 yards to Namath's 206 in eight fewer passes. MVP Richard Dent played a great game, as did Willie Gault, as did Mike Singletary, as did William "Refrigerator" Perry, but McMahon dictated the tempo on and off the field for two weeks; he dealt with the pressure in his own unique fashion and when the game came he was up to it.

The Bears may have trashed Chicago's reputation for choking, but Illinois's reputation remained firmly entrenched. "Champaign" Tony Eason, the Fighting Illini alumnus, reacted to the Bears' rush the way a flower reacts to the first breezes of winter: he cringed, he tucked the ball in, and as the Bears blew about him he folded up like a bulb and prepared to take his punishment, thinking—already—of next year. He was waiting to be planted in the ground, and he was. Eason's behavior was not atypical for the Pats; coach Raymond Berry tried to alter his team's offensive persona to adapt to the Bears' defense, and when they were snuffed in the first series and had to settle for a field goal their spirit was broken and the game was just about over. (When McMahon marched the Bears downfield to tie the game on the next series, the game was over, and when the defense forced two turnovers for two quick scores the game was a rout.) That was the difference between the two teams—their quarterbacks and the way the squads as a whole reacted to the pressure, and the brazen Bears won the most one-sided game in Super Bowl history.

Now we speak of dynasties. The Bears have a defense unlike any the NFL has ever seen, both in personnel and in strategy. Buddy Ryan has been idolized unlike any other assistant coach in football history, but he will move on to be head man in Philadelphia, and who can blame him? The Bears' defense ought not to be affected: they have the players who will do the job regardless. So like all the recent dynasties—the Pittsburgh Steelers, the Minnesota Vikings, and the Miami Dolphins in the '70s, the Green Bay Packers in the '60s, the Dallas Cowboys in both eras—

the Bears have begun with defense, but they also have the catalyst that makes the entire team go—the quarterback Jim McMahon. We knew he would be great when he pulled into Chicago as a rookie and stepped from the limo with his dark sunglasses on and a Stroh's in his hand. McMahon is a gamer, he is going to get even better, and with him at the helm the Bears should be very good—and very entertaining—for as long as a football team can expect to stay together.

It turns out that, on the other side of the score, the words are not much different; only the inflection is changed.

"Wait until *next* year."

Da Coach Outcoached

January 9, 1987

HUBRIS MAY have had something to do with it, but this was hardly the stuff of tragedy, this early decline and fall of the Bears' dynasty. It was, rather, something we had been warned about but hadn't believed. If we hadn't actually expected it, we had dreaded it the way we dread our dreams, when the small faults of characters align themselves in a conspiracy of self-destruction we hope will never happen in real life. Well, in real life it happened to the Bears, and we watched. They were outplayed and outthunk but mostly, I believe, they were outcoached. It was a team loss in that everyone played poorly, but if anyone should accept the responsibility alone it's Mike Ditka.

Not because he started Doug Flutie. That was a gutsy move typical of Ditka, a move that affirms our faith in him as a coach, faith to follow the Bears into next year anyway. Oh, Jim McMahon was right, to be sure. Sending an inexperienced quarterback into the playoffs was like sending Bambi outside to play during the hunting season, but it was the best choice available. It made its own kind of sense. Mike Tomczak, whom Flutie replaced, was equally green. Steve Fuller was McMahon's first choice and the choice of the television second-guessers, but that choice was wrong. Anyone who saw Fuller's starts earlier in the year saw a quarterback who, for one reason or another, had lost what little poise he had to begin with. McMahon, being the basically lazy sort that he is, liked Fuller above Tomczak and Flutie because Fuller offers the least competition. A team with Fuller at quarterback is a team awaiting the return of McMahon. No, Ditka made the right choice, but in doing so he risked the Bears' chances this year against those of next year, mortgaging this year's crop for next. Unfortunately, the locusts came three weeks before harvest. Flutie, however, not only offers the brightest future for a McMahonless Bears team but in the meantime motivates McMahon to get cracking. Any talk of Flutie being the starting quarterback going into training camp should be taken with this in mind, because I don't believe Ditka is ever going to allow McMahon to be traded. The problem was that Ditka was thinking about motivation rather than a game plan.

Ditka didn't outcoach himself, however; he didn't have to. There was somebody on the other side of the field more than willing to teach him a few lessons. The Washington Redskins and Joe Gibbs came to town with a game plan so beautiful it can be appreciated again and again, although we probably won't be watching this game as often as we watched Super Bowl XX. Last Sunday, while the rest of the football world watched the New York Giants lay claim to the Bears' abandoned throne, I was watching the tape of the Bears-Redskins game. The Redskins' unstoppable offense—so nightmarishly inexplicable the day before—suddenly made sense. The Redskins spread out the Bears the way a teenage lothario spreads a pair of thighs—with a little enticement and a lot of simple game playing, prompting responses and anticipating them—and like a teenage lothario when they saw an opening they waited for nothing. In the words of Alex in *A Clockwork Orange*, they practiced the old in-out, in-out. They went to wide receivers on sideline patterns, then they ran straight at the Bears. They went wide to Art Monk, then they went straight with George Rogers. Once this pattern had been established, they played little variations off it. They went wide, they went straight, they ran Kelvin Bryant off tackle. They threw over the middle into Mike Singletary's zone and got away with it. In short, they knew how to attack the Bears and they did it. They had a game plan. Mike Ditka, meanwhile, had nothing. The Bears' game plan was the lottery special. Let's try this, let's try this, and if that doesn't work let's try this. Flutie was forever throwing downfield. He threw none of the short, ball-control passes we might expect a coach to put in the game plan simply to give the kid confidence. The Bears threw on the first play from scrimmage, but the patterns were not simple but complex; the pass was incomplete. Finally, when the Bears led early and had the chance to put the Skins down by more than a touchdown—which would have changed the game drastically—Ditka was his usual cautious self. The Bears settled for two field goals, one of them when they had a first down on the five-yard line and they ran between the tackles three straight times. How any coach can be so blustery off the field and meek on the field is beyond us.

The Redskins' preparation and the Bears' lack of the same says two things: one on offense and one on defense. First, Jim McMahon is essential for the Bears not only as a steady quarterback, not only as a dynamic presence, but because he is the only one who will overrule Ditka on the field. How many times in the Bears' championship season did Ditka send out a cautious play only to have McMahon go for broke? Many times that we know about, still more that we can assume. Second, the Bears' defense is not overrated, but their new defensive coach is. The Bears have defensive players who will make any coach look good, and it's true that under Vince Tobin the Bears cut their points-allowed statistics. Yet, there was a change in attitude and tempo under Tobin that made the Bears vulnerable in the playoffs. Buddy Ryan was a genius because he approached defense the way most coaches approach offense. He came up with game plans to exploit the opponents' weakness; he went on offense even when he didn't have the ball. The defense would change not only from week to week but from quarter to quarter as the score changed. The Bears, this year, played defense, and they played it as well as defense had been played, but they were always playing defense. They were always waiting for something to react to, trying to stop the other team from doing what it did best rather than forcing the issue themselves. It gave the Redskins something to work on that they knew would be solid. The Bears were set in their ways.

Now, the game itself. The Skins' early game plan had worked for a touchdown in the first quarter when quarterback Jay Schroeder read a Bears blitz and hit Art Monk with a beautiful pass. Monk gave the Bears' cornerbacks no end of trouble all day. Deep in Bears territory, Gary Fencik came to the line, leaned over it like a child reading over his father's shoulder, then turned away—even as Schroeder audibled—as if he had been unimpressed because the book had no pictures. Schroeder wasn't fooled. Fencik turned again and charged with the snap and Schroeder tossed the ball directly into the spot Fencik would have occupied. Monk ran under the pass for a touchdown. The Bears came back when Flutie completed three straight passes, the last a beautiful playground pump-and-go to Willie Gault for a touchdown. They then settled for two field goals to lead 13–7 at the half.

The critical moments occurred in the third quarter. Flutie gave the Skins an interception at the Bears' twenty-five-yard line. This was his first costly mistake and it was to be expected. He wasn't going to have a perfect day. The Bears' defense knew this, and they stood strong, stopping a run and then expecting the pass on second down—incomplete. On third and seven, however, again expecting the Redskins to go outside—as they had all game—the Bears were crossed up. Monk ran a pattern seven yards upfield and faked to the outside. Mike Richardson accepted Monk at his word and came in to prevent the first down. Monk, however, turned upfield again and Schroeder threw an easy pass for the score, 14–13.

Yet Dennis Gentry had troubled Washington all day on kickoffs, and he did so again. He ran the kick back to the Skins' 43, and the Bears' offensive line went about saving this game the way it had saved the game against the Detroit Lions last month: it beat up the defense. Neal Anderson went around end for twelve yards. Calvin Thomas went off tackle for fourteen. The Bears were on the Skins' eighteen-yard line, a go-ahead field goal assured, a coup de grace touchdown possible.

Walter Payton fumbled.

Now, watch this drive. Gibbs had probably been waiting all day to throw this sequence into the game. Each play leads into the next within the scheme the Redskins had already established. Pass wide right, pass wide left to Monk for a first down at the forty. Straight ahead for two yards, followed by Bryant on a delay for a first down at midfield (the Skins' linemen anticipated the penetrating Bears linebackers and picked them off one by one to free Bryant). Then wide left to Monk followed by straight ahead with Rogers through a big hole to the Bears' thirty-three. Then straight ahead with Rogers for four, followed by the inevitable pass wide left. The Bears read this one, however—incomplete. Then, on third and six, Dan Hampton went offside. The pass was incomplete, but the penalty made it third and one. Everyone knew it would be straight ahead—that was the Skins' game plan—but the best game plan is one that builds on itself. Schroeder faked to Rogers straight ahead and rolled out on the old-fashioned bootleg for an easy first down.

As the fourth quarter began, Monk again burned Richardson, and Richardson, in scrambling back to deflect the pass, was called on pass interference in the end zone, giving the Skins a first down on the one-yard line. Rogers tumbled into the end zone two plays later. The Bears' defense had been humbled, the Bears were beaten. The rest was academic.

The Book says turnovers and penalties are the signs of a poorly coached football team. The Bears aren't the Indianapolis Colts or the Tampa Bay Buccaneers when it comes to such things, but neither are they the Bears of last year. Ditka profited last year by setting the Bears free and letting them play, but this year they were a little too loose for good sense. What it says when stars like Payton and Hampton are committing the costly mistakes, I don't know, but I believe the Bears need a little more direction next year. Next year, what we're waiting for now.

Bear Furnishings

January 19, 1989

WRITING ABOUT the Bears can be difficult, because of the thick media veneer that covers the entire organization, from the lowest defensive back to Mike Ditka and on up through the ownership. They are, after all, the Bears, and this is—as painful as it is to admit—a Bears town. While the Cubs and White Sox and Bulls and Blackhawks are worshipped in (progressively diminishing) circles, they remain human beings. But there is something about the Bears that makes them not exactly larger than life, not exactly phony, but superreal. Perhaps it's the gladiatorlike game they play, perhaps it's the candy-ass treatment they receive in the media (especially television), but the Bears always seem to walk a little taller, talk a little bolder, and act a little more as men should act than any of us normal people do. It's the same sort of treatment John Wayne received from John Ford—a sort of instant mythification—and it's best seen when it's taken away—as when Willie Gault and Doug Flutie became suddenly human after being traded, or when William Perry and Jim McMahon were brought low this year.

In examining the Bears' loss to the San Francisco 49ers in last week's NFC championship game, the initial stage of the postmortem is not the mere analysis of strategy, but rather the stripping off of this high-gloss media finish. We make them human, then we look for faults.

This line of thinking first raised its ugly head with a painful realization: great as the Bears have been this decade and as well as individual players have performed—with a few clearly destined for the Hall of Fame—this is nevertheless not a great Bears team. The great Bears of the early '30s won championships in 1932 and 1933 and then went undefeated in 1934 before losing to the New York Giants in one of the most famous of the pre–Super Bowl title games, the one in which the Bears led at the half before the Giants switched to tennis shoes and scored twenty-seven second-half points to win on an icy field. The great Bears of the early '40s—the Monsters of the Midway—peaked at the end of an

184

eight-and-three 1940 season to whip the Washington Redskins 73–0, then repeated in 1941, and then went undefeated in 1942 before losing the title game shortly after George Halas entered the Navy. No doubt the Bears of the '80s, with their added speed and strength, would thrash these teams soundly if placed on the same field, but the fact remains that they did not dominate their era as previous Bears teams had. They didn't get the job done. In a cursory glance through the Bears' history, we do not see anyplace else where the Bears lost three out of four home playoff games; we don't even see anyplace else where they lost back-to-back home playoff games.

We went to the Lincoln Park apartment of Dr. W. late last week for the official postmortem. Dr. W. appeared to be watching a soap opera as we entered, but, appearances aside, he was prepared to be hostly, with diet soda, a case of beer, a frozen pizza in the refrigerator, and the game tape already inserted in the VCR. We settled in.

One impression we'd been struck by while watching the live broadcast the previous Sunday was that Jim McMahon had a bad day, and surely his poor statistics don't lie. Yet it should also be remembered—as was obvious on a second and more even-tempered viewing—that he had a number of passes dropped. His arm also appeared to be in good shape. If he was rusty from inaction—which he himself denied—the manifestation was that his passes lacked their usual touch. They zinged on a beeline to the receiver and—more than once—right through or off of his hands.

McMahon in no way had a good game, but he should not be the scapegoat either. If he can be blamed for anything, it's for not improvising off the Bears' dull game plan, for not sticking to a running game that appeared to be there, between the tackles, whenever it was called upon, and for not overruling a second-quarter rollout pass after the Bears had run the ball up to midfield; they went to the air on second down with three yards to go, and the pass was intercepted.

And the Niners drove for a touchdown to go up 14–0. Championship teams exploit whatever errors the other team commits, and the Niners played the role of a championship team all game long. Let's be clear: that interception should have been harmful only in that it deprived the Bears of field position and possibly points. The Niners took that slight shift in momentum and drove it home, with the key plays being a trap on third and ten, in which fullback Tony Rathman bounced off three Bears to make a first down, and of course the excellent, off-balance Joe Montana peg—like a shortstop throwing out of the hole behind third base—to Jerry Rice on a quick post pattern for Rice's second touchdown.

Dr. M, the Boomer, has been fixated all year long on the cliché that a game shifts on three plays. If that's the case, the three plays in this game were: (1) Mo Douglass's fifteen-yard penalty in the first quarter, after the Bears' defense had snuffed the Niners on their first possession: it deprived the Bears of field position on the fifty-yard line after the Niners' punt. (2) Rice's first touchdown catch, a seemingly innocent down-and-out in which he burned Mike Richardson with a quick shimmy for a sixty-one-yard score. (3) Rice's wide-open catch down the sideline during the Niners' critical drive to open the second half, which put the Niners inside the Bears' ten and set up their third touchdown.

That drive is what crushed the Bears, and to be sure there were several plays critical to the march. Montana did not allow a third-down pass to fall incomplete until later in the third quarter, with no fewer than three third-down completions coming in this possession: on the fourth play of the half, he hit Rice on a slant-in on third and six for a first down; at midfield on third and three he slipped, steadied himself with his left hand on the ground, and hit Rathman out of the backfield for a first down; and he threw a touchdown pass to a secondary receiver, tight end John Frank, on a third down. The pass to Rice, however, was the killer, because Rice is the Niners' primary weapon, and the Bears knew it, and still he was wide open. How he got open illustrates how the Niners won and why the Bears lost.

Rice and the Niners' other wide receiver were lined up on the same side of the field, with Rice on the outside about a yard behind the line of scrimmage. The Bears lined Vestee Jackson up opposite Rice, with Richardson covering the other man. Rice, however, went in motion, crossing behind his teammate, back toward the center of the field. The Bears were in a zone defense, not a man-to-man, and they tipped this off when Jackson and Richardson switched men instead of crossing over, with Richardson now guarding Rice and Jackson taking the other receiver. Rice hopped around Richardson's inept bump-and-run, went downfield, and cut outside to an utterly vacant area of the Bears' zone defense. What this shows—besides the fact that the Niners had a weapon, the Bears knew they had a weapon, and yet the Niners managed to use their weapon anyway—was that Niners coach Bill Walsh had noticed predictable tendencies on the part of the Bears' defense, and he exploited those tendencies.

Or, to put it in layman's terms, the Bears got outcoached.

Mike Ditka is the glowing symbol of the Bears on the television screen, and this, it is commonly said, has been his finest year. He took a team said to be on the decline, a team decimated by injuries, and while overcoming his own woes, in the form of a mild heart attack, he led them to the best record in the NFC, home-field advantage in the playoffs, and the conference title game. It's difficult to look at Ditka—so smooth, these days, in front of the cameras, chiding stupid questions, using all forms of the media to motivate (read "embarrass") his players, and in the process entertaining these cynical and often unentertainable reporters, who snigger and guffaw over his ludicrous, facetious statements—it's difficult to look at this man's image and not believe that here is a person good at his job, skillful in its applications, adept at its fine points. He trains his tiny button eyes on some questioner, his mouth drops ever so slightly open, and he says, with only the slightest hint of sarcasm, "Oh, I'm very concerned that we haven't scored in the third quarter this year. I'm concerned because reporters say I'm supposed to be concerned, and I know reporters know everything" or some such drivel.

Look, Ditka, we're going to put this in a way that might get across to you: You're right, it's not important, in itself, to score in the third quarter of football games; but when you consistently fail to move the ball after halftime, that's not a disease in itself, but maybe it's the symptom of some greater ill. Maybe, just maybe, it shows that you're not adjusting to what the other team is doing as well as they're adjusting to what's become predictable in you. When you lose three out of four home playoff games, and you're outscored in the second half of each of those losses, maybe it's not that you're overconfident one year, and not that you're simply not good enough another year, and not that injuries finally caught up with you in another year; maybe—just maybe—it's because you're being outcoached down on the field.

Tale of the Tape

October 26, 1989

LAST WEEK, for the first time in years, I dusted off the Super Bowl XX video and put it in the VCR. Nostalgia had little to do with it. Like a coach, I wanted to study the things that had made the Bears successful; like any fan, I wanted a glimpse of the glory days to get me through the present darkness; and, like a cheap detective, I wanted to examine a picture of the troubled family in better times, thinking that it would provide clues to the current problems. Because right now the Bears are a team—as Mike Ditka himself admits—in disarray. As one member of the Bears put it recently, where other teams used to come into Soldier Field fearing for their lives, they now come in nursing an armload of past offenses, thinking it's payback time. It's a story as old as the decline of Rome; the barbarians are at the door, chaos lurks on the other side of every game. Last Monday's fiasco at Cleveland, played before a national TV audience, confirmed the worst.

The fans have changed their attitude toward the Bears, and the old "everybody knows you when you're up, nobody knows you when you're down" line doesn't fully explain the change. Clearly, the team doesn't excite as it did four, three, or two years ago, or even as it did last season. The departure of Jim McMahon is not the sole aggravating change here, but it is the most noticeable and the most telling. For many fans—myself included—it was the last straw, coming as it did on the heels of the Bears' shabby treatment of Willie Gault, Wilber Marshall, Otis Wilson, Al Harris, and Todd Bell (the last two doubly done over by the Bears). When McMahon left, he said a number of things about the Bears and Ditka, with varying degrees of fairness, but his harshest, most direct, and most pointed attack was on Ditka's belief that it's good coaching, and not good football players, that wins games. McMahon said it would be a relief to be away from that sort of crap. The fans believe his version of events, and for good reasons. Look at the 1989 Bears compared with the 1985 championship team, and in every position where a starter has been replaced, the new man has a diminished personality, less character, and usually less ability. Mike Tomczak for McMahon, Neal Anderson for Walter Payton, Brad Muster for Matt Suhey, Ron Morris for Gault, Ron Rivera and Jim Morrissey (the latter now injured) for Marshall and Wilson. James Thornton for Emery Moorehead at tight end is the only position where the Bears have improved themselves in four seasons, and even that can be debated. Is it the Bears' persistently poor drafting position—dictated by their success—that is responsible, or is it Mike Ditka cleaning house?

Ditka has taken more than his fair share of the blame for the Bears' newly arrived hard times; that's only fair, as he never received his share of the blame for the Bears' playoff losses. Three times the Bears lost in the playoffs to teams of inferior ability—equal talent at best, as in last year. Each time, Ditka was outcoached. The irony is that there may be something to Ditka's contention that it's coaching and not players that win football games. His blindness is that he fails to see that good coaching could find a way to exploit a few great players against another team's superior overall talent (e.g., Bill Walsh's use of Joe Montana and Jerry Rice). Yet Ditka has taken the most flak recently not for his coaching but for his personality. Unfair as this is, it is not without cause. Ditka has plastered himself all over the television, making himself ubiquitous. He has done ads (and these are just the ones that come quickly to mind) for a fast food chain, an antifreeze, an airline, a bank (no, make that a savings and loan), Japanese cars, car-rust protection, soup, and—last but not least—a very bad sitcom now in syndication. This in itself shouldn't affect his coaching, but when he cites Midway Airlines for the same qualities of loyalty and teamwork that he supposedly champions himself—especially in light of his treatment of Wilson, released after suffering a severe injury last season—that tarnishes both the product and the coach.

So I got out my copy of Super Bowl XX the other night and put it on—again, no sound. Where I used to play Bruce Springsteen in the background, now I play some new industrial funk by a Wax Trax group called Meat Beat Manifesto or rap by Public Enemy or N.W.A. Even in that near cacophony, the 1985 Bears dominate the scene. What a team they were (for peak value, the team of the decade). They were the team that brought us back to football and instilled in us the criteria of what makes the sport worth watching. Football is a brutal game; one of the things we forget when two mediocre clubs face one another is that it's a sport in which one team should establish its dominance, physically, against the other team. That player's recent remarks about how other teams now come in with chips on their shoulders is really just glorified nostalgia, because in Super Bowl XX the New England Patriots came out scrapping. There were some early pushing bouts after the whistle had blown, and then, play after play, the Bears lined up to once again show who was boss of the field that day; the Patriots didn't just surrender to the Bears, they were beaten into submission. What a defense the Bears had. Look at their front seven: Dan Hampton, William Perry, Steve McMichael, and Richard Dent up front, backed by Marshall, Mike Singletary, and Wilson. In all of football history, not even the Steelers of the last decade can match that group man for man. (Of course, the Steelers had defensive backs like Mel Blount, so overall they still get the edge.) There wasn't a team in football that the Bears couldn't beat up that year, and the amazing thing is that there wasn't a team in football the Bears didn't beat up over the next three years. The shame is—and it's made fresh by watching the game again—that the Bears should have won one or maybe two more Super Bowls and that they never even got to another.

That's Mike Ditka's fault, I believe, because the other thing Super Bowl XX shows is that the Bears had a potent offense. Their offensive line was at the peak of its ability, Payton was still a force, and Gault was amazing and—it should now be pointed out—essential. Wendell Davis and Ron Morris may have terrific hands, and they may know how to run a pattern, and they will probably put up better stats for most of their careers than Gault amassed that championship year: Gault caught only thirty-three passes, for only one touchdown during the regular season. Yet he does so many things that Davis and Morris will never do; he changes the other team's defense with his mere presence on the field. McMahon, meanwhile, was a marvel, and he knew how to use all the weapons in his arsenal. Overruling the plays of the cautious Ditka, he drove the Bears to lay it on thick, understanding that, in football, momentum and initiative are precious and must never be relinquished. When the Bears lost McMahon—whether or not it's true that he could no longer do what he had done on the football field—they lost the last great individual they had who could counterbalance Ditka.

Look at the Bears of last Monday night, with the defense rocked back on its heels by turnovers and the cautious play calling of the offense—when there was any play calling. The Bears again showed their trademark, lack of any noticeable game plan, the failure of one play to match up strategically with the one before. There were moments when they followed a couple of passes with a run up the middle—exploiting the active defensive rush by the Browns, which tended toward the outside—and these were broken for some big gains. Yet beyond that tactic—and a very elementary point it is—the Bears didn't have a clue about what they were doing on offense, about what they had to achieve to beat the Browns' defense. They came out and passed the ball with a bullheaded persistence throughout the first half, even when it became apparent that Tomczak was off his game. There is no truth to football wisdom such as "the run establishes the pass" except in how a team makes that wisdom work for it on any given day; it seems obvious that—with an admittedly talented but somewhat rattled quarterback (feeling the pressure from the coach, his teammates, and the fans, as well as the other team)—a game plan based on establishing the run and then going to the air is only common sense. Ditka and his play caller, coach Greg Landry, seem to have forgotten that what made the Bears great—and what allowed them to defeat the Minnesota Vikings and Cincinnati Bengals to open the season—was the old, theoretically antiquated seven-minute drive, based on short, sturdy runs and the occasional pass.

There will be debate, no doubt, about what the source of the Bears' trouble really is: the injuries on defense, the number of young players, the lack of an experienced quarterback, poor planning on the part of the coaching staff. Whether it's good players or good coaching that wins ball games, the point, in one way, is moot, because the players the Bears have now are what they're stuck with until the college draft next spring. So the team, at this point, needs a certain amount of good coaching. It's not getting it. What can a fan, or a player, say about a team that, after a time-out has been called and after the quarterback has returned to the huddle, is still shuttling players in and out of that huddle? About a coaching staff that, after the team has run up the other team's middle to get to third down and goal to go from the one-yard line, calls for a wide run and then a pass on fourth down, losing the football? About a coach that tells a 4–2, first-place football team, "I don't know if we'll win another game all year," after it has suffered a particularly difficult loss?

Mike Ditka has never been much of a strategist; his primary strength as a coach has always been that he was a good motivator. After the way he's treated his players, from Gault through Marshall to McMahon—and in view of his increasingly petulant and unpredictable behavior—one has to wonder whether he can motivate his veteran players at all. But the worst thing one can say about Ditka is that he squandered the team of the decade.

Soldier Field's Inner Beauty

November 6, 2003

LIKE so much of Chicago, the rehabbed Soldier Field puts its best face toward the lake. Seen from the east, the curved glass exterior of the stadium bowl is contained by the distinctive columns of the old stadium. The effect is jarring, but the separate parts almost unite, in the manner of an elegant new office building rising above the classic old library next door. Unfortunately, there's nothing yet between the stadium and the lake but the torn-up runways of what used to be Meigs Field. Most people see Soldier Field from the west, where some have compared it to a spaceship landing on the old stadium; to my way of thinking, the west grandstand bulges out over the columns like some great metallic blob pouring over the wall to engulf Lake Shore Drive. I suppose one could defend retaining the old exterior as a quaint ground-level facade that gives the building character, like the first floor of Louis Sullivan's Carson Pirie Scott building—but really, why bother? What about those bland old Doric columns was worth preserving? The new Soldier Field almost single-handedly debunks postmodernism.

Given the mishmash of the outer Soldier Field, nothing prepared me for the interior I glimpsed Sunday before the Bears' game against the San Diego Chargers—not even early endorsements from soccer fans who'd seen the Chicago Fire return there. Where the old Soldier Field made the field of play seem a postage stamp, the new stands almost swaddle the action. The 100 level cozies up to the field, and two sections are stacked above it. The soaring grandstand in the west contrasts with the skyboxes that cap the stadium in the east; similarly, the stands rise high behind the north end zone—the old "bleacher" section—but are more moderate behind the south end zone. "There's not a bad seat," said a fan as I stood admiring the place while the Bears warmed up, and though that's easy to say from the 100 level, where we were, it did appear to be the case. Like so many Chicagoans, the new Soldier Field is ugly on the outside—it doesn't really care how it looks—but warm and functional within.

Thanks go to the Cubs for (if nothing else) distracting me from the Bears when they came out this season looking ugly, before emerging over the last two weekends as a team as pleasant as its new home. Thanks also to the National Football League's scheduling computer. The Bears dropped five of their first six games, including the bitterly one-sided Monday night loss to the Green Bay Packers that christened the new stadium, but then they sandwiched home-and-home games against the even more woeful Lions—the second this weekend in Detroit—around Sunday's game against the equally awful Chargers, who came in at 1–6. The Bears were coming off a 24–16 win over the Lions that had seen them mix old blood with new. Graybeard quarterback Chris Chandler had replaced newcomer Kordell Stewart and made assistant coach John Shoop's offense seem almost respectable, with the help of some fine play by rookie wide receiver Justin Gage. The defense, meanwhile, had finally produced critical turnovers, with rookie pass rusher Michael Haynes forcing one bad throw that was picked off by rookie cornerback Charles Tillman, leading to a touchdown. The final minutes even found the Bears catching a break, as an onside kick apparently recovered by the Lions was called illegal in a dubious overruling by the replay official. The question was whether the 2–5 Bears could keep that little bit of momentum going.

With Purdue product Drew Brees having a miserable day at quarterback for San Diego, they could. Diminished competition or not, the Bears just plain looked good Sunday—as unexpectedly good as the inside of their new stadium. The first play was well designed and a complete success, as Chandler threw over Dez White, drawing double coverage, to an open Gage deep down the sideline. Chandler hit White with a perfectly timed square-out, and then the offensive line, which has begun to gel in recent weeks, swept en masse in classic Southern Cal "student body left" style for a big gain by the revitalized Anthony Thomas. Even when the drive stalled, it stalled on a nice play: White ran an out-and-up and would have been open, but he was pushed out of bounds by the defensive back. Paul Edinger's thirty-eight-yard field goal put the Bears up 3–0.

The Chargers found running and receiving room for the dangerous LaDainian Tomlinson on the next series and marched to the Bears' twenty-six. But in the two critical plays of the early going, rookie line-backer Lance Briggs combined with end Phillip Daniels to stymie Tomlinson on third and short, and rookie Joe Odom blocked a forty-six-yard field goal attempt. (Unfortunately, the fans didn't see a replay on the grand new stadium TVs because they were playing an auto ad from a Bears corporate sponsor.)

Again the Bears showed that they had actually prepared for the game. Chandler ran a quarterback draw from a no-backs formation eleven yards almost to midfield, and he kept finding White open. On a critical third and three he caught the Chargers in a zone defense, and White found an empty space just beyond the chains for a first down. On an-other third and short, Thomas burst through a huge hole in the middle of the line for a fifteen-yard gain to the San Diego six. Thomas doesn't improvise well, but when the hole is where it's designed to be he hits it, and that was the case again on the next play, when he gained five yards to the one. Then Thomas went in for the score that gave the Bears the 10–0 lead they held at halftime.

Dick Jauron usually stood by himself on the sideline. In his Bears cap and khaki pants, his shoulders hunched under his Bears jacket, he looked less like the team's head coach than its traveling secretary using his headset to make plane reservations to Detroit. Yet his team looked crisp and impassioned—as when R. W. McQuarters cleaned Reche Caldwell's clock on an incomplete pass late in the half. Returning punts, McQuarters aroused memories of Ron Smith, the '70s-era player who absolutely refused to take a fair catch. McQuarters even returned a dan-gerous punt deep in Chicago territory just before halftime, when a more judicious player would have made sure his team took its lead into the locker room. As it was, the Bears were warmly cheered by the faithful as they trotted off the field at intermission.

Jerry Azumah, who had returned the opening kickoff of the second half for a touchdown in the Bears' win over the Lions the previous week, ran the ball to the Bears' forty-five this week. The drive stalled, but it had given the Bears field position, and after a nice defensive series—Alex Brown penetrated to knock Brees's arm on third down—McQuarters returned a punt to the Chargers' fort-five. On third and one, with every-one expecting a run, Chandler called a play-action pass and lofted a perfect toss to Stanley Pritchett coming out of the backfield, but the ball bounced off Pritchett's face mask and out of bounds. The Bears went for it on fourth down and Thomas got the yard. Chandler then made a lovely pump fake, turned, and threw to tight end Desmond Clark, who was tackled at the two. But Thomas was stifled twice and White couldn't make a grab over the back of a San Diego defender. The Bears settled for a field goal, and the Chargers, down only 13–0, had a chance to seize momentum.

Fortunately, the Chicago defense was inspired, and Brees couldn't have grasped momentum if it had been handed to him in a bowling-ball bag. On one play, Tillman smacked a San Diego receiver the instant the ball arrived and swatted it to the ground. On another, Briggs met Tomlinson one-on-one in the flat and brought him down with a lovely tackle after a harmless three-yard gain. After a punt, the Bears were marching toward midfield at the end of the third quarter. But Chandler pulled his pump fake one too many times on a White out-and-up and underthrew the ball so badly it was intercepted.

At that point, San Diego head coach Marty Schottenheimer switched to forty-one-year-old quarterback Doug Flutie, the Boston College miracle man ("Bambi" to the Bears faithful after he cost them their 1986 bid to repeat as Super Bowl champions), and he aroused both the crowd and the Chargers. Azumah nicely broke up a pass but then badly missed a tackle, allowing a big play down to the Bears' thirty-one. As ever projecting moxie and confidence from that little body of his, Flutie scrambled to the fourteen. Tomlinson burst through a big hole to give the Chargers first and goal and scored on the next play to make it 13–7. On what had been a near perfect football afternoon, cloudy but comfortable, the skies in more ways than one began to darken.

Conventional wisdom called for running, but the emboldened Bears came out with five wide receivers and Chandler hit White over the middle for nineteen yards into San Diego territory. The drive stalled on a third down when the Bears again spread everyone out but Chandler's pass was deflected. Yet Tillman made a spectacular play on Brad Maynard's punt. He covered the ball all the way, pinched it to the turf just short of the goal line, and rolled into the end zone to allow others to down it at the one. Flutie scrambled for one first down, but then the defense held—Flutie throwing into double coverage on third down and Azumah swatting the ball out of bounds.

Again eschewing a fair catch, McQuarters took the punt and slashed through a hole in the coverage for a thirty-six-yard return to the San Diego twenty-one. The Bears ran the ball to a first and goal at the nine, and Thomas ran to the five at the two-minute warning. He ran it again to the two and a half, then again to within eight inches of the goal line. It was like Zeno's paradox, except that the Bears had only one more play to go and not an infinite number. Logic called for them to take a field goal and put the game out of the Chargers' reach. Yet Jauron rashly decided to go for it—a call the fans endorsed. As he later explained, "It seemed to us the only way we could lose the game was to get a kick blocked." For the man who approaches risk like an insurance agent, even his boldest move was dictated by what was most judicious. In any case, Thomas got in for the score that made it 20–7. Flutie led the Chargers to midfield in time for a Hail Mary, but with safety Mike Brown exhorting the fans in the south stands to scream their loudest, Bobby Gray calmly smacked the ball aside in the end zone.

In the closing minutes, fans sang along with the Beastie Boys' "(You Gotta) Fight for Your Right (to Party!)," then with "Bear Down, Chicago Bears," and they gave the players a warm reception at the gate to the locker room. Chandler, the grizzled veteran, trotted through it, but rookie Briggs ate it up, smiling and nodding all the way. I was down on the field with other members of the media by that time, and was struck by how intimate this outsize stadium suddenly felt, everyone right on top of the action.

Mensches of the Midway

February 1, 2007

WHAT STRANGE Super Bowl team is this?

Chicago fans are thrilled, of course, that the Bears will be playing in Super Bowl XLI Sunday against the Indianapolis Colts in Miami, but I get the feeling they're not sure what to make of this new breed of Bears. Following the lead of head coach Lovie Smith, these Bears are diplomatic and soft-spoken off the field and rely on speed and guile on it. One might argue they're hardly Bears at all.

The winners of 1986's Super Bowl XX retain an unbreakable hold on the city's sports consciousness because they were every inch the Monsters of the Midway. They were ferocious, outspoken, larger than life; they took the irascible qualities the franchise has always embodied and exaggerated them. Owner-coach George Halas built a series of combative teams known for tough players who took no prisoners, from Bronko Nagurski—a name that still screams not just leather-helmet football but what Nelson Algren lovingly referred to as Chicago bohunk—on through Doug Atkins, Mike Ditka, and Dick Butkus. The Bears won the 1940 NFL title against the Washington Redskins 73–0, and on the rare occasions they were upstaged with a title on the line it took artifice— such as the 1934 Giants switching to sneakers on the frozen field of the Polo Grounds—to do it. Even in the lean years, such as the Abe Gibron era in the '70s in which Butkus retired, the Bears were proud denizens of the NFL's "Black and Blue Division." The '85 Bears were built in Ditka's image, and for all his legendary conflicts with Halas, Ditka was very much Halas's heir: the two men battled so much because they were so much alike.

I dusted off my videotape of Super Bowl XX last weekend and was again amazed at just how brash and oversize and, yes, just plain great those Bears were. They rubbed their opponents' noses in it. There was quarterback Jim McMahon with his headbands for the Juvenile Diabetes Foundation and POW-MIAs—worn in defiance of a league edict—and another for sponsor Adidas worn coquettishly around his neck; add the gloves he sported indoors at New Orleans's Superdome and he had the look of someone dressed up to pose for Manet. There was game MVP Richard Dent forcing two fumbles in the first half—at one point prying the ball from Craig James's hands—and Dan Hampton rising to brandish one of the fumbled balls in what has become an iconic image from the game. The Bears' defense pounded New England Patriots' quarterback Tony Eason into early submission, and only because the scrubs allowed a late touchdown was the final 46–10. The Bears didn't just use defensive tackle William Perry as a running back—they had him attempt an option pass the first time they got down close to the goal line. Considering the score was tied at 3 at the time, that was brazen.

Off the field the Bears were equally brash, as their legendary exploits on Bourbon Street the week before the game attested—not to mention McMahon's mooning of a helicopter during practice.

The Bears who won the NFC championship over the New Orleans Saints two weeks ago seemed another breed entirely. If the defense, playing like the old Bears in shirtsleeves in the snow, was fierce it wasn't feral. My grandfather, who was the legendary Bernie Bierman's line coach, used to say it all comes down to blocking and tackling, and these Bears block well—especially left guard Ruben Brown pulling to the right—and they're sound tacklers, even as they gang-tackle trying to strip the ball. But they stick a tackle; the '85 Bears buried ball carriers. The most notable offensive play of the season for this year's Bears was Devin Hester's 108-yard return of a field goal attempt by the New York Giants: he faked downing the short kick in the end zone and then ran it all the way back. Speed. Guile.

The differences were most striking after the New Orleans game. The '85 Bears spoke their minds to a fault and flaunted their dominance. These Bears spoke in clichés to conceal their thoughts and emotions, a trait no doubt handed down from Smith and most recently adopted by embattled quarterback Rex Grossman. Asked if the faith shown in him by the coaching staff had been important in his development and in helping him deal with the media criticism and boos from demanding fans, Grossman simply said, "Yeah, it was huge," and went on to another question. Asked if he'd been psyched up by Reggie Bush's taunting somersault into the end zone on a score that put the Bears' lead in jeopardy at 16–14, middle linebacker Brian Urlacher said, "We didn't pay any attention to that," when clearly they did. (The Saints didn't score again and lost 39–14.) Asked what he said to Grossman after the game when he sought his quarterback out for a high-profile embrace, Smith said, "I just hugged him and told him I loved him." Can anyone imagine Ditka saying anything of the sort—least of all to a quarterback?

These Bears were classy, at least when they were in Smith's realm. Off-field conflicts such as last year's to-do between linemen Olin Kreutz and Fred Miller were put behind them, and even defensive tackle Tank Johnson, no stranger to police blotters, was never less than humble and eloquent while addressing the media in the locker room.

During the hype of the last two weeks, the Bears were matched in class by the Colts under Tony Dungy. Like Smith, who was his assistant when he coached the Tampa Bay Buccaneers, Dungy is soft-spoken and diplomatic. The '85 Bears reflected a big, brutal, combative era in sports. These Bears—and the Colts—say something different about today's sports environment. Both teams play a more precise, more sportsmanlike kind of football, and Chicago fans are suspicious of it. These Bears aren't one of those Chicago teams that don't even have to win to be celebrated. But me, I'm taking them.

[Wrong, as it turned out. Sparked by Hester running back the opening kickoff for a touchdown, the Bears took an early 14–6 lead, but it was all Peyton Manning and the Colts after that, as they claimed a 29–17 victory. The lasting legacy of the '85 Bears remained unchallenged.]

Ridiculously Beautiful

October 25, 2007

WHEN THE ball is in Devin Hester's hands, the game of football opens up and flowers. A sport that has entangled itself in ever more complicated strategies over the decades becomes again simple and beautiful. It returns to its origins, a man with the ball trying to elude all others. No wonder every punt and kickoff brings calls to come watch. At home, in a bar, or on site at Soldier Field, this is no time for a bathroom break. This is not to be missed.

It was one thing when he was doing it at the University of Miami— see him now in the "Devin Hester Anytime" collection of highlights on YouTube—but it's quite another to watch him outclass NFL players as well. These are the fastest athletes for their size—and in many cases the orneriest—in the world. Even so, with the opponents focusing everything on stopping him, Hester finds a way to run free. It's what he did with the opening kickoff of the last Super Bowl, what he did when he almost tiptoed through the punt coverage before exploding into the open for an eighty-nine-yard touchdown last week against the Minnesota Vikings, and what he did to score on an eighty-one-yard bomb from Brian Griese to briefly tie that game in the final minute and a half. The Bears' radio play-by-play man, Jeff Joniak, has put it best: "Devin Hester, you are ridiculous!"

Unfortunately, Bears fans have never been comfortable with offensive pyrotechnics. They like bone-crushing defense, because defense means winning, or at least losing with honor. The wonders of a Gale Sayers scoring six touchdowns or Walter Payton rushing for 275 yards in a single afternoon in otherwise unmemorable campaigns offer little solace by comparison. Bears fans like hitting, and for them the pleasure of seeing someone elude that hitting—even one of their own players—is fleeting.

So while Bears fans expected quarterback Rex Grossman to fail after his increasingly flighty performances last season, right up through the Super Bowl, and were willing to throw him under the bus once Griese, his backup, had rallied the Bears to a win in Green Bay against the archrival Packers and almost pulled off that comeback against the Vikes, it was the plight of the defense that really hurt. It was the defense that let the Dallas Cowboys' Tony Romo go wild in the home loss the third week of the season, signaling that things this year would not go the way they did last. It was the defense that one week later gave up an incredible thirty-four points in the fourth quarter in Detroit, the defense that put the Bears in a hole in the first half in Green Bay, and the defense that couldn't stop Vikes' rookie Adrian Peterson from running for 224 yards against the Bears' vaunted linemen and linebackers, making safeties Adam Archuleta, Brandon McGowan, and Danieal Manning, though not Hester, look ridiculous.

The thing about Hester is that as a return man he can be avoided. The Philadelphia Eagles proved that Sunday by kicking away from him. He didn't have a single return yard all day. The result was a game that reduced coach Lovie Smith's team to the Bears of the Dick Jauron era. The defense bent, but at first refused to break. The Eagles were dominating the first half in time of possession, but a pair of field goals gave them only a 6–0 lead. Peering out of his helmet, shoulder pads hunched, Griese— who bears a striking resemblance to Steppenwolf's Gary Cole—looks less like a quarterback than an actor playing a quarterback. But he rallied the Bears with a couple of nice passes to tight ends Desmond Clark and Greg Olsen, and Chicago got on the scoreboard with a field goal toward the end of the half. The defense gave it right back and the Eagles led 9–3 at intermission.

The Bears began to win this game of attrition in the second half. Griese drove them for three more field goals—the last after a pair of Tommie Harris sacks had helped earn them good field position—to put the Bears up, 12–9, but then the defense, which had bent throughout the day, broke in the fourth quarter. Philadelphia quarterback Donovan McNabb caught them in zone defenses time and again and found receivers in the open spots, finishing a drive with a touchdown toss between, of course, the safeties to tight end Matt Schobel. The teams exchanged possessions but the Eagles gained field position, and—again kicking away from Hester—they punted the ball out of bounds at the Bears' three-yard line with a minute and a half to play.

What happened next—well, it cheered Bears fans, no doubt about it, but it hardly chased their angst. Griese marched the Bears the length of the field, with Hester making a couple of key catches and acting as a decoy on other plays, including the touchdown toss to Muhsin Muhammad in the back of the end zone. The Bears had already stolen a win in Green Bay, and they stole this one, 19–16, to keep their season alive at 3–4. Staying alive was nothing much to boast about, not with the defense scuffling and Hester's big-play game neutralized. But if Griese's heroics cemented Grossman's place on the bench, that was something a fan could hang his big, furry, growling, ear-flapped Bears hat on.

4

Cold Steel on Ice (Metaphorically, Not Literally)

Hearing the Hawks

February 22, 1985

HOCKEY DOES not translate well to television. Its sounds and its rhythms, its unique pace and the chaotic, unpredictable quality of its play, get lost in the circuitry. Where in baseball a double can be fragmented into its components, because each player has his specific duty to perform correctly, and where in basketball the relatively small area of half court can be adequately covered with two or three cameras, in hockey the play is both patterned and free, and the rink is much larger than a basketball court, allowing the players room to improvise with or without the puck, on or off camera. Hockey is Ornette Coleman to baseball's Louis Armstrong and basketball's Charlie Parker. Perhaps most important, however, is that television has made little effort to capture hockey's aural excitement. The sound of bat on ball is always precise, and the grunts and cussing of seven-foot centers under the boards are common TV fare these days on weekend afternoons, yet some of hockey's most dramatic moments occur in times of sudden silence, in the way a player demands a pass—tapping his stick on the ice in the manner of a baby tapping his spoon on a high chair—or in the dap, dap, dap of a skater running on his toes to get up a quick head of steam. Hockey must be experienced first-hand.

The Chicago Stadium is known as one of the noisiest arenas in the nation, yet it's uncanny the way the din will suddenly part and allow these small sounds up to even the second balcony. Hockey fans seem to know when to expect something, and the things they expect and prepare for lie in the finer points of the game. Certainly, a fight or the loud, rolling sound of someone being pounded into the boards will bring the fans to their feet in a roar, but these are the lower elements of the game—necessary, but not requiring much of the spectator—and not coincidentally they are the parts of the game television covers best, so that sheltered fans receive this as their picture of the sport and never bother to attend games because hockey, after all, is rather barbaric, you know, one rung up from fighting, which it, by the way, frequently descends to.

Try explaining to them the satisfaction of a crisply passed puck—the two sharp reports as it is slapped by one stick and received by another an instant later—or the beauty of a Denis Savard rush up ice, and the point is more often than not lost, which in a way is not surprising, because there are times when the point of a rush up ice seems lost on Savard himself. He is the closest thing the Blackhawks have to a hockey genius, but he is that sort of genius whose mistakes are indistinguishable from his brilliancies. Last Sunday afternoon, playing against the Detroit Red Wings, he scored two goals, the first a rather routine affair in which— while the Hawks were pressuring the Wings, who were for the moment rattled—he found himself in front of the net just as the puck was passing by, and he backhanded it into the goal with an absentminded grace, the way Chaplin would kick a cigar butt into an ash can. That goal put the Hawks ahead 3–2 in the second period. His second goal, in the third period, which tied the score at 4, which is where things wound up, was a more impressive effort: he got a barely legal pass at center ice from linemate Steve Larmer, then skated in on the net with a Red Wing in hot pursuit and lifted the puck over the goalie's left shoulder. Yet both these pale when compared with typical Savard rushes—none of which was successful on this afternoon, but that is beside the point—in which he skates up ice carrying the puck with abandon, is met by defensemen at the blue line, loses control of the puck, kicks it out from the gathering of skates without losing his speed, pirouettes, skates backward with his face to the center of the ice looking for someone to pass to, abruptly changes direction, goes behind the net and comes out the other side looking to stuff it in the corner—but the goalie is prepared for such shenanigans and is pressed against the goalpost—and is finally fallen upon by the same two defensemen, who have been tracking him at a distance all along.

Savard is one of the few constants on this team, which changed coaches not long ago and is now making an attempt to pull itself together in time for the Stanley Cup playoffs, where momentum frequently over-rules quality. The Hawks are certain to make the playoffs, in spite of their losing record, and in new coach Bob Pulford's experimenting there is an obvious attempt to find the sets of players who play most confidently together. Pulford began the game by reuniting the Savard-Larmer-Al Secord line, whose amazing success two years ago carried the Hawks to the Stanley Cup semifinals. Secord, however, was injured for most of last year, and the magic has been lacking this season on the occasions when former coach Orval Tessier allowed them to play together, as it was lacking in this game. The threesome did not play sharply at the start, and Pulford broke them up during the first period, replacing Secord with Curt Fraser and putting him instead on a line with Troy Murray and the Olympic teenager, Eddie Olczyk, a grouping that produced the Hawks' first goal. Secord, as usual, was in the middle of the play even as he was on the fringe; he was in the midst of a battle for position in front of the Red Wings' net, and when the puck slid out to defenseman Behn Wilson, who was manning the right point, all Wilson had to do was skate around the tangled group in front of the net to have an open shot on goal, and with a small deke to get the goalie on the ice this was nicely executed.

Unfortunately, while the Hawks were playing nice hockey, the Red Wings were getting lucky, or at least that's the way it seemed. The Hawks had to work twice as hard to score the same amount of goals, an impression that is borne out by the Hawks' accurate shooting with few results: they put fifty shots on goal while the Wings had only twenty-nine. Ron Dugay, who would wind up with a hat trick, scoring three of the Wings' four goals and assisting on the other, tipped in a slap shot near the net, deflecting it past Murray Bannerman, midway through the second period, to tie the score. Bannerman is a fine goalie who deserves our support, but he went about deserving our contempt a few minutes later, when he panicked with the puck near the net, belly flopped on the ice, and left the goal wide open when he failed to snare the puck. The Wings had an easy score to take the lead.

This seemed to inflame the Hawks, who pressured the Wings in their attack zone and forced a goal, scored by Rick Paterson, and Savard's simple backhand followed. It seemed as if the Hawks would hold the lead going into the final period. All looked well until Dugay broke free down the right side, skated past defenseman Doug Wilson, and put a slap shot over Bannerman's shoulder, a goal that, begrudgingly, was earned.

Detroit had the momentum, and, if that wasn't bad enough, Bannerman injured himself during the second period, and Warren Skorodenski, our backup goalie, was forced into duty for the third. Skorodenski is capable enough, as he was to show, but we have to wonder about a goalie whose only nickname can be "Skoro," as in "Oh no, we've been Skoroed upon." The Wings' intensity and our cold goalie combined right away to the wrong end, as the Wings dumped the puck into the Hawks' zone, where it bounced off the boards and directly out in front of the net, and who should be there, outhustling our defense, but Dugay, who poked it past Skoro without much effort.

Making Savard's tying goal all the more admirable, as the Wings were ready and working hard to preserve a victory. Yet Savard was, as he sometimes is, unstoppable, and the Hawks, with renewed fervor, went about stealing the win right back. The last few minutes were dominated by the Hawks, although Skoro was called upon to make some fine saves, but we were, unfortunately, not in tune with the cosmos. Pulford made a move that, if not daring, was at least sentimental, putting Secord back on the same line as Savard and Larmer, and the three worked hard and to greater effect than in the first period, but in the end they had nothing to show for it except a Secord fight with ninety seconds left in regulation. The one close shave was with this group and defensemen Doug Wilson and Bob Murray on the ice and the puck in the Hawks' attack zone. They were, again, pressing the Wings, and with things quite tangled in front, the puck came back on the point to Wilson, who is known throughout the league as one of the better offensive defensemen. Wilson wound up and let loose a ferocious slap shot, and the Detroit goalie, Greg Stefan, never had a chance. In fact, we never saw the puck either, only knew that it was whizzing past the players and on toward the goal and in that one moment we felt, with the rest of the hockey fans in the stadium, that something was about to happen, and it did. In the moment of silence, when air is gasped between one yell and another, we heard the puck go bouncing off the post, producing an awful, discordant sound, at once both flat and sharp, echoing on up into the second balcony and beyond, the sound of a good effort gone bad, the sound of a hockey team desperately trying to salvage a season.

The Bleachers in Winter

February 14, 1986

I HAVE SEEN the Wrigley Field bleachers in winter, and they are in the second balcony of the Chicago Stadium during Blackhawks games.

There is, of course, no sunshine in the stadium; going shirtless is frowned upon but not unheard of. Yet the two places have the same Dionysian atmosphere, the same concentration of fanatics, and for good reason. The action is seen at a comfortable distance, a distance that encourages a fine appreciation of the game and its nuances, a distance where the game is seen on a large level, where the crowd becomes part of the event, a distance that permits a lower price for the ticket, and, finally, a distance that requires a loud voice. The second balcony, like the bleachers, is not a place for introverts.

In fact, I was watching Hawks games from the second balcony long before I sat in the bleachers of Wrigley Field. As I climbed the five flights of stairs from street level to the upper reaches of the stadium last Sunday, I recalled seeing a playoff game as a youth with my family. My father got four tickets in the second balcony instead of the usual two in the first balcony, and the entire clan went off to sit with hoi polloi for one of the biggest games of the year. The difference between first and second balcony was great then, and it remains the difference between fans and fanatics, between middle class and working class, between the social drinker and the occasional drunkard. It was wild. The place was jammed, the fans were loud, the language was foul, and the beer flowed on and on. When a fight broke out down in the mezzanine, it nearly sparked a riot in the second balcony, as if nothing they could do in the rich seats couldn't be duplicated on a larger, earthier, more authentic level in the second balcony. My mother, to my knowledge, never went to another hockey game. I was remembering this as I followed a father, carrying his son, up the stairs. He set him down and let him walk up the last flight, and there, at the top, was a beer vendor, encouraging him. "Come on, one last step.

There you go," he said, and then, lifting his head and his volume, "Cold beer, no lines, no waiting."

This was long before the game started, just as the Hawks and the Philadelphia Flyers were leaving the ice after warm-ups, and this was a Sunday matinee, the second of the season, yet already the outer aisle was lined with fans who had bought standing-room tickets. I had bought my ticket only two days before, but because I bought only one I got a leftover seat, and I found it just as the person in the next seat was explaining how it came to be empty. He was a big, bearded guy, with a heavy Chicago accent, and he was speaking with two women in the row below us. "Yeah, Lance had ta give up his seat, but he's here tidday. He's downstairs lookin' for a ticket. He'll probably hafta pay twenty-two bucks for somethin' down there," and he gestured toward the mezzanine. Everyone seemed to know everyone else, although from group to group it was a cool, distant knowledge, acquaintances rather than friendships. Later, I asked this fellow why his buddy had to sell his season ticket. "He got a job at the *Tribune* a couple months ago. He works nights." On the presses? "Yeah, he's one a those scabs they hired." Too bad, I thought, fidgeting a little in my seat.

It was Sunday afternoon, and after the usual roaring rendition of the national anthem the crowd settled, for a time, into a relatively mellow mood—mellow by stadium standards. "Have a beer," said a guy behind me. "C'mon, this is party time." His buddy answered, "I gotta recoup from last night." The listless audience was reflected by listless play on the ice. Both teams were slow to start, slow to hit, slow to mix it up, in contrast with the National Hockey League norm. (Studies have shown that the team that draws the most penalties in the first period usually wins.) These Sunday afternoon games are difficult for the players, who were in different cities only the day before. The Hawks, in fact, had lost their first matinee of the year, the previous Sunday, to the lowly Toronto Maple Leafs, after playing Saturday night in New York. In addition, the referee dallied all day long; he stood above the face-offs without dropping the puck, and he chased impatient centers away as if they were children bothering him while he had more important things to do. "C'mon, ref, I gotta go to work tomorrow," the guy behind me yelled. When the Flyers scored first, on a shot by defenseman Mark Howe that trickled off goalie Bob Sauve's stick and into the net, the crowd got irritated. "Wake up!" "Church is over!" "Where did you guys party last night?" The fellow behind me said, "They musta had a lotta suds last night." "A bucket o' suds," his buddy said contemplatively.

Yet the Hawks followed the fans into consciousness, and they scored a beautiful goal, a fine example of midseason hockey. Darryl Sutter took a pass from Keith Brown just short of center ice, and he and Tom Lysiak skated in quickly for a two-on-one. Sutter and Lysiak then executed a neat little give-and-go, clearing the Flyers' defenseman and allowing Sutter a clear shot on Flyers goaltender Bob Froese. He scored easily. Having earned the tie, the Hawks kept the pressure on and later scored a terrific goal on a more patterned offensive play. The puck slid out to the left point and Doug Wilson, who passed across ice to Steve Larmer, just outside the right face-off circle. Larmer drew the defense before crossing the ice again with a pass to Denis Savard. Savard was standing in the center of the left face-off circle, and he wound up for a slap shot straight off the pass. It was on goal and it was in goal—as easy as lacing a boot.

The fans responded with the "woof woof woof" cheer of the Bears and their fans, but the Hawks weren't able to stay in that company for long. The players settled into a defensive mode, and if Sauve hadn't been having an outstanding day they would have quickly fallen behind. On the afternoon, the Flyers outshot the Hawks 46–26. After a particularly good save, organist Nancy Faust began playing the theme to *The Untouchables*. Even when the Flyers were penalized and the Hawks had a man advantage, they played cautiously. "Dey oughta decline dis power play," the guy next to me said. "Decline da penalty." "Looking dumb! Looking dumb!" the guy behind me yelled. As it was, the Hawks held the Flyers scoreless through the second period and went into the third still up 2–1.

Between periods, they have a "Shoot for Travel" competition, in which the goal is blocked off with a board except for three small slots on the ice. Three persons try to slide the puck through the slots from the blue line, with airline tickets as the prize. The second player was a man in a three-piece suit. "Go back to the office," someone yelled. He missed the goal completely. "Pretend it's golf," someone else yelled, and he again missed the goal. And again. "You suck!" someone screamed, and he left the ice without falling down.

The Hawks continued to play it close to the vest in the third period. Coach Bob Pulford had perhaps dictated such play, for his coaching was tactical in a reserved sort of way. In spite of having the home-ice advantage, allowing him to change lines last to match the Flyers' tactics, he kept his best line—Savard, Larmer, and Al Secord—off the ice for the first five minutes of the game. He might have been thinking of saving his best skaters for late in the game, when the ice might open up with the teams weary from too many games in too short a time period, but if that was his thinking it backfired. Defenseman Behn Wilson, who is so disliked he is referred to as "Gentle Behn" by the faithful, took a cross-checking penalty. Although the Hawks had killed each of their penalties in the game and had even endured a five-on-three disadvantage for a minute at one point, Sauve finally gave up another goal. Defenseman Bob Murray failed to clear the puck when he had the chance, and the Flyers pressed it in on goal. Sauve went down and made another brilliant save with his leg pads, but Ilkka Sinisalo pounced on the rebound and plugged it in the net.

The Hawks came alive on offense and forced the puck into the Flyers' zone, but the Flyers aggressively stood their ground; the goalie swung his stick at a Hawks player. Secord—the team's enforcer and, with this year's decision by Doug Wilson, the last Hawks player to go without a helmet—came roaring across the ice and smacked a Flyers player, causing a fight in which he held his own, but in effect took himself off the ice for the rest of the game. When Savard swung his stick at the Flyers' bench as he came off the ice shortly thereafter, earning a misconduct penalty, two of the three players Pulford had been saving were gone. So were the Hawks' hopes of breaking the tie.

As the five-minute overtime period leaked out and the Hawks held a Flyers rush and responded with an ineffectual rush of their own, the guy behind me kept yelling. If a normal loudmouth is leather-lunged, this guy was leather-larynxed. His throat vibrated with his screams, to the point where he seemed about to tear his vocal cords out and send them fluttering down upon the ice. "C'mawn, c'mawn. Get on 'em, get on 'em."

"No voice tomorrow for dat guy," said the guy next to me.

Blacked-Out Hawks

March 28, 1991

IT'S COMMONLY said that there are 17,300 Blackhawks fans in the Chicago area—no more, no less. That's because the Chicago Stadium seats 17,300 for a hockey game, and while the Hawks have played to sellout crowds for decades (with lulls here and there), it always seems to be the same people going back game after game. Everyone knows one or two Hawks fanatics, but these people always seem to be on the fringe of society: the young man who takes legal briefs from office to office, or the guy who always wears tennis shoes and jeans with the mandatory office necktie. Hawks fans are an intense, loyal, vocal lot—borderline normal. After all, they're the ones who can't keep themselves under control for even a brisk rendition of the national anthem. It's comforting to think, however, that as noticeable as they are—and noticeable they are, in their shiny black jackets and their jerseys with the cool Chief Black Hawk in the center—that there are only 17,300 of them.

Think again.

Over the last month or so, I've done some research in the city's bars, stopping in for a drink or two during home games. These games are blacked out—even on SportsChannel—by the Hawks' money-grubbing Wirtz ownership, the city's reigning tightwad sports dynasty ever since "Papa Bear" George Halas died. The Wirtzes have always sought, even in good years, to fill the Stadium to capacity for hockey games. The one way to ensure that, they've always believed, is to prevent the games from being televised, so that anyone who wants to see them must be in attendance. (There are rumblings that some home playoff games will be televised on WGN this season, but I'll believe that when I see it.) The cable generation, however, has found ways around the blackout policy. A regular little cottage industry has sprung up around certain bars and their satellite dishes, which enable them to pick up visiting teams' broadcasts from the Stadium. This violates the little "This broadcast is only for the use of . . ." admonishment delivered by the announcers at every sporting event, but it's so common that no law-enforcement agency has been willing to crack down. Some bars even advertise that they show Hawks home games, and even beer companies abet the bars by giving away signs reading, "Hawks here on satellite," *satellite* being the code that means "including home games."

Because this practice, though prevalent, is, after all, illegal, I'll keep my neighborhood satellite tavern anonymous here. (If any agency ever cracks down, it's sure to start with the bars that have advertised or otherwise become notorious.) In layout, it's a typical shotgun bar with a big room in the back. It has bands in on the weekends and a small marquee out front to advertise them, but otherwise it's just like thousands of other neighborhood places in the city—right down to the home games on satellite. Which are very well attended, I should point out.

Last Sunday afternoon, I stopped in for a late-season matinee (they start scheduling them after the football season ends), and the bar stools were already packed at the end where the two televisions were tuned to the game. (The two TVs at the other end of the bar were devoted to the NCAA Basketball Tournament.) By the end of the first period, the stools were packed all up and down the bar, with fifteen to twenty guys watching the various TVs—and I mean *guys*. The only female was a girl of about nine or ten there with her younger brother of about six. When they got bored, they'd go to their father, get another couple of quarters, and run back to the video games. Once, the boy cadged a quarter off the bartender. "Do you promise to come back in fifteen years?" he asked. "Whattaya mean?" said a guy at the bar. "He'll be back next Sunday." Off the kids went. A fellow strolled along the bar behind all the men with their backs to him and said, "I can't get a seat here. I feel like a hockey coach walking up and down the bench."

The image was echoed on the screen, as Blackhawks coach Mike Keenan looked out over the ice from behind his seated players. Keenan looks and acts like a cousin of Mike Ditka's, and they bring similar philosophies to their respective sports. Both believe it's their personal system—and not the quality of the players—that makes the team competitive. Both are driven and demanding men with short fuses. Keenan has become the dominant member of the Blackhawks organization—from the front office, where he has assumed the duties of general manager, to the ice, where he has run out all the players who didn't play his way. Among them was Denis Savard, a pixie-sized wizard of a hockey player, known for his dashing style and his pirouettes, dispatched to Montreal last summer for defenseman Chris Chelios.

Savard was very popular in the city, and Keenan probably would have been run out of town if the Hawks hadn't already turned around so abruptly under his leadership, becoming one of the strongest teams in the National Hockey League this season. Keenan prefers defense and "dump-and-chase," a style of play ugly on the surface but eminently functional when it's played right. The puck is dumped from center ice into the corners, then Hawks forwards make chase, hoping to beat opposing defensemen to the puck, which they can pass to a teammate in front of the goal. The system attempts to put all five Hawks skaters on the offensive—even as they remain in position to shift to defense—and all five opposing skaters on the defensive. It is stripped down and unpretty, and it didn't appeal to Savard at all. He preferred precision passing and three-man rushes up the ice, a la traditional hockey and the great Wayne Gretzky Edmonton Oilers of the '80s. That's why Savard was popular and that's why he's gone. Keenan aside, who doesn't prefer that dashing hockey to dump-and-chase? The Hawks do, however, play dump-and-chase in a very precise, scientific manner. I've never much cared for it, but even I have to admit they make it work and work well, and the emphasis on fundamental defense, first and foremost, has helped make rookie Ed Belfour the best goalie the Hawks have had since Tony Esposito was in his prime.

I first stopped in at this neighborhood place about a month ago, for a game between the Hawks and their archrivals, the Saint Louis Blues. The Hawks came out storming and opened a big lead; the only suspense hung on whether Belfour would earn a shutout and stop the scoring streaks of the Blues' Hull-and-Oates combination, Brett Hull and Adam Oates. Belfour has a nifty mask with a pair of bald eagles painted on the sides, but he has a slovenly way of blocking a shot. He frequently gets down on one knee and lays his stick across the ice, like a charwoman stooping to use a dustpan. Like the Hawks' functional, unpretty style of offense, however, it works; while he did allow a goal, Hull and Oates were not involved, and the Hawks won handily. Unfortunately for the fans, however, the out-of-town television announcers threw a wet blanket on the Hawks' play, complaining about uncalled penalties and mouthing excuses for the Blues. Moaned one guy at the bar, "It's depressing watching them win with these announcers."

Watching a hockey game on satellite is sometimes closer to seeing a real game than watching the official coverage on SportsChannel. There are no ads—this is the virgin feed going out of the Stadium—so the viewer watches the players standing around the face-off circle during short breaks and, of course, the Zamboni cleaning the ice between periods. In fact, on the night the Hawks played the Blues, the fans' shooting contest between the second and third periods sent the guys at the bar off on a tangent. This contest, where the goal is blocked off except for a little opening in the center and fans are led out to take shots from the blue line and the center red line, is a Stadium tradition. The contestants, in fact, are always the same demographically: there's Joe Blackhawks Fan, complete with gut sticking out under his jacket, his twelve-year-old son in tennis shoes, and finally the woman in either miniskirt or spandex tights, but always in spike heels, tiptoeing across the ice. The guys at the bar started reminiscing about the infamous "Boston feed," where a camera operator had zoomed in on "that chick in the leather miniskirt. They showed her heels, then her legs, and then the skirt, but they never went above the waist!" Hyuck, hyuck, hyuck. These Hawks fans feel the most important cold steel on ice is the nearest tapped keg.

This may not sound like everyone's idea of a nice atmosphere in which to spend a Sunday afternoon, but when one is watching a hockey game on television it seems entirely appropriate. The bantering last Sunday began during the national anthem and went on from there. The goaltender for the Minnesota North Stars left his position on the blue line before the anthem was over and skated to his net. "Aw, ya commie," said one guy. One particularly beat-up Minnesota player had adhesive bandages all around his lips, where he had apparently been cut in a previous game, but one guy said, "Looks like he found the wrong girl last night."

The Hawks have developed a tendency recently to rough things up, especially at home. Their Saint Patrick's Day game with the Blues erupted into several fights, with over four hours of penalties assessed during the sixty-minute game. The referees took instant control of the game with the North Stars, however, penalizing Keenan for mouthing off in the first minute. Penalties throughout the first period kept the Hawks on the defensive and the general pace of the game excruciatingly slow. The Minnesota announcers passed on a comment from a fan within earshot: "Hurry up, I gotta go to work tomorrow." In the second period, however, the refs let the two teams play a little more, and the Hawks exploded for five goals. Mike Hudson broke the ice with the first of two scores, including the most noteworthy goal of the day: he fanned on an open shot, barely brushing the puck, fell on his ass, then deflected it as the Stars' goalie tried to fall on it, poking it into the net. "He assisted on his own goal!" one amazed guy said, and two others broke out in perfect timing, aping the Stadium public-address announcer, "Chicago goal by number 20, Hudson, assisted by number 20, Hudson," and burst into laughter.

The Hawks laid back and played defense through the third period, and the Stars rallied to 5–4. With the slow pace, one guy said fearfully, "Overtime, it's a five-hour game."

"Hey, it's good for business," said another guy, lifting his glass. The Hawks, however, held on, and the bar filled with cheers before it emptied.

But the highlight of the day? Hearing Harry Caray sing "Take Me Out to the Ball Game" during the WGN-TV broadcast between the second and third periods. That's the problem with hockey: just when it's beginning to get interesting, baseball comes along.

Blackhawks Family Values

November 26, 1998

LET'S GET one thing straight before we go further: love is not finite. As any parent knows, a new offspring comes along and the family grows to embrace the child (more often than not, anyway). Money and time may be limited, but not the ability to care about someone or something new. The same goes for the sports teams we say we "love," so it's not quite right to suggest that the American Basketball League's Condors have a better chance of making it because the National Basketball Association owners are locking out their players. It's not as if some specific amount of affection either is spent from season to season or else spills over from one sport to another when a team or sport alienates its fans. If that were true, more people would be attending the games of the Condors and the Blackhawks and perhaps even the Bears. Yet, with the Bulls and their Chicago fans still waiting for the lockout to end, fewer people are attending Hawks games than at any time in memory.

What can I say? The Hawks are a tough team to love playing in a tough place to love in.

These vague and abstract thoughts—abstract by sports standards, anyway—occurred to me in large part because I bid the Hawks adieu before their first long road trip of the season while sitting high up in the United Center in a section filled with kids. I had gone down that night and bought the cheapest ticket possible, $15, and been seated in the very last row of what they'd have called the second balcony in the old Chicago Stadium. At the ends of the arena were vast expanses of empty seats extending from the top to the bottom of the 300 level, yet they had thrown me into the back of a rather crowded section, presumably to generate some camaraderie—which, believe me, I appreciated. To my surprise, however, I wasn't surrounded by the old blue-collar fans who used to populate the upper balcony at the Chicago Stadium, nor by the South Side yuppies who have replaced them, treating the UC like their regular weekend gathering place and watering hole. Around me were huge families filled with young kids—most of them, believe it or not, girls between the ages of five and ten. One group of five girls and their father sat down just to my right, followed by four more girls, their parents, and their three-year-old kid brother in the next row down, and then another family of boys and their father a couple rows down from there. Everyone seemed to know each other, and the girls got to chirping about their classes and teachers, and I all but expected Mary-Kate and Ashley Olsen to stroll in wearing Blackhawks jerseys and waving to everyone.

It was the strangest thing, and I couldn't get over it. Here were the Hawks at a low ebb in popularity—they couldn't sell sixteen thousand tickets to their send-off, their last home game for weeks, and they'd lost nine of their previous ten games, with the tenth a measly tie, and the beefy guy in shorts I'd bought my copy of *The Crease* from outside the stadium had said, "So, it was here or stay home and watch the Bears, huh?" Yet these families had decided to invest hundreds of dollars in taking their kids to see the Hawks—on a school night, yet. Had they gotten the dates for the circus mixed up and decided to stick around after driving all the way from Beverly or some other Catholic enclave (to judge by the size of these families)? Or was some deep filial love of hockey involved? Had that thin, short-haired, and attentive mother been one of those Blackhawks babes—in the big hair, satin warm-up jacket, spandex pants, and high heels—who smoked cigarettes in the Chicago Stadium stairwells fifteen years ago, and had she met her now somewhat apathetic husband at a Hawks game? What was the deal? All I knew was that there was something life affirming and bizarrely hockey affirming about it all.

Bizarrely hockey affirming because few of these people paid any real attention to the game—and I can't say I blamed them. The Hawks, under new coach Dirk Graham and general manager Bob Murray, have put together a miserable team. It's reminiscent of the California Angels squads of the late '70s and early '80s, when baseball's free agency was new and Angels rosters always seemed to comprise overpriced stars past their prime and overrated young talent, all put together pell-mell. Having missed the playoffs last year, the Hawks raised their payroll to $35 million, fifth in the league, but their two biggest additions, center Doug Gilmour and defenseman Paul Coffey, are thirty-five and thirty-seven and appear well into end-of-career declines. It's an old, slow, plodding team, and though disciplinarian Graham set out to instill a solid system—the Hawks opened with four wins and a tie in their first six games—the system soon broke down and the Hawks began losing games by disgraceful scores such as 10–3. On this night, trying to halt that ten-game winless streak against the only slightly less mediocre Ottawa Senators, they practically moseyed out of their locker room, past their bench, and onto the ice as Frank Pellico played "Here Come the Hawks" on the organ. Where was Keith Magnuson when a fan and the team really needed him—or at least Chris Chelios? (Out with a knee injury, unfortunately.)

The publishers of The Crease, the renegade program, had thoughtfully tucked a barf bag into its pages, but nobody in the UC was going to get worked up to the point of nausea. The screaming and yelling that went on over the national anthem was pro forma, and the fans were, if anything, even less involved in the game than the players. There was very little hitting on the ice, but when one nearby fan yelled, "Hit somebody," it was with all the gusto of a vendor droning, "Beer here." Why had we come? It had to be love, but of what sort? Was it a married love based on memories—nostalgia for those wonderful, character-driven Hawks of the '60s, or the beautiful, intricate teams of the early '80s—or something else entirely? I only know that Graham and assistant coaches Denis Savard and Lorne Molleken—in their stiff suits and tight ties, shifting their weight from foot to foot behind the Hawks' bench—had the look of ushers at a wedding where no one is optimistic about the prospects. Looking around at the empty seats and taking in the antiseptic UC atmosphere, I was reminded that Joni Mitchell began her recent performance there singing, "They paved paradise and put up a parking lot." Who knew Joni was a Hawks fan so well versed in the history of the old Chicago Stadium?

Yet if instead of the game one watched the nearby people, there was some sense to be made of how this event had enticed us. The first period ended in a scoreless tie, and during the shoot-the-puck contest the boys from a few rows down got a hockey game going in the back aisle, using their feet as sticks and a plastic cup as the puck. They made the UC seem a little like a neighborhood rink. People talked and visited, and as play resumed we all watched the Bears score, posted at intervals, climb from

14–3 in favor of the Detroit Lions toward the 26–3 final. Somewhere there were Chicago sports fans much more miserable than we were.

The Hawks kept intruding, however. They couldn't put two passes together. They got called on a stupid penalty early in the second period, and though a forechecking Alexei Zhamnov forced the Senators into an equalizing penalty, what good was that? The Hawks don't have anyone who skates well enough to be considered a good four-on-four player, and when Senators defenseman Lance Pitlick seized the initiative for a quick rush, he got a shot on goal and it went in past Mark Fitzpatrick.

The Hawks managed to get it back moments later. Coffey, making his home debut after missing the early season with injuries, snapped a wrist shot that was tipped by Eric Daze. Ottawa's Damian Rhodes stopped it, but Tony Amonte, the only bright spot of the season in Chicago, tapped in the rebound for his league-leading twelfth goal. "Go Hawks!" said a dad down the row to his daughter. Early in the third period the crowd was actually getting into the game a little, with the help of the three-man tom-tom club that roams the upper balcony, and things looked good when the Hawks went on the power play. They had Gilmour and Coffey at the points, with Amonte, Daze, and Zhamnov up front—a promising group that hadn't gelled yet. They didn't gel here, either—not until it was too late. Gilmour let the puck hop over his stick, and Ottawa's Shaun Van Allen pounced on it and skated the length of the ice for a breakaway and an easy shorthanded goal. "We're outta here!" threatened the dad down the row, but for the moment he stayed put. The go-ahead goal did leave the Hawks still on the power play, and moments later Gilmour atoned for his muff. He captured the puck just inside the left point and, as I was moving to clap and cheer derisively, slapped a shot on goal that Daze tipped in. It shut me up.

Having scrambled back to tie the game at two, the Hawks almost blew it when they drew another dumb penalty with just over five minutes to go. The seconds ticked down as the Senators methodically attacked the Hawks' net, and an Ottawa player in the corner passed through traffic to an open teammate in the slot who fired the puck past Fitzpatrick just as the two minutes were about to expire. "All right, let's go!" said the same dad. He and his daughters stood in the aisle as the referees reconsidered and finally waved off the goal for an Ottawa player being in the crease.

Regardless, the dad chased the girls down the aisle and homeward; it was a school night, after all.

The game ended with a lethargic five-minute overtime. Both teams seemed content to escape with a 2–2 tie, and that's the way things ended. Shortly before the end, however, the thin mother looked over her shoulder at a discreetly cozy couple sitting side by side in the last row. She looked down the row at her husband several vacant seats away— their daughters were visiting with friends for the time being—and she motioned for him to come sit beside her. At first he was reluctant. "The stuff," he said, pointing to the pile of coats on the seat next to him, but then he got up and trudged over. And so it was we all sat there, in an antiseptic stadium watching a rather poor contest, feeling the peculiar anguished, overflowing, evanescent, blissful pleasure of the company one sometimes keeps at a hockey game.

So Beautiful, So What?

March 30, 2000

LOOKING DOWN from the United Center press box onto the section of seats just below me before Sunday's Blackhawks game, I saw a couple of Eddie Belfour jerseys, a Jeremy Roenick, and a Chris Chelios, but nary a one for a current Chicago player. That's a sign of trouble—when fan jerseys of departed players outnumber those of current "stars." But it was still early—I'd ridden down on the Damen bus past Sunday-morning joggers and churchgoers—and as the noon game time approached the more hip and savvy (if bleary-eyed) Hawks fans started showing up, many of them wearing Tony Amonte jerseys. In fact, four season-ticket holders, two of them wearing Amonte's number 10 jersey with their own names on the back, sat right in front of the press box and struck up conversations with the beat writers.

"You guys are loyalists," said one reporter.

"What can I say?" replied one of the guys. "I couldn't stay home with the wife."

They then proceeded to dine on prepackaged bagels, cream cheese, lox, and pickles, demonstrating that some Hawks fans know how to adapt to these early Sunday matinees late in the season. Meanwhile, down a couple of sections, a more stereotypical Hawks fan brandished a beer and called out, "Breakfast of champions!"

Let the record show it is now thirty-nine years since the Hawks and their fans could truly call themselves Stanley Cup champions.

As bad as things have gotten for the Hawks—and they are about to miss the playoffs for the third straight season—I still love their fans, and I still find the team's faintly mystical pregame scoreboard presentation—a montage of details from the Chief Black Hawk logo, followed by historical highlights set to Aaron Copland's "Fanfare for the Common Man"—quite stirring. The Hawks' fans still do a pretty good roar during the national anthem too. Yet there are now vast tracts of empty seats for most games, and on this (barely) afternoon, attendance dwindled to a mere 16,998. Not long ago the Hawks became the first National Hockey League team to average twenty thousand for a season. The once proud franchise has fallen on very hard times.

Yet there have been signs of progress. The media guide from the beginning of the season is of little use now, the Hawks having shuffled their management and turned over what seems like half the roster since October. When it became apparent the Hawks were once again doormats, general manager Bob Murray was sacked and replaced by Michael Smith, a rare outsider for this most insular of Chicago franchises. Bob Pulford, old Whitey himself, was booted downstairs from his senior vice president position and awkwardly made head coach, for he didn't replace Lorne Molleken but simply shouldered him aside. Molleken was given the title "associate coach," and he still stands with Pulford behind the bench and handles the more distasteful coach's duties, like the post-game media conference. The Hawks took to playing a recognizable system, and they've encouraged chemistry by instituting a relatively fixed array of lines and defensive tandems. Smith recently traded away old favorites Dave Manson and Doug Gilmour for prospects. All things considered, the Hawks have improved. They enjoyed a six-game unbeaten streak in mid-March, and went into Sunday's game having won five of their last seven, seven of their last eleven, and ten of their last seventeen. For their last twenty-nine games they were ahead of the league at 14–13 with two ties. Of course, before that they'd amassed a miserable record of 15–24–6.

Having launched my personal boycott of this moribund franchise early in the season, I decided to give the Hawks a second chance by seeing how they'd fare Sunday against the best team in the league, the Saint Louis Blues. I wound up sorry I'd ever been away.

Don't get me wrong: the Hawks were outclassed and outplayed. But Amonte gave them an early lead, and goalie Jocelyn Thibault clung to it like a mountain climber gripping a piton. He entered the game having recovered from an early season crisis of confidence to lower his goals-against average to 2.89. It's true, the overexpanded National Hockey League is going through a defensive trend, with teams playing conservative systems to rein in the sport's few true stars—a style that suits the Blues as much as anyone—but 2.89 is a respectable GAA, especially given

Thibault's early troubles, and he'd recorded his second shutout of the season the week before against Roenick's Phoenix Coyotes. Thibault, it's worth noting, has a cool mask, which is half the appeal of a goalie. The top features a full frontal facial portrait of Chief Black Hawk—a marked contrast with the profile seen on the jerseys—and the neck guard spells out his nickname, "Ti-Bo."

He had his work cut out for him this afternoon. Amonte, the Blackhawks' one true star-caliber player, has been teamed on a line with the re-invigorated Alex Zhamnov and the old enforcer Bob Probert. Zhamnov has never lived up to being traded for Roenick, but he looks inspired these days, and he came into Sunday's game with twenty-five points in his last twenty-one games since returning from a pulled hamstring. In the current NHL environment, averaging more than a point a game (either a goal or an assist) is enough to rank a player among the league leaders. Amonte has always played inspired hockey, though he doesn't look as dashing since he cut his hair and dyed it peroxide blond. Sunday the two of them were the team's only effective offensive players. They dashed to and fro, while the lummox Probert played menial steward to their two musketeers, doing the dirty work like digging the puck out of the corners. Saint Louis lacked its top scorer, Pavol Demitra, from what has become known as its "Slovak Pak" line with Michal Handzus and Lubos Bartecko, and Demitra's place was taken early by Jamal Mayers. The line served a lethargic first shift on the ice, and Zhamnov and Amonte took advantage, with Zhamnov beating the defense to a loose puck and feeding it to an open Amonte in the slot. He scored with a sharp wrist shot from the face-off circle to the right of the goalie. (Probert was penciled in with an assist alongside Zhamnov, but where he touched the puck in that sequence I never saw, despite the several replays shown on the stadium scoreboard.) Thibault had the lead, and all he had to do to claim the victory was hold the Blues scoreless the next fifty-eight minutes or so. Once the Saint Louis defense was shaken awake, the Hawks weren't likely to score again.

The Blues looked bigger, stronger, and faster, but Thibault kept the Hawks in the game. In the second period he kicked out a one-timer, smothered another in his pads, then snatched a third out of the air. The fans were slowly responding to his effort, as chants of "Let's go Hawks" and "Ti-Bo, Ti-Bo" started first at one end of the arena and then at the other. During breaks in play Thibault took off his mask, turned, and leaned his elbows on the crossbar of the goal, like a heavy drinker at the neighborhood tavern in the process of forgetting a rough day's work. Ace defenseman Anders Eriksson went into the penalty box after being called for hooking, and organist Frank Pellico picked up on the anxious atmosphere by playing the music to *Jaws*. Thibault made another great save, really getting the fans involved, and the Hawks killed off the penalty and took their 1–0 lead into the final period.

The Blues picked up the pace in the third period but the Hawks responded nicely, dumping the puck into the Saint Louis end whenever they got it and forechecking persistently. I was reminded that one of the sublime joys of hockey is the way tension builds, gradually during the second and third periods of a one-goal game and sharply during penalties, peaking when the losing team pulls its goalie for an all-out onslaught at the end. Unfortunately, this game never got to that climactic stage. Thibault stopped the Blues' Bob Bassen point-blank, exciting the crowd even more, and after extended end-to-end action halted with icing on the Blues at 7:18, the crowd cheered. Then came what seemed to be the critical sequence of the game. During a Saint Louis barrage, Thibault slid to the side and got caught in a tangle of players as the puck slipped through to Mayers on the other side. He missed the open net, and when Thibault sprang to his feet out of a pack of players it was without his stick and deflecting pad. He had a bare hand and a mitt. He made two great kick saves before the Hawks could control and clear the puck, then recovered his stick and arm pad in time to make another glove save following a Saint Louis rush. He held onto the puck and stopped play, as if to give the overdue applause a chance to rain down on him. The Blues put the pressure back on but Thibault survived another flurry, and the Hawks iced the puck with 2:06 to play. But the Blues won the face-off to the left of Thibault, and defenseman Chris Pronger took a pass back at the point and slapped a slightly screened shot just over Thibault's glove and into the net. All those great saves, and then he got beat on a shot from just inside the blue line.

The overtime period, played four on four, did not suit the Hawks' strengths, not even with Amonte and Zhamnov on the ice together. It was all Thibault and the Hawks could do to hang on to the 1–1 tie, but hang on they did, even after defenseman Bryan McCabe lost the puck right in front of the net, giving the Blues' Jochen Hecht a clear shot on goal. Thibault stopped it, and another in the final seconds from defenseman Al MacInnis, who led the Blues in shots on goal with a series of blasts from the point but could never get one past Thibault. Thibault preserved the tie, even though the Blues outshot the Hawks 36–11 for the game. It just didn't seem fair. Thibault should have gotten the victory on style points alone.

One of the ironic things about hockey is that for a very beautiful sport beauty has little to do with the outcome. This was a well-played late-season game, with crisp passing—crisper on the part of the Blues than on the part of the Hawks, of course—few offside calls, even fewer icing delays, and no fights. The two teams glided back and forth, and through it all Thibault stood firm. Sometimes, it's true, there is so much beauty one can hardly stand it; then again, sometimes there is only just beauty enough.

5

Further Afield

Memories

November 18, 1983

MY GRANDFATHER coached football. He won the first Sugar Bowl, fifty years ago this coming New Year's, when Tulane beat Pop Warner's Temple team; you can look it up. As a child, I knew this, and I knew him as the man sitting in the comfiest chair in the house, cigar in one hand and drink in the other, watching television and telling stories about those days and before, but to me the stories were a confusion of names and places—Cooper, Bierman, Stillwater, Baton Rouge. Not that my grandfather was a boring old man—he never was and never will be, for the stories have been honed by years of being told and retold, and although they wander to include the details he remembers at the moment, they come to points precise as wedding silver—but that I was incapable of associating the man telling the stories with the events of so long ago. It was as if he were making the stories up as he went along, or—worse yet—as if he were the sole surviving biographer of a man long since gone.

That is a spooky thing, watching someone pack and unpack memories like so many furnishings, enough to intimidate any child, but it is a quality he shares with many of his age, I think, and with many of his generation. In the days before the tape recorder, the instant camera, eight millimeter and videotape, before jet planes, before convenient air travel in general (Knute Rockne went in an airplane long before Buddy Holly did), the only thing you could rely on to fill the hours spent on trains, going from game to game, was either your skill as a storyteller or your ability as a listener—and usually both. The stories my grandfather tells are almost completely true—this is what makes them great; they never arouse disbelief—but they are also finely crafted, as if in exchanging them again and again with the very friends who were in those same stories they lost extraneous details, were embellished in the subtlest manner, until a finished version was reached. And after the stories were completed and repeated, there was always Negative Bull.

Negative Bull, my grandfather explains, is a game played by a group upon an unwary subject, although games of solitaire are not uncommon— played by one person upon a subject. Today, it is practiced, unknowingly, everywhere, but it was perfected as an art in the long hours of train travel. The object, as the name dictates, is to get the subject to bullshit, eventually prodding him into such a state that he will get up out of his seat to make his point. The person who agitates the subject into a standing position wins. In solitaire, the winner achieves the simple satisfaction of outsmarting the subject, but with the added risk of having to calm him without help.

In a game with Toby Pearson—his good friend of recent years, a 1916 graduate of Alabama and, to boot, a Coca-Cola distributor in his region of West Virginia—he could begin by asking, "So what is it that makes this Bear Bryant such a good coach?" and have him already on the edge of his seat. Toby, however, could accept the gambit without losing control—a rare quality—and for years they would meet regularly for an afternoon-long lunch, "with only two rules," he says. "One, that you couldn't say you'd heard the story before. And two, equal time."

There are few stories showing Negative Bull in detail—there is a limit to everyone's memory, after all—but I have no trouble picturing them, this group of coaches and writers, friends and wives, playing Negative Bull in a railroad car or hotel lobby or speakeasy (it seems a game well suited to drinking) and so flustering a victim he goes off muttering about these simpletons without realizing he is the biggest ass of all. It is a game of elites played upon the rest of the world one at a time, and as some of the best participants were sportswriters—especially Fred Russell from the *Nashville Banner*, he says—it shows what a peculiar relationship players and coaches had among themselves by today's standards.

It is a familiarity that is foreign to me, both as a journalist and as a grandson. Once, when he visited during the summer, we were sitting and watching the Cubs, and he was talking and trying to get me involved in the game. I, full of adolescent petulance, would have none of it. To almost everything he said or noticed—Ron Santo's soft hands, Don Kessinger's long reach—I said, "I know." My grandfather is, I think, a happy man, of good disposition, but he could get serious quickly; moments like that reminded you suddenly of his great size and his years as a football coach, that he had played both sides of the line at the University of Minnesota and had set a Big Ten track-and-field record that still stands for throwing the hammer of that era's size and weight. In such moments he never threatened you physically—not in the slightest—but it seemed as if he were leaning on you, or preparing to. "Now look," he said, "old people have lived a long time and they have a lot of things to talk about. They don't get a chance to talk about these things very often. So do me a favor—don't say, 'I know,' because that's the worst thing you can say to an older person. No kidding," and he twisted his head sharply for punctuation and went back to watching the Cubs. I don't think I've said "I know" to him more than a handful of times since.

We journeyed out to Wheeling, West Virginia, more Thanksgivings than not, my family and I, before I went to college, until watching the Detroit Lions play in the mud became almost as much a ritual as Thanksgiving itself. Last year, I went out myself, and now that I too had some stories I was trying to preserve as truthfully as possible—I am compulsive to a fault with memory, but as my grandfather says, you don't learn these things from strangers—my grandfather's stories became clearer than they had ever been, clearer in their intent and in what they were trying to salvage. He talks often of the 1923 game against the Fighting Illini, favored to win "by thirty or forty points, no kidding." The Golden Gopher defensive line, including himself and his future best man, Conrad Cooper, held Red Grange to minus yardage, however, and Minnesota won. Yet, the point he lingers on is not a single memory of throwing Grange for a loss, nor anything specific about the game, but that it was the first game played at Minnesota's Memorial Stadium, that they had dedicated the stadium Minnesota still plays in with an almost impossible victory.

Last weekend, along with my father, we drove back to Wheeling on the turnpike, past farms and tilting columns of smoke, the smell of burning leaves seeping into the car and lingering for miles. We spent Saturday—all of Saturday—watching college football, three games in all: first UCLA and Arizona, to scout the Bruins for the Rose Bowl only to watch them be virtually eliminated, then Auburn and Georgia, two teams in the top five in a spirited game, and finally Tennessee and Ole Miss, in which Ole Miss pulled the second upset of the day. This is the

behavior of a football fanatic, but I didn't mind. I listened to them—
my father and grandfather—tell stories, correcting each other on what
details mattered. Toby Pearson is dead in the last couple of years, and so
is Conrad Cooper and many other close friends of my grandfather, so he
does not get much of a chance to exchange the stories he spent a lifetime
gathering, but I could listen to them as long as he is willing to speak.

He is an old man, eighty years old, and does not feel fit enough to
attend the fiftieth Sugar Bowl, but he sent in his place a letter to be included in the program. In it, he described the biggest play of that first
game, when, down 14–3, Tulane's "Little Monk" Simons ran a kick back
for a touchdown, and they went on to win in the second half. My grandfather wrote that five key blocks broke Simons into the clear, but that he
would never tell who threw them because that way any member of the
team could claim responsibility for turning the game around. Looking
at me as he explained this, he said, "Yeah, no kidding. That's important."

My grandfather is a person who understands just how important
memories can be.

Harbor Lights

April 11, 1986

LIKE ITS bridges and its ballparks, the city's lakefront is beautiful and uniquely Chicagoan, and it quite literally shines in the spring, during the two weeks of smelting season. We remember, in years past, riding along Lake Shore Drive, with the smelters' lanterns along the lakefront tracing the shoreline. Last year, on one of the warmer nights of the season, we walked down to Belmont Harbor and sat on a bench, our backs to the city, and watched as they pulled in their nets of bright, flashing silver until, one by one, they wrapped up the nets, dimmed the lanterns, and went home. Next year, we vowed, we're going to do that ourselves.

John came by between 6:30 and 7 Saturday night. We had been working indoors all day. The weather was warm, and the front door stood open. Clouds had passed over in patches during the day, but it had cleared later in the afternoon. The evening, we knew, would probably be brisk. "C'mon, what's taking you?" said John, who was only slightly less late than normal. We packed as he talked. "My landlord was hanging around today," he said. "He asked me what I was doing tonight. I said I was doing what all yuppies do in the first two weeks of April—going smelting. He said that wasn't yuppie, that was ethnic."

"Obviously," I said, "he hasn't heard that yuppies are into ethnic. Yuppie and ethnic are one and the same thing nowadays. Like bowling. Bowling and smelting are in."

"First pull's supposed to be at seven," John said.

We packed the beer, ice, and various other provisions—chips, cheese and crackers, oil and a pan for frying the smelt—into the car and drove up to Montrose Harbor. John's boss had told him that he had set out four lines, just down from the refreshment stand, earlier in the day. We pulled in shortly after seven and found a space in the parking lot. We locked the car and walked down along the harbor looking for his boss, Owen. We got well on down past the stand—no sight of him. Walking back, we found four untended lines running into the water. Whereas most smelters had run their lines down into the water and attached them to the railing, which stood waist high, these four were arranged with boards standing upright. A smelter throws an anchor, which is not unlike a grappling hook, into the lake. A rope, of course, is attached. The net runs down into the water, carried by a trolley rig, a wheeled weight that clips onto the rope and rolls down along its length into the water. A line that is raised will increase the angle of the net in the water, covering more space, while making it easier for the trolley weight to slide down the rope. These four lines had been raised above the railing with thin boards, about seven feet long, specially cut at the top so that the rope was held in place by a divot in the wood. "These must be Owen's," John said. "No one else would go to this much trouble." The boards were held in place with bungy cords at the base and at the top of the railing. "The nets aren't even in the water yet." We went and got chairs and some of the provisions and came back to wait.

If the view from Lake Shore Drive was the spectator's view, looking out on the smelters and the lake beyond, we now had the participant's view, the smelter's view. We were on the east side of the harbor, looking back toward the city, and the skyline was gorgeous. The wind was brisk and out of the west, making the air crisp and clear, and as the horizon darkened the buildings along the drive became etched against the reddish backdrop of the sky, the glow of the city's amber-colored streetlights. Farther south, the red lights of the Sears Tower and the Hancock building flashed in diverse rhythms, and among all the confusion of apartment lights the white headband of the Hancock stood out like a straight line drawn on a chalkboard cluttered with writing.

Owen arrived with his group not thirty minutes later. They had been parked in a bar waiting for night to fall. He said hello and set right to work. He was wearing a sweatshirt that read, "If you love something, set it free. If it comes back to you, it's yours. If it doesn't come back to you, hunt it down and KILL IT," but he was really a nice fellow in spite of that. The nets were tightly wound, and he tried to figure them out and spread them on the sidewalk. We tried to help.

"Have you even looked at these since last year?" John said.

"Nah," Owen said. "Takes all the fun out of it."

He explained that the best way to do this was to grab the net by the weights and pull slowly. Each net untangled a little bit easier than the one before, and soon we had all four in the water.

"We're in," Owen said.

"Now the best part," John said. "Fishing is creative use of leisure time."

Owen brought a cooler from the car, we put the beer on ice, and we sat down to talk. Drinking in the park is, of course, illegal, but this, of course, is not a law that is well observed in Chicago—not by the smelters, who drink religiously, and not by the police, who patrol the area occasionally and ask only a bit of discretion. I asked John who he liked in the baseball races. "I never read anything until the season starts," he said. "Last year I read everything I could and I lost a lot of money betting on games. So I never read anything. So I don't know." I said that, like everyone else, I liked the Mets in the National League East, and I was picking the Reds in the West. I was a little surprised that so many other people seemed to be on the Reds. The Royals, I thought, were a good bet to repeat in the American League West, and my token surprise was the Baltimore Orioles. The Orioles would be good this year, I said. They'd beat the Royals in the playoffs and the Mets in the World Series. "I feel good about the Orioles." We agreed it didn't look so great for the Cubs and Sox. Cubs in second, I said, Sox in third, although if the Royals die the Sox have as good a chance as anyone in that pathetic division.

Owen suddenly realized we had no charcoal, and John didn't want to give up his parking space, so we walked back along the harbor toward the bait shop, hoping to find some there. Almost every post along the railing was occupied by a smelting rig, but no one seemed to be having much luck. On the other hand, no one seemed too upset about it. Smelters as a group are not really ethnic, but in no way are they yuppies. Back in the parking lot, a few vans had been equipped with televisions, but that was only a few. Down along the harbor there were no televisions, only radios turned to every station imaginable but mostly heavy metal and country stations, depending on the age of the group. "Helter smelter," one fellow said to another, laughing, as we walked by. The Blackhawks were popular too. They were, at that point, in the process of blowing a game to the Saint Louis Blues, putting their first-place position in jeopardy. (They won the following night, however, to clinch the division title.)

They had no charcoal at the bait shop, but they did have fishing licenses, which John and Owen needed, and we walked back hoping to barter for some briquettes. Smelters, however, aren't terribly interested in charcoal. Almost every group had a fire going, to stay warm, but when we asked these people if they had any spare charcoal, they looked at us with contempt: first of all, they seemed to say, "Charcoal?" as if we didn't know that wood was the only thing to burn, and secondly they couldn't get over our stupidity, going smelting without something to light on fire. Finally, down by the parking lot, we found someone willing to give us the few left at the bottom of the bag. We paid them in beers, and later we figured that, on a monetary scale, we got taken. Money, however, has no value to smelters—only beer, wood, and fish.

When we got back, we checked the nets, drawing in the line slowly, returning the empty nets into the water by allowing them line and jiggling the rope to encourage the weight to drop. The first three were empty, and the last one had two, which would wind up being half our take for the night. We were not going to be eating smelt. A fellow from the group next to ours came over to commiserate. "We were here on Tuesday, on opening day, and we got more in one pull than we've got all night," he said. "Water's too cold." We nodded our heads.

"This is why I moved to Chicago," John said, sitting back. "To live the life of a sportsman."

Owen took up a collection and got in his car to get some Polish and Italian sausages and some more charcoal. We started the fire with the little charcoal we had and huddled close. It was getting cold. Still, the park remained busy. Cars passed by, bumper to bumper, on the street, their passengers looking at the smelters and the view. We crossed the street and walked down to the lake, where some smelters had set up their rigs. We sat down and watched as, overhead, planes passed one after another on their descent into O'Hare. The evening was so clear we could see them lined up in the sky, a moving constellation that came north over the lake and turned west just above us.

The evening passed, Owen returned, the traffic subsided, some of us went home. A few authentic yuppies walked by, ending their evening out. "That's what's driving the fish away," John said. "It's the sound of those high heels on the sidewalk." One woman stopped to talk to the group next to us, four guys dressed in hats and heavy coveralls who were, by this time of night, quite tanked. To impress the woman, one guy got to biting the heads off the few smelt he had. He held a fish up to his mouth, bit the head off with a quick snap of the wrist, and spit it out like the end of a cigar. "Just like sushi," he said.

After midnight, after we had cooked the fine, hot sausages Owen had brought back, not even the yuppies bothered by anymore. The few groups that were left were gathered around their fires. We got ready to leave, and even the four guys next to us began to ignore their nets. They piled the fire high in their garbage can and sat right next to it, their backs to the wind. They talked and talked and occasionally laughed a drunken laugh. They seemed ready to stay all night. They would return to their homes, smelling of smoke, as the sun rose, perhaps as their wives dressed their children for church. Behind them, bars of light glimmered on the surface of the harbor, and the apartment windows darkened, one by one, in the buildings beyond.

That's Cricket

March 17, 1988

WHEN WE told friends and family—whom we were visiting in Adelaide, South Australia—that we planned to see a cricket match, they usually responded with a single syllable: "Hmmm." Australians have produced a hybrid culture from elements garnered from Britain and the United States, a unique culture that, in many ways, defies attempts to divide it into U.S. and British elements, but in their use of *hmm* Aussies tend quite heavily toward their British roots. An Australian can remain aloft in any conversation simply by resting on *hmm* and its various upswings and downdrafts. When we asked about cricket, most persons seemed somewhat embarrassed about it—as if it were bad enough that Australians have adopted this most British of games, so why would an American be interested—but in dismissing the sport they were at their most British. They didn't attack it, as an American would, but instead let the whole thing slide in a particularly British fashion. "Hmmm," they'd say, tracing a small, descending melody in the air, in the manner of a bird warbling pessimistically to itself in a tree. "Yes. Well. The Oval is quite beautiful."

The Adelaide Oval is, indeed, beautiful. The oval itself is large enough to accommodate any of several different Australian football games—from Australian rules to soccer via rugby—and it is well manicured and tended, a lush green without bare patches. It is bounded by a short fence of wide, colorful advertising billboards. A grandstand follows the oval down one stretch and around the corner; it is of a single level, with the roof a soft-brown terra-cotta shade, offering protection from the sun for those below and a nice backdrop for "those yobs" sitting across the oval, on the slightly pitched bank that surrounds the rest of the field. Viewed from the grandstand, the Oval offers, to the left, trees at the far end, then a hand-operated scoreboard with characters in yellow and white on a black background. Behind the scoreboard rise the spires of Saint Peter's Cathedral; on Sundays its bells chime out above the play. A line of trees follows behind the bank of grass along the back stretch. To the right, above the grandstand at the far turn, rise the skyscrapers and cranes of growing downtown Adelaide—a sore point for our host of the day, Arch Campbell, eighty-four, of Adelaide, who also happens to be a new grand-father I obtained in a recent transaction. He is a spry, lively, ageless gent, with a glint in his eye that is odd not so much for his age as for his former profession—schoolmaster. (Obviously, somewhere along the line a little puckish energy got passed in the wrong direction.) He proved himself knowledgeable about cricket and willing to instruct a couple of ignorant Yanks, but when he spoke of how beautiful the Oval was he ended by looking off to the right grandstand and the rising skyline beyond, and squinting he said, "They've quite ruined it, putting up those tall build-ings," with that glint showing through to distort the seriousness of the remark.

That remark reflected an attitude—joking or not—most Cubs fans can recognize, with our reverence for Wrigley field; the Adelaide Oval, with its hand-operated scoreboard and its embankment of grass "bleachers" across from the grandstand, has charms that should be equally familiar. Except, of course, that the Adelaide Oval has no lights.

Arch gave us the basic idea of the game, but underscored it with one basic piece of advice. Watching cricket, he said, "is a slow and slumber-ous way to spend the afternoon." He also called the game "somnolent," and advised us that it was certainly all right to drop off now and then, because everyone did it and when you woke up no one would be the wiser and the game would hardly seem to have changed.

It was good advice. We were entering upon the third day of a four-day match between the home South Australian team and the visiting Tasma-nians. This was not a test match between nations but a state match in the Sheffield Shield standings. Six of Australia's seven states have cricket teams, with the winner at the end of the season awarded the Sheffield Shield. It was summer approaching autumn in Australia, and the season was coming to a close with Tasmania at the bottom rung and South Australia not much better. This inherent lack of interest in the match was augmented by Tasmania's scoring a whopping 592 runs in its first innings, which took over a day and a half to complete. The crowd was small and dominated by elderly spectators.

For those not well versed in the slow, slumberous, somnolent ways of cricket: each player on the team bats once an inning, with two batters—one at each end of the twenty-two-yard-long pitch—on the field at any given time. A batter remains on the field until he is out, which means until he hits a ball that is caught on the fly, until the bowler breaks his wicket, or until he is found to have illegally blocked a ball that would have hit the wicket, usually by deflecting the delivery with his shin pads instead of the bat. Also, if the batter runs and fails to make it to the next wicket before the ball is fielded and returned, that too is an out.

What is called the perfect balance between offense and defense reflected in baseball is never so apparent as when the game is compared with cricket. The offense has all the advantages in cricket, especially when the game is played on a pitch as true as the one at the Adelaide Oval. The bowler attempts to throw the ball at the wicket, and he may skim the ball off the ground in an attempt to get it past the batter—in fact, it's the way most deliveries tend to go. Yet the batter need only deflect the ball away from the wicket in any direction—there is no fair or foul territory, and the fielders are arrayed all around in the manner of a constellation—and once the ball is deflected the batter still need not run. He can sit there deflecting the ball this way and that in five-foot taps all afternoon if he so desires, and that's exactly what the South Australian team did, picking their spots for the big swings that would deliver three and four runs at a blow. (If a hit reaches a boundary, it is four runs; if it clears the boundary, it's six.)

Arch called it "slow cricket"; it was the game played at a pace where every delivery was like a solitary tick off a clock that is not running. The pitch was true, and South Australia had every hope of catching the 592 runs scored by Tasmania, but to do so they had to play cautiously and not squander any outs. Both the first two batters—Bishop and Hilditch—were well on their way to centuries (scoring one hundred runs), but neither was taking any chances. They had begun batting the previous afternoon, and when we arrived just after 11 A.M. they had just begun the day's action. Bishop was the first to one hundred, and Arch said, "Now's when they get cocky and make a mistake." He made an out at 101, deflecting a ball straight back to the wicketkeeper (the catcher) in what we might call a foul tip. It was almost 1 P.M. and time for lunch.

In spite of the game's almost utter lack of time clock (an element it shares with baseball), the sport is extremely regimented, as if it exists in a dreamworld but with specific boundaries that are unhesitatingly stuck to. The day begins at eleven in the morning, then at 1 P.M. everyone breaks for lunch. At 1:40 the game begins then pauses at 3:40 for tea. At four the game resumes for its final session, which concludes at six. On top of this, there are breaks for drinks for the fielders (nonalcoholic, or so we imagine) midway through each session. Arch ushered us downstairs for lunch, to the club lounge, where we dined on a smorgasbord of cold meats and salads, with just a dab of hot English mustard—the single spiciest element of the day.

The pleasant pace should not give anyone the idea that cricket is a simple or simpleminded game. The battle between batter and bowler offers all the intricacies of baseball's battle between pitcher and hitter, but instead of the struggle lasting five or six pitches, with one pitch setting up the next, the batter-bowler conflict has no set end, and a bowler may be looking ahead two overs (sets of six pitches apiece) in delivering a certain pitch.

This realization made us all the more sympathetic to the Tasmanians, even though we were rooting for S.A. The Tasmanians were led by Dennis Lillee, who we were informed was one of the greatest of Australia's fast bowlers and had recently come out of retirement at age thirty-six to accept Tasmania's captaincy. Lillee would march off, then return on his run. He showed the ball briefly by holding it forehead height just as he neared the far wicket, as if to say, "Here it is, try to hit it." He then skipped, hurling himself forward, and allowed the arm down and then up over the shoulder for the delivery. (The elbow is not allowed to be bent or flexed in any fashion.) Time and again, he and the various other Tasmanian bowlers did this, and each time the S.A. hitter deflected the ball away and remained standing, or skittered it into a small gap and the two hitters changed places, then waited patiently as Lillee marched off his run again. The frustration became apparent, once, when the silence was broken by a piercing group of shouts. Lillee threw a high bouncer, which deflected off Bishop's replacement, O'Connor, and was caught by the wicketkeeper. The umpire ruled, however, that the ball had bounced off O'Connor's shoulder and not his bat and that he was not out.

S.A. continued to score in dribs and drabs. Hilditch completed his century just after lunch, but O'Connor was a much greater culprit in slowing the game. He blocked the ball here and there but rarely far enough to get more than a run or two; two hours later, he and Hilditch were still batting, but O'Connor had only thirty-some runs to his credit.

The excitement was too much for my traveling companion; she went home just after lunch. Arch and I stayed on, however, chatting through the afternoon. He called it a day at the tea break. Just after I returned to my seat and the game had resumed at 4 P.M., a large flight of gulls came over the far trees. They circled once over the oval and settled down like the snow in a paperweight. From then on, whenever a ball was hit into the farther reaches of the oval, a fielder had to go tearing after it, sending gulls fluttering into the sky with every step. It added something of slight pageantry, an exotic, tropical air to the game. Wrigley field may have ivy, but I've yet to see an outfielder scare up gulls or even pigeons in pursuing a baseball.

Hilditch finally went out in this session, fouling one back to the wicket-keeper, who caught it on the fly. He retired with 185 runs and with S.A. amassing 335 on its first two outs. The Tasmanian tally of 592 was looking more and more within reach, especially as one of the team's best batters, Hookes ("Hooksie," one nearby gent called him), was coming out. Hilditch, however, received the applause with nary a sign of recognition as he left the field; having made an out, one is evidently not to show an ounce of glee, no matter how many runs he has chalked up.

Hookes was in good form, and he used the oval's pitch to whack some long balls off the boundary. The score climbed higher into the 300s by five, when I left. I walked home to where we were staying with relatives, through downtown Adelaide, stopping at what seemed the halfway point, the King's Head Hotel, where I had a Coopers (a heavy ale much like Belgium's Chimay, especially in that it is fermented in the bottle) and watched the end of the day's action on television. Nearby, people watching the match were amazed at the scoring. Bishop and Hilditch are like the Dernier and Sandberg of S.A., and while both are fine players neither is expected to routinely go out and rack up a century. Listening to the talk of the S.A. fans was like sitting in Murphy's after a game in which both Dernier and Sandberg had hit three home runs. It wasn't your everyday occurrence. The following day, Hookes too completed a century, and S.A. went on to win 673–592 in a match called after first innings (normally, there is time for each team to bat twice in the four days). This we learned in Monday's paper, for one day of slow cricket goes a long way.

After finishing the Coopers I trudged on home, recalling, in particular, one especially sharp memory. Midway through the day, a shadow appeared near a fielder in the comer of the oval; it was too big to be a gull, too slow to be a plane. Looking up, I saw a pelican high in the sky above the field. It hung in the air without a beat of its wings, as still as a pendulum that has come to a stop. That, to my mind, was cricket.

Tyson at the Auditorium

July 7, 1988

LOUIS SULLIVAN's Auditorium Theatre has arcs of large, bare light bulbs overhead, lined up along the rafters. Down front, the stage is framed by a golden facade, open in the middle, inscribed with the names of the greatest composers—Verdi, Mozart, Beethoven, Berlioz, Haydn, Schumann. At the top of the facade is a wall painting, apparently some sort of Christian allegory; the overhead lights are mainly for ornamentation, and in the dimness the painting can be barely made out. Only figures, not specific persons or characters, can be distinguished; the figures march in two rows—one to the left, one to the right—toward the center, but even in the dim light a person below can make out that one of the figures carries a cross. The low lighting is meant, I believe, to create an atmosphere of reverence, a quiet tone in the audience, although a more coarse individual—a fight fan, for instance—might say it is meant to give the Andy Frains an excuse to use their flashlights. Outside, in the lobby, the tile floors and wall lamps are only slightly less ornate than the fittings in the theater proper, and the atmosphere—on this evening—is a bit more abrasive. Even the bathrooms, as I recall, are impressive in this place. I say "as I recall" because my previous visit to the Auditorium had been to see Mikhail Baryshnikov, several years ago, while the purpose of this visit was to see the Tyson-Spinks heavyweight championship fight, on closed-circuit television, which—as we all know by now—lasted a mere ninety-one seconds, leaving no time at all to allow oneself to get caught remarking on the bathroom fixtures.

We had wanted to see this fight as much as we had wanted to see any sporting event this year, and its shortness, its abrupt and seemingly easy end, should not allow us to diminish its impact or its importance. This was the heavyweight fight of the decade, easily eclipsing Spinks-Holmes, because both these fighters had beaten Larry Holmes and neither had lost to anyone else. Likewise, we knew, before the fight took place, that only an upset victory by Michael Spinks could keep the bout from retaining its title as heavyweight fight of the decade, because after Spinks there was and is nothing for Mike Tyson. Spinks was the only man on the planet believed capable of even merely challenging Tyson, and the brevity of the bout and its indisputable end serve, again, not to diminish the match but to elevate Tyson to greatness.

We played our seats very cool, however. Ticket sales, we heard, were slow, and so we felt comfortable waiting to join the last-second rush. Boom-Boom called around Monday morning the day of the fight, in fact, to get the prices and a feel for the various sites we could choose from. Ditka's, we knew, would be $100 or $150 a seat—this price was well advertised—and the other "VIP" location, Park West, would be equally bad. The Vic, our early choice, turned out to be $75—still not right. The Stadium was $30, we found, but when the Boomer called to say that not only could we see the fight at the Auditorium Theatre but seats were a reasonably priced $40, the choice was made. "Great, I saw Baryshnikov there," I laughed, and the sense of displacement was as deliberate as the joke, because given a choice between seeing Mike Tyson fight or Baryshnikov dance I'll pick Tyson every day of the week.

Because Tyson, like Baryshnikov, is at the top of his field—he does what he does better than anyone else—except that Baryshnikov's claim to this position is probably now in a bit more dispute than Tyson's claim to the same rank, both because Baryshnikov is older and a bit past his prime and because the main benefit to ranking boxers as opposed to ranking ballet stars is that ballet's standards are aesthetic and subjective while boxers rank themselves.

And according to boxers' rankings, there is no doubt these were the two best fighters on the planet. Don't dismiss Spinks for his quick demise. One of the main attractions of this fight, for me, was that although I favor Tyson over all other boxers, I've always liked Michael Spinks too. Spinks was winning an Olympic gold medal when I was getting my driver's license, and I've always liked his awkwardly effective style. If there was anyone to give Tyson a decent bout, I believed it was Spinks. He matched up well. His spidery attack was meant to fight Tyson—if any style of attack is—and while he's no graceful "float like a butterfly, sting like a bee" sort of boxer, I believed he could use stick-and-run guerrilla tactics for several rounds and perhaps, if he was savvy enough and strong enough and lucky enough, come away with a decision (my pick, however: Tyson by knockout in the eighth to tenth round).

Spinks is an admirable boxer, even in light of his performance against Tyson. After the Olympics, he established himself as a pro but then halted his career, choosing to help his brother Leon in Leon's pursuit of the heavyweight crown. When Leon pissed his short-lived title away, Michael—almost by design—set about capturing the light-heavyweight crown and then moving up a weight class for the big one—a move that had never been accomplished. Yet he whipped Larry Holmes twice to claim the title—a title he then had unceremoniously taken from him. Remember that, throughout twelve years as a professional boxer, not only had he never lost but he had never even been knocked down. He had every right to claim he was still heavyweight champ, which made the Tyson match perfect for both contestants.

The circus atmosphere around Tyson, meanwhile, did not complicate this fight—nothing, it turns out, could complicate it—so much as embellish it. Tyson seemed as comfortable with his newfound position of magazine cover boy as some of his fans seemed looking at the ornate interior of the Auditorium. The question was whether the distraction would hurt his performance. In their usual fashion, the media went about first building Tyson up, then questioning the buildup, which only built him up more, and then outright attacking him from below. (When his wife, Robin Givens, was shown on the screen at the Auditorium, the response was reminiscent of the sort of treatment Yoko Ono used to get at campus screenings of *Let It Be*.) To put this in simple perspective, Tyson was fighting his most difficult opponent amid the most trying conditions the media could create—almost as if to establish a true test of his greatness.

Our seats, bought that very morning over the telephone, were extraordinary: on the aisle, eight rows off the orchestra pit. The screen was set in the center of the facade, and it was huge, twenty feet high maybe, although I imagine it was still a squint from the balcony. The tickets said 8 P.M., with Tyson-Spinks set to go off at 9:50, and the fights of the undercard were already under way when we got there, shortly after eight, with announcers giving that hurried, quickened commentary that puts one immediately in the mood for boxing. We adjourned, briefly, to the lobby for cigars and drinks (Studs Terkel doing likewise nearby). The crowd was an odd and—in this town, at this time—welcome mix of white and black, the dress everything from suits to sweat suits. It was, of course, a very male crowd, but with a smattering of females, including a few pairs on an unusual girls' night out, and one or two boss fight chicks in miniskirts out of the Victoria's Secret catalog.

The crowd was, if not subdued, at least calm. It was a crowd that liked the favorite, Tyson, but that respected the challenger, a crowd that wanted a good fight. I think they got it.

We went back in to watch the end of the Trevor Berbick–Carl Williams fight (to establish the top challenger, it was said). The two typified everything boxing was before Tyson came on the scene: they huffed, they puffed, they threw a few punches, but mostly they hugged and beat each other about the kidneys. Then came the long prefight production, including taped interviews with Tyson and Spinks, and then the actual coverage of the usual prefight rigmarole.

No member of the Spinks entourage was present when Tyson had his hands taped and gloved, and although this oversight was entirely the fault of Spinks's men, Spinks's manager used the incident to hold up the fight fifteen minutes. Our crowd was impatient, its responses tinged in sexual metaphors: "Let's do it," "Let's get it on." At the actual fight site, this was the usual garbage, but the usual garbage is what fight ritual is all about, and it was hard not to feel present at the meeting of the tribes—our best man against yours—when Spinks and then Tyson came out, each amid his men, and they pressed through the crowd to the ring. Instructions were given. Tyson has looked meaner and more menacing; he looked, in fact, calm, and I thought for a moment that perhaps all this prefight commotion had taken something away from him. But it was a gambit.

A rumbling filled the Auditorium Theatre, a rumbling unlike any Baryshnikov or his artistic cousins have ever heard. We drummed our feet against the wood of the floor, and the bell rang. Tyson came out in the most unusual fashion, on the jog, with an exaggerated, almost cartoonish gait, his legs lagging slowly behind with each step. Then his face curled back (imagine the way a cat pulls back its ears when fighting) and he launched an amazing offensive, throwing himself directly at Spinks with a hurried, spinning, unfocused combination of blows. Boomer later said it was like a buzz saw, and in this case the cartoon cliché fits. People have said Spinks panicked, that he never got to his strategy of stick-and-run, but he really had no chance. Tyson subjected him to a full onslaught from the get-go. There was no hiding from it; the only alternative would have been to sit against the ropes and hope that, like a tornado, it would pass.

Spinks, however, was trying to hustle into his strategy double time like the good ex-Marine he is. He, too, was throwing punches—although they were being outnumbered two to one—and he spun off Tyson and toward the corner. Here, Tyson's two main strategic strengths became evident. We know he throws as vicious a punch as anyone has ever seen in boxing. Yet he also cuts off a ring—trims it down into various sectors that he can cover—with the skill of a mathematician, and his hand speed is amazing, especially when combined with his immense power. Quite simply, he outcounterpunched Spinks immediately. Spinks set up, led with a right, but Tyson came in under it with a punishing left uppercut, and we were on our feet without realizing it.

There was an instant, too, when we suddenly perceived that Spinks was slowed, perhaps hurt. "He caught him, he caught him," I remember saying out loud. Before Tyson himself could realize this, he hit Spinks with a right to the body, and Spinks lost his air and went down on one knee. Replays later showed that after that first punch Tyson probably could have blown him over with a puff of breath.

Spinks took a good many counts—seven, I believe—before rising. Tyson went right at him. He swung a left hand, Spinks ducked to the right, and Tyson swung a right that blew Spinks over and flattened him like a field of tall grass in the wind.

It was over so quickly our first impression—and the false impression of a good many, I imagine—was fix. Then came the replays. Tyson punches so quickly and so effortlessly that the amount of energy he expends on his blows—if delivered by anyone else—wouldn't seem to amount to much. On the replays, however, their impact was felt, and it was telling. The initial left uppercut did the damage; everything else followed like night the day. Yet the final right-hand punch was so effortless even in replays that its effect was disguised. Then there came a shot from near ringside, from behind Tyson, in which it became apparent that Spinks's feet were lifted off the mat. Then, finally, a bird's-eye camera shot out of Hitchcock—with all its connotations of fate and impending doom—that showed Spinks ducking directly into Tyson's final right hand, which connected squarely on the side of Spinks's head, and how he rolled over on his back, legs quivering, and how his eyes—wide open—rolled to the left to stare at the bright light as it dimmed.

Writers like Bernie Lincicome who suggest Tyson blew his career by finishing Spinks so quickly show an utter lack of both understanding of the sport and empathy with its practitioners. This is a most dangerous sport, with no room for mercy. To point out that the sport demands a measure of ruthlessness is like pointing out that ballet demands beauty and grace. Meanwhile, fight fans knew beforehand that if he won, this would be Tyson's last good fight for two or three years. (It will take that long for the next Olympic champion to be determined and then to gain his professional footing, and even then—in my opinion—it's not likely he'll have much of a chance against Tyson.) There are no $20 million paydays on the horizon for Tyson, but he still has his series of cable television fights on HBO, and people will watch because they are relatively free and because he is the greatest boxer of this generation and one of the five best of all time. In the long run, poor competition didn't diminish Joe Louis, and it won't diminish Tyson. In fact, I believe the occasional bum going seven or eight good rounds against him will, eventually, become an essential part of the Tyson myth—provided, of course, he doesn't follow through on his threat to retire (a threat, it seems, deliberately meant to counter the sort of doubt expressed by Lincicome. Don't bet on it, not even at 5–1).

As we left the Auditorium, talking about the fight under the marquee lights, Boomer said the one abiding emotion he felt was fear—fear that someone could be at once so destructive and indestructible, unharnessed and yet entirely focused. I had a different feeling. Much as I admire Michael Spinks, and as much as I wanted him to do well, I left the theater laughing and exhilarated. Mike Tyson is one of the great athletes of this century. He towers above the rest of his chosen field, like Babe

Ruth or Bobby Jones or Wayne Gretzky. In other words, he does what he does better than anyone else in the world, he is a marvel to watch, and we are lucky to be on the planet at the same era in time. I imagine ballet fans feel the same way after seeing Baryshnikov.

King Versus Simeon

March 16, 1989

DURING A BREAK in the first half of last Sunday's Public League championship basketball game, the public-address announcer read a list of the
five previous champions. "Nineteen-eighty-four Public League champion—Simeon Vocational," he said. Screams, hoots, and applause came
from various sections of the crowd. "Nineteen-eighty-five champion—
Simeon." Same response, a little bit louder. "Nineteen-eighty-six Public
League champion—Martin Luther King High School." All the previously
quiet areas of the Pavilion at the University of Illinois at Chicago—which
is where the game took place—suddenly came alive. The response was
not as loud as that for Simeon, but it was more intense. Boos came from
the Simeon areas. It was like hearing the separate small skirmishes on
a large battlefield. "Nineteen-eighty-seven champions—King." Same responses, only louder. "And 1988 champions, defending champions of the
Chicago Public League—Simeon." And now everyone was screaming in
one way or another, hooting or booing, clapping or razzing, in that shrill,
high-pitched tone familiar to us all from high school assemblies.

Then the players from King and Simeon high schools broke from
their huddles, took the court, and resumed the 1989 Public League
championship game.

The rivalry between King and Simeon has become one of the richest
in the city. By that I mean not one of the richest in Public League basketball, nor even one of the richest in citywide high school sports, but simply one of the richest, most interesting clashes the city has to offer—right
up there with the Cubs fans versus the White Sox fans, Lincoln Park
versus Hyde Park, Carson Pirie Scott versus Marshall Field's, and black
Democrats versus white. As is the case with all these other conflicts, the
clash between Simeon and King is a clash not merely of personalities but
of styles and techniques. It is amazing how well the battle is played out,
right down to the smallest details.

Undefeated Simeon took the court first for its warm-up session. Dressed in white-and-gold sweat suits, the players split into two groups, ran down the sidelines to the far end of the court, high-fived one another as they formed concentric circles, then swung back to the other side of the court—the two groups running figure-eight patterns—where they repeated the high-five procedure. Then the King players came out, dressed in darker, black-and-gold sweats, a figure of their mascot jaguar on the back, and the two teams formed two tangent circles almost automatically and slapped one another's hands as they passed. Simeon's rooters obviously outnumbered those from King, but the King fans were a sturdy lot, loud and proud, and they were backed up by a band, which punctuated the events in a very partisan manner throughout the early evening.

King's fans, its players, and its coach all adopt the attitude of the outnumbered outsider. Simeon, meanwhile, has the confident elegance of a basketball-court boulevardier. King, coached by the irritable, brazen Sonny Cox, had bypassed the usual early season showdown between the two teams when it declined to play in the Mayor's Tournament this season, accepting an invitation to another holiday meet. Simeon had, as a result, rolled through the mayor's tourney and through the rest of the season. King, meanwhile, had slipped once, making them underdogs in Sunday's title game. Now, not only had the two teams won the last five Public League championships, but twice during that stretch they had met in the title game, with King winning in 1986 and Simeon last year.

While the Simeon Wolverines appeared in their home whites, with the now-classic broad blue, gold, and white stripes down the sides (echoed in the piping around the shoulders), King appeared in villainous black, the dappled spots of its jaguar mascot suggested by a stylized gold-and-white pattern down the sides (which actually suggested nothing so much as sunlight shining through a thin stained-glass window). The King players left the bench with their shirttails out, while most of the Simeon players started with theirs in. The one piece of the uniform common to all players: the Patrick Ewing T-shirt beneath the jersey.

The two teams' star players were, likewise, of divergent styles. Simeon's tall, thin senior center, Deon Thomas, dictates a half-court game stressing set plays and getting the ball inside. He had been unstoppable during the regular season. King's Jamie Brandon, meanwhile, is a junior forward of medium height (six foot four and, we assume, growing), who excels in an open court. His style of play is best depicted simply by pointing out his number, 23, famous for being worn by another popular Chicagoan.

(Michael Jordan, by the way, made the scene, acting as color man for the television broadcast on WGN. His appearance in a dapper double-breasted suit during the national anthem gave the song a manic intensity that would, no doubt, have cheered the vets in front of the Art Institute had they been there to see it.)

Thomas and Brandon, however, were different players at different positions. Even on the same court, they rarely met one another face-to-face; their confrontation was the sort created by newspapers and television commentators. For anyone watching last Sunday's championship game, the pivotal battle took place at the guard position, where Simeon's Jackie Crawford matched up against King's Victor Snipes.

Crawford is a short, muscular, scrappy guard, the sort who—in his every aspect on the court—reflects an attitude of deprivation and transcendence. In short, he sets out to make each opponent pay for the gods' neglect in not granting him an extra six inches of height. Listed at five foot nine, he may be more than three inches shorter than that, but he is—nevertheless—a fine player. He displayed his character in the first quarter, when he drove the lane, stopped, took the open shot, popped, and then guarded Snipes, chest to chest, all the way back up the court, jawing at him, talking dirt, and giving him a bit of verbal in-your-face the whole long trip. He's a tenacious defender, a real fyce dog—hiking up his shorts, pursing out his lips, getting low to the ground, and yapping all the time—and at the end of the first half he found himself guarding Brandon after a switch-off and hounded him into a bad shot to end the period, holding King to a 30–24 lead. The mustache he was working to grow was only slightly darker than his closely cropped scalp.

In style and temperament, Snipes could hardly have been more different. At six foot two and thin, he has an elegant carriage. He is relaxed and efficient as a ball handler, reminiscent, in some ways, of Sleepy Floyd, the former Georgetown star now with the Houston Rockets. His facial expressions bring to mind Spike Lee's Mars Blackmon: bewildered, faintly anxious, but belying an inner calm. Crawford and the other Simeon guard, Cody Butler, came in with reputations as ball hawks, but Snipes denied them, drove the lane, hit the open shot, and dished out a total of ten assists (a fine day's work in a thirty-two-minute, sixty-seven-point game). It wasn't the sort of performance that draws attention to itself, but take it from us: he dominated.

The confrontation between the two was most clear when someone else was shooting free throws. They'd be standing out at midcourt, away from everyone, but Crawford would be pressed against Snipes, head butting up against chin. Crawford was trying to be fierce, talk a tough game, intimidate, but Snipes had all the composure of a big dog silently watching a butcher cut chops while a smaller dog yelps at his heels. The matchup was a near draw in the first half, but in the second half Snipes's composure won out; he didn't humiliate Crawford so much as force him into a place where Crawford humiliated himself. Toward the end of the game, Crawford completed a frustrated series of thrown elbows and nasty fouls with an incident in which he fell to the floor, losing the dribble and the ball, and then—from his prone position—tried to trip a passing King player. Demonstrating once again that there is a thin line between the intense player and the bush-leaguer.

Snipes was our unanimous most valuable player, because his play reflected the play of the team. While he was quietly, efficiently denying Crawford, King was quietly, efficiently denying Thomas and, in effect, Simeon. King came out in a box-and-one zone defense, in which four guys remain stationed pretty much at the corners of the free throw lane, and one guy roams free, covering Thomas wherever he goes. Damian Porter acted as Thomas's shadow, and he did his job well. On the rare occasions when Thomas did get the ball inside, the box collapsed and three men were clawing at him. They allowed him only four shots from the field and eleven points for the game. King also jangled Simeon's rhythm by throwing in an occasional full-court trap defense and then falling back into the dependable box-and-one for the half-court game. Simeon went down remarkably meekly. They didn't play poorly; they just got beat.

If Simeon had hit any of the many fifteen- and eighteen-foot jump shots they had open, if they had played with more aggressiveness and a swifter trigger finger, they might have gone downstate as undefeated

Public League champions. As it was, King made the open shots—both Snipes and his off-guard sidekick, Ahmad Shareef, hit their opportunities, with Shareef displaying a cool, gunslinger's hand-and-finger gesture whenever he scored—and King then opened the game up offensively, so that by the fourth quarter they had set up Brandon for show time and he went wild, ending with thirty points on the way to an easy 67–57 victory.

We were sitting in the first row of the balcony, at center court, and the main King cheering sections were across the floor, one near each hoop—the band at one end, the pep club–type kids at the other. As the clock ticked down, they grew increasingly ebullient. The band threw in bursts of everything from Paul Simon's "You Can Call Me Al" to Kool Moe Dee's "Wild Wild West," and the pepsters answered back with the various rhythmic chants common to high school sports, finishing with "We're going downstate!" My companion for the day—an old political/media pal I've known since the days earlier in the decade when we were both, for a time, court reporters—was no more familiar with the scene than I was. In fact, neither of us had been to a high school game since, well, since we had been there ourselves. It all came back, though—at once familiar and, now, quite distant—the easy emotionalism, the intense self-involvement, the feeling of being part of something larger (even if it is only your damn high school). The game over, the Simeon players slouched on their bench as the King players gloried at center court. Crawford broke into sobs, we're sorry to point out, but was consoled with a brief embrace by Snipes. Only a couple of minutes later, though, there he was, dancing at center court as the team lined up to accept its trophy. Snipes stood out in front of them, between the team and the presenter, and he grooved to the brassy band music. He kicked one leg, then the other; he threw an arm over his head and straightened it out, then the other; and then he tipped forward and fell into the arms of his teammates.

Kevin Garnett

March 16, 1995

HIGH SCHOOL basketball is a game of stars. The talent is so diffused at that level that one great player can dominate. Yet because the talent is diffused, high school basketball is also a great team sport. A fivesome in sync can concentrate on stopping that one player, then methodically grind down the other team on offense. A star might ride roughshod over a conference during the regular season, but if he's in effect a one-man team he usually runs into trouble along about March in the playoffs.

Yet there are stars and then there are transcendent talents. Over the last decade of attending the Chicago Public League semifinals and finals off and on, we have never seen anyone like Kevin Garnett, the center on Farragut's city championship team this year. Deon Thomas, Jamie Brandon, Rashard Griffith, Kiwane Garris—all were players with star ability, outstanding talents. Garnett, however, is something altogether different, much more special and much more rare.

Garnett is a six-foot-eleven-inch-tall will-o'-the-wisp, a spindly giant made of gossamer and set free to fly on the basketball court. He has an uncanny feel for the action, along with the coordination to maneuver himself through it as if he were some sort of fallen angel. He has a soft shooting touch, a sense of comfort and ease on the dribble, a creative flair for passing, a slashing, waspish manner around the defensive basket, and above all, unbelievable quickness for a big man. He's there and not there, a mirage—a talent package too good to be true.

Yet there he was last weekend at the UIC Pavilion, preaching to the converted. Given the uncommon attention surrounding Garnett, along with the widespread interest prompted by the hit documentary *Hoop Dreams*, it was no surprise that tickets for both the Public League semifinals and finals sold out for the first time in our memory. (All praises to our buddy Buck, a good friend and a fine gentleman, for having the foresight to go down to the Pavilion on Friday and buy tickets.) Yet the normal crowd hysteria, the screechy cheers and jeers of high school, seemed toned down from previous years as the aficionados moved in.

The upper deck, where we were sitting, was as usual crammed with the basketball faithful. On Sunday, the yuppie pilgrims sitting in front of us even brought a pocket television so they could check out the NCAA tournament pairings as they were announced during the game. We were all there to examine whether Garnett was for real, and he made an immediate impression. With his long, flapping, gownlike shorts hanging down below his knees and his warm-up jacket zipped to the chin, there was an air of the abbey to Garnett, a feeling he later emphasized by sometimes clasping his hands together as if in prayer when running downcourt after a particularly good shot. Seeing a player like that at such a stage of his development—a period of boundless promise—was an almost religious experience.

Early in the championship game Sunday against Carver, Garnett was posted up low, his back to the basket. Two weeks ago, we wrote of the Bulls' Toni Kukoc in that position making a move where he shows the ball over his left shoulder then spins quickly to his right. As a tall, thin player of versatile talents, Garnett has many similarities with Kukoc, and here he tried a similar but even more amazing move. He did the same spin, only without the fake. He simply spun to his right, but so quickly he left Carver center John Smith standing there as Garnett leaped and dunked the ball through the hoop. Just as amazing was the crowd response: a few immediate claps and hoots here and there, sure, but beneath that a mass sustained "Oooh," followed by murmurs of "Did you see that?" and "Damn!" and "Jesus H. Christ." We were all of us believers by then.

Even so, miraculous as Garnett proved to be, he was still prone to the usual star shortcomings when faced with opponents stressing a team concept. The Farragut Admirals trailed in the third quarter against both scrappy Dunbar in the semis and more talented Carver in the final. In both games Garnett played well, but not well enough to win by himself. In both, it wasn't until Ronnie Fields took control in the second half that the Admirals asserted their dominance. Garnett and Fields demonstrated that quality great teammates have for developing a dynamic to bail each other out.

Dunbar, even with its victories in the Public League playoffs, had somehow reached the semifinals with a pitiful record of 14–14—an indication of just how disastrous its season had been. The Mighty Men were now playing as a team, however, and they had a game plan in place to upset Farragut. That plan consisted of spreading out the offense to draw Garnett away from the basket, and getting back on defense to keep Farragut from turning the game into a dunkfest. The importance of this strategy was emphasized when Farragut's first three baskets came on a breakaway jam by Garnett, a breakaway jam by Fields, and a jump shot from the free-throw line by Garnett.

That jump shot Dunbar was prepared to accept. The Mighty Men were out to harass Garnett near the basket, allow him whatever points he could get outside, and then keep Fields from beating them. That they did early on. Dunbar kept Fields under wraps and stayed close through the first half, which ended with Farragut up 28–24. Then Dunbar came out determined to steal the game in the first few minutes of the second half. On offense, they kept isolating players on the weak side of the court, keeping Garnett and Fields on the other side, and they beat their men to the hoop time and again. On defense, they turned up the pressure and forced the Admirals into turnovers. Dunbar opened a 40–29 lead in what looked to be the biggest upset in Public League history. Yet by straying from the hoop and playing aggressive defense, Garnett led Farragut back into the game. Now Dunbar was rattled, and Farragut ran off fourteen straight to take a 43–40 lead. That, however, was when Garnett was hit with his fourth foul.

With Garnett on the bench, Fields took over—both in running the offense and in applying the defensive pressure—and he was suddenly beautiful. Leading a small lineup, he padded the Farragut lead to 50–44 before Garnett returned with six and a half minutes to play. Then, just as Dunbar was rallying its forces, Fields exploded past his man and drove untouched to the hoop for a dunk. That made it 53–49. A few minutes later he raced open downcourt on a two-on-one break, and his teammate led him with a perfect alley-oop pass. The dunk made it 57–50. While Dunbar rallied one last time to close within 59–57, Farragut scored the final points to win 63–57.

Carver's semifinal victory over King was much more impressive, if only for the sheer mechanical grind-it-out quality it had. Carver was led into the game by Nick Irvin, a sophomore, the youngest in a series of athletic Irvin brothers. Irvin continues to carry a bit of baby fat on his body, giving him a Mark Aguirre build, but he is clearly a player. King was out to stop him; Carver aimed to do the same with King's Leonard Myles, a '70s retro player complete with Afro, headband, mustache, sideburns, and knee-high athletic socks. Both teams succeeded in shutting down the other's star, but that done, Carver prevailed, mainly on the strength of its alternating big men, starter John Smith and backup Alvin Robinson, who actually got the bulk of the playing time. They also had an outside sharpshooter to complement Irvin in Jason Garcia, and an excitable small forward in Marcel O'Neal. O'Neal had actually been enduring a rough playoff season until he led Carver with fifteen points against King. He got the fans going early on with a skywalking dunk (he just barely made it; his legs were kicking him up through the air all the way), punctuated by a trademark gait down the court, as his fists pumped up and down at his sides. It was something we would see several times during the game, and one last time when it was over, just before O'Neal leaped into the arms of his teammates on the bench as time expired with Carver a 60–49 winner.

We did not see it at all last Sunday, even though Carver led 25–17 at halftime and seemed to have the game in control. O'Neal kept Fields in check early on, and the rest of the Carver players swarmed on Garnett whenever he got the ball low, forcing him into several turnovers. Toward the end of the half, Carver went to a small lineup with good success, and it clearly had Farragut on the run. Garnett dragged his warm-up jacket off the court at halftime, then dragged it back on after intermission.

Once again it was Fields who turned the tide. He and Garnett opened the half with baskets, then Fields went down the lane, was fouled, and forced a shot up and in to tie the score at 28. Garnett jumped on Fields's back and lifted his own feet off the ground, yet Fields walked around as if Garnett were no weight at all. Fields is an exceptional talent, but he is a much more conventional player than Garnett. Fields is a Michael Jordan wannabe, complete with a shaved head and number 23, the only player on either team to go to black shoes for the playoffs. Yet, while he missed the ensuing free throw, he was also clearly feeling in the zone all of a sudden, and that made all the difference for Farragut. With Fields driving and either shooting in the lane (he finished with twenty-two) or dishing out assists, Carver could no longer swarm on Garnett. When Fields wasn't chewing up Carver, Garnett was hitting a series of smooth and effortless turnaround jumpers (he finished with thirty-two). After being held to seventeen points at halftime, Farragut scored fifty-four in the second half. Garnett put them ahead on a pair of free throws at 32–30, and they never trailed again.

Not that it wasn't a great game. Irvin, after a subpar performance in the semis, kept Carver close almost single-handedly in the second half of the final, scoring sixteen straight for the Challengers at one point. He hit a last-minute three-pointer to make it 45–38 after three quarters, stole the ball and converted a layup to open the fourth quarter, added a three-pointer from across the Eisenhower Expressway, and then made a Chet Walker Jr. move, bouncing off a Farragut player in the lane and throwing the ball up and in. But as Carver increasingly resorted to a one-man attack—the Challengers never went back to that small lineup that worked so well in the first half—Farragut played more like a team, with predictable results. Farragut won, 71–62.

Still, all eyes were on Garnett right up to the end. He is an open, emotional player, a quality that came through in abundance on the court as he mixed scoldings with hugs where his teammates were concerned. As the clock ticked down and the city championship neared, he was hugging everyone—big hugs with his boa-constrictor arms in which he clasped the recipient's head to his breast. Even Irvin got one as he left the game in the final minute.

Garnett is the closest thing to a Wayne Gretzky–style basketball genius we have seen in the city's high schools, but the future is far from certain for him. Dick Versace, the former Bradley and Indiana Pacers coach who's now Chicago's top basketball expert, says he thinks Garnett could go straight to the pros. Garnett might have to, as he is said to have the usual academic problems. Still, he doesn't seem quite big enough yet for the National Basketball Association, while his prodigious talents would be squandered at some low-profile junior college.

Whatever happens, Chicago has been privileged to have him this season. Garnett, who is reported to have a fairly troubled family life, moved here from South Carolina last year just to play with Fields after the two developed a fast friendship at a basketball camp. So it was appropriate that Garnett saved the longest hug for Fields at the end of the championship game. He wrapped his arms around Fields's head at center court, right in front of the scorer's table, and then he leaned into him so that Fields slowly backpedaled as Garnett staggered forward, their feet in step. They were dancing the dance of champions, and at last it seemed there truly had to be some flesh and blood to this player almost too good to be believed.

Chicago by Canoe

August 31, 2006

HUCK FINN said, "It's lovely to live on a raft." It ain't so bad on a kayak or a canoe, either—not to live on one but to float on one through the city. I'm not talking about kayaking downtown, though I understand the appeal: to paddle the same waters as Jean Baptiste Point Du Sable and look up at the canyons of skyscrapers that have grown up around the Chicago River. But I prefer the north branch of the river, which seems like a tributary of the stream in the old kids' TV serial *Journey to the Beginning of Time* in the way it takes one back to the days of Du Sable and his canoes while remaining part of the contemporary environment. I remember crossing the Irving Park bridge on a bus and looking down at the river to see a heron flying—another country. That feeling is even more pronounced when one is on the river, paddling its placid waters.

On a recent afternoon I rented a canoe at Chicago River Canoe & Kayak, which does a burgeoning business allowing people to get away from it all without really going anywhere. It's at 3400 N. Rockwell, just south and west of Lane Tech and a stone's throw across the river from Hot Doug's, where I'd fueled up beforehand. The five-year-old business, which rents its vessels for $14 an hour, $10 on weekdays, has grown every year; the day I was there, owner Ryan Chew had to rush out for reinforcements, but was back in ten minutes with more canoes and kayaks stacked on a trailer. (He'll be open weekends through October.) I went north against the current, thinking I'd paddle for an hour, then turn around and have a relatively easy trip back.

Trees lined the river on both sides, blocking the city off and muffling its noises, but a factory loomed up behind them as one last reminder of the surrounding urban environment. The factory rattled and churned at a steady rhythm, and someone was paged on a loudspeaker.

Just beyond it, however, calm settled in as tactile as a mist rising from the river. Turtles sunned themselves on fallen tree limbs. A cardinal flitted across the river as if swinging from a clothesline strung from side to

side. Ducks and geese paddled by, unruffled by the scent of the foie gras
sausage I'd just had, but then I spooked a great blue heron. I'd seen it up
the river from a hundred yards back, unfurling its wings like someone
shaking blue sheets to be folded, but when I rowed up in its direction I
lost sight of it. Then it took flight with a squawk and a few loping flaps
of its wings, dragging its legs like regrets, circled far down the river, and
came back to perch in a tree overhead, where it ruffled its throat feath-
ers at me as if delivering a silent scolding. On an earlier kayak trip I'd
seen kingfishers in the trees, sitting there looking like the old White
Sox player Walt "No-Neck" Williams, their big, bill-heavy heads growing right out of their bodies. But on this day they were missing—perhaps
hiding in the shade somewhere to get out of the midday heat.

Every once in a while I paddled past someone fishing from the shore.
Fish jumped occasionally or hovered just under the surface of the water—
mostly carp with silver-dollar scales and bloated bellies. I saw a few floating belly up, too, including one bass—a good sign, but for it being dead.
Yet I never saw anyone onshore catch anything, and the anglers rarely
raised a greeting. It must've been the innate jealousy of those on land for
those at sea, because everyone else in a canoe or kayak—and there were
several groups heading in both directions—all smiled and said hello.

I paddled on one side, then the other, dropping the oar every few
strokes to steer. A motorboat came by, leaving a wide, low wake, and
just to be safe I turned at a diagonal to meet the waves head-on. The
canoe nodded like a horse at the mild excitement and continued on its
peaceful way.

I crossed under the Irving Park bridge, where traffic hummed above as
if it were the city's respiration, and the loose joists on either side clanked
in that familiar way one hears on the bus when it hits them. A pair of
boots sat on a cement platform under the bridge, as if someone were
tucked in nearby having a nap—and perhaps someone was. Dragonflies
hovered momentarily alongside the canoe before continuing on, patrol-
ling for mosquitoes.

Some 1950s apartment buildings sometimes poked through the trees,
but there were also beautiful town houses with cedar siding. Other
homes had docks and boats, and rough stairs leading down to them. It's
one thing to live in the city and have a sailboat at Monroe Harbor or a

speedboat at Diversey and head out on the water at the end of the day; this was humbler and more homey, a boat behind one's own house to sit on or, if the inclination strikes, to motor down the murky waterway for a while. A beautiful gold-brick house nestled next to the Wilson bridge, which has its own stately elegance. Further on, a CTA train rattled across its own bridge on its way down to the street-level tracks that conclude the Ravenswood line—another reminder that just beyond the trees the city bustled away.

I paused under the Wilson bridge before turning back. The wind blew up the river and actually pushed the canoe back against the current, which left a line of dented whorls in the surface of the water as it brushed by the prow of the canoe. Some exotic bird came hurtling upstream. What was it? A kingfisher? A smaller heron? No, just a pigeon, heading for its nest under the bridge.

A few days later I was back on the Irving Park bus looking down at the river. It no longer seemed like a different place. No, it was my river, our river, for all those willing to discover and cherish it.

Bloom of the Rose

March 1, 2007

LAST YEAR's Public League boys championship game was all about Simeon's Derrick Rose proving himself a great basketball player. This year's was about Simeon, in Rose's senior season, proving itself a great team.

It was a rematch of the 2006 title game, but this time the details seemed to favor Washington, the underdog, which last year looked intimidated playing on the Bulls' home floor at the United Center. A crowded events schedule at the UC pushed this year's title game back to the UIC Pavilion, where it had flourished for much of the '80s and '90s, and Washington's Minutemen seemed much more comfortable in the humbler setting last Saturday night, especially with attendance held down by the threat of a winter storm and by the televising of the game on Channel 26. Washington came in a hot team, having won fourteen straight to go to 21–4. Simeon was 24–2, but the referees weren't blinded by the Wolverines' star quality. They hit forward Tim Flowers with a foul on the game's first possession, though from my seat in the second row I clearly heard him slap all ball as he blocked a shot. Then they hit Rose with two fouls in the first quarter. He stayed in the game, but another foul in the second quarter sent him to the bench, and an offensive foul midway through the third quarter sent him back again. By then, however, the game was all but over. Simeon's senior starters took their curtain calls in the fourth quarter, and at the end Rose was back on the floor with the ball in his hand, dropping it as time ran out with the dispatch of a workman putting down his tools at the stroke of five on a Friday.

Simeon simply stomped Washington in every facet of the game. They did it by playing fine team basketball, and also with pure talent. Of the Washington players, only DeAndre Liggins, the lean six-foot-six junior who did such a good job at both ends on Rose throughout the game, could have cracked the Simeon starting lineup. Rose and Flowers have been Simeon's stars since ascending to the varsity as sophomores, and the focus was on them as Washington took the early lead. Rose fed Flowers a no-look pass so slick the normally soft-handed forward wasn't ready for it, so a few possessions later Rose fired a bullet pass down the lane he dared Flowers to drop, and Flowers converted it into an easy layup. Rose then hit a three to put Simeon in front 10–8, and the Wolverines never looked back.

It was how they did it that impressed. Even after Rose drew his third foul, he calmly dribbled up the court, stopped, and drilled a three to put Simeon ahead 32–23 before he and Flowers sat down for the final two minutes of the first half. Washington tried to rally, but center Kevin Johnson, who at six-six has height Flowers lacks, hit a lovely turnaround jumper in the low post, then cleaned up a missed lay-in on a fast break to put Simeon up 37–29 at intermission. When play resumed Simeon went into a zone defense to put pressure on Washington, and the Minutemen responded by going to a running game. Yet that only played to Simeon's talent advantage. Cruising the floor, Rose dished the ball out to start a textbook three-man break that Bryant Orange finished with an easy layup. On defense the Wolverines kept getting back, filling the passing lanes, and getting their hands on the ball. Simeon scored the first thirteen points of the second half to go up 50–29, and even after Rose sat with four fouls there was nothing Washington could do.

Orange came to the fore—he would lead the team with twenty-one points—and having established his jumper tossed up an apparently bad shot that turned out to be a perfect alley-oop pass to Johnson flying down the base-line for a slam. "Oooooh!" went the crowd. Johnson returned the favor, dealing a lovely pass off the hip to Orange for a fast-break lay-in, and Orange soon added a three to make it 61–35. Having stormed down the lane for a crushing dunk, Johnson then hit a couple nice midrange jumpers and it was 67–41. He'd finish with nineteen points and nine assists. Rose returned with 5:45 left to shepherd the win home and add a little French pastry—something Washington, to save face, meant to deny him. Liggins fouled Rose on an apparent breakaway. "That's like, 'No show time,'" said a fan sitting in the front row. Then Rose drove the lane windmilling the ball but couldn't finish. But backup senior guard Deon Butler put Simeon ahead 87–57 by hitting a three, as if to declare "no prisoners," and Rose added the exclamation point. He passed to Butler on a give-and-go, Butler lofted a perfect alley-oop, and Rose's dunk made the final score 89–57.

Simeon broke out the preprinted championship T-shirts at center court as the players celebrated. They would actually be a step down in wardrobe for Rose, who arrived wearing a sweatshirt that said *Lottery Pick* across his chest, a reference to the NBA draft. What separates great players from the merely very skilled is that great players tend to make those around them better. Rose lifted not just Flowers this season but also Johnson and Orange, who credits Rose with raising his confidence and urging him to look for his shot.

The only games Simeon lost during the regular season were to Farragut in a holiday tournament and to Rice out of Harlem in New York City, and the Wolverines avenged both after a fashion, beating Farragut and defeating vaunted Oak Hill Academy of Virginia in a nationally televised game. They look to be odds-on favorites to repeat as state champs, which would establish them as not just Derrick Rose and his supporting cast but a great all-around basketball team, one of the best in Illinois history.

[Simeon didn't lose again that season, and did indeed go on to win a second straight state championship, finishing 33–2.]

Acknowledgments

THESE PIECES were written for the *Chicago Reader* between 1983 and 2008, when I had a regular column called "The Sports Section," which ran every other week, for most of that time in rotation with Jerry Sullivan's "Field & Street." So the first person to thank is Larry Doyle, my old friend and first roommate out of college, who was the one who went to the trouble of getting the *Reader*'s guide for freelancers when we were both struggling young writers trying to find our way, and who drew attention to how the *Reader* had a heading set aside for a regular sports article, but no one writing it.

That was just about the time I found myself looking at sports with what amounted to a fresh set of eyes. Like most American boys, especially in the suburbs of Chicago, I grew up loving sports, infected as I was by the trials of the 1969 Cubs, to the point where for several years I read nothing on my own but sports books and the backs of trading cards. When I went off to college, however, like many stuck-up aspiring intellectuals, I put sports aside. College football and basketball were fine as diversions, almost essential in that regard at a Midwest land-grant institution like the University of Illinois, but not for serious consideration. Back home, on my parents' couch, between assignments and spending a lot of time acquainting myself with the wonders of cable television, I found myself watching sports in a different way, especially the Blackhawks on what was then SportsVision, one of the first local cable sports stations. What a beautiful team that was in the early '80s, with Denis Savard whirling to set up Al Secord and Steve Larmer. The sportswriting of the time, like much of the journalism, reacted to television by surrendering the visual; it didn't attempt to paint pictures so much as it tried to convey gossip and capture gotcha moments on and off the field. Yet it always seemed to me that good writing was visual, that it conjured up images and impressed them on the mind or preserved them in memory, and that there was enough to write about on the field of play without

273

delving into soap opera shenanigans in the locker room or errors committed in the larger culture. The merest game had elements of drama to be tapped, if one only looked hard enough at the details and depicted them well and accurately.

That approach found an immediate home at the *Reader,* and I have to thank Pat Clinton as the editor who enthusiastically greeted those first columns and said to keep going. Bob Roth and Mike Lenehan were no doubt instrumental in making a regular place for "The Sports Section," and over the years Michael Miner shepherded most of these pieces into print. Later, Alison True remained committed to a typically contrarian *Reader* approach to sports—written in many ways to appeal to people who didn't like sports at all—and Kate Schmidt contributed an unerring eye for what worked on the page for both fans and nonfans alike, while rekindling my love for the Sox just in time.

Compiling these columns reminded me of what a joy it was to write them—almost as much fun as the actual game experience, in some cases. How could a writer fail to spin such moments into gold when they were golden to begin with, both the triumphs and the tragedies? So I think every sportswriter owes a debt—usually unstated—to the athletes. The one thing I absolutely could not tolerate in all my years in the press box was a sportswriter complaining about how this or that athlete was a bad quote. It takes almost unfathomable reserves of skill, practice, and dedication to master a sport, and while there's a special place reserved for those who can attain that level and also speak eloquently about it, it's not something an athlete should be obliged to excel at. Athletes give enough of themselves in the arena, and if they can't express what that truly feels like—or even if they simply don't care to—well, I always considered it my job to attempt to put it into words in any event.

Mike Levine, at Northwestern University Press, was captivated by the idea of a "Sports Section" compilation from the moment my good friend Miles Harvey first suggested it, so I have them both to thank, as well as Anne Gendler and Marianne Jankowski for seeing it through to completion, inside and out. Words can't express my debt to Tony Fitzpatrick, both for his foreword and for lending me the use of *Joe Crede of Chicago.* This book was a longtime dream of mine, and thanks to all of the above it has come out almost exactly as I imagined. Any and all flaws in the concept and execution are mine.

Finally, I have to thank my wife, Catherine, and daughters Sadie and Meg. They endured years of my being not only out at games, but holed up on Sundays to write my "collums." Yet I couldn't have done it without their love and their unwavering support. It warps a person, in some ways, to be a sports reporter; you're at these amazing games, with fans screaming and players trying to perform under the pressure, yet you're expected to be dispassionate, to obey the ban on "no cheering in the press box." So it was a different kind of joy, when the column ended, to share the 2010 Stanley Cup Champion Blackhawks with Meg as a true fan, to have thrown off the notebooks and tape recorders and the objectivity to, in a way, come full circle and revel in the sheer joy and exhilaration, much in the manner of Patrick Kane flinging away his stick and gloves to gallop into the air above the ice.